WHO SHALL LIVE?

ECONOMIC IDEAS LEADING TO THE 21st CENTURY

Series editors: Lawrence R. Klein *(Univ. Pennsylvania)* &
Vincent Su *(Baruch College, CUNY)*

WHO SHALL LIVE?

Health, Economics, and Social Choice

Expanded Edition

Victor R. Fuchs

Stanford University

World Scientific
Singapore • New Jersey • London • Hong Kong

Published by

World Scientific Publishing Co. Pte. Ltd.
P O Box 128, Farrer Road, Singapore 912805
USA office: Suite 1B, 1060 Main Street, River Edge, NJ 07661
UK office: 57 Shelton Street, Covent Garden, London WC2H 9HE

British Library Cataloguing-in-Publication Data
A catalogue record for this book is available from the British Library.

ISBN 981-02-3201-2

Printed in Singapore by Uto-Print

To

*L.H.F. and the memory of A.F. and F.S.F. —
with gratitude and love*

CONTENTS

HEALTH, ECONOMICS, AND SOCIAL CHOICE

PREFACE TO THE
EXPANDED EDITION

The French have a saying: "'Plus ça change, plus ça la même chose''—the more things change, the more they remain the same. Despite dramatic technological and institutional changes in health care during the past quarter century, the major themes of *Who Shall Live?* are as applicable today as when the book first appeared. Indeed, the central theme—the necessity of choice by society and by individuals—is more widely recognized now than ever before. All over the world there is increasing acknowledgment that no nation can provide all its citizens with all the health care that might do them some good. Resources must be allocated. The challenge to every society is to allocate those resources as fairly as possible and to do as much good as possible. This book provides a framework for addressing that challenge.

Although the need for choice is not new, public acknowledgment of that need by political leaders, physicians, and others involved in health policy is more recent. *The First International Conference on Priorities in Health Care* (Stockholm 1996), which attracted participants from dozens of fields and over 50 countries, was a major milestone on the road to better health policies. The conference left little doubt that the economic perspective employed in this book is a necessary, albeit not sufficient, guide for this journey. Also required are insights from many other disciplines ranging from biology to psychology to law to ethics. Moreover, each society, in keeping with its own values and traditions, must reconcile attempts to achieve efficiency and equity in health care with other goals such as democracy, personal freedom, and social solidarity.

With regard to health outcomes, the book's emphasis on the importance of individual behaviors such as cigarette smoking, alcohol consumption, exercise, and diet continues to be warranted, especially if we want to understand why mortality rates vary within and between countries. Although the ability of medicine to intervene decisively has increased greatly since the early 1970s—new drugs, improved surgical procedures, more precise diagnostic techniques—the contribution of care *at the margin* remains relatively small because the more effective medical innovations have usually been widely diffused. Thus, the answer to the question ''who shall live?'' is still more likely to be explained by genetic, environmental, and behavioral factors than by differences among populations in the quantity or quality of their medical care.

An additional quarter-century of experience with national health plans shows that universal coverage does not eliminate or even substantially reduce mortality differentials across socioeconomic groups. In England, for instance, infant mortality in the lowest socioeconomic class is double the rate of the highest class, just as it was prior to the introduction of the National Health Service. The relatively homogeneous populations of the Scandinavian countries not only enjoy universal coverage for health care, but also have many other egalitarian social programs. Nevertheless, life expectancy varies considerably across occupations and there is no evidence that this variation is diminishing over time. Of course, the failure of national health insurance to reduce socioeconomic differentials in mortality is not a decisive argument against its adoption. As I stress repeatedly in the book, health professionals provide important caring and validation services even when they do not change health outcomes. Moreover, many countries believe that national health insurance contributes to social solidarity.

The most striking changes in American medicine in recent years have been organizational, driven by pressures from private and public purchasers to slow the rate of growth of health care spending. When I was writing *Who Shall Live?*, most insured patients could choose freely among available providers, physicians' decisions were rarely questioned by insurers, most physicians practiced solo or in small groups, and they were reimbursed fee-for-service. Today most Americans are enrolled in a managed care plan, which means that the purchasers selectively contract with providers, patients face financial penalties if they seek care ''out-of-plan,'' fees and prices are negotiated in advance, physicians' decisions are subject to outside review, and providers often share in the insurance risk.

Managed care organizations seek to control spending by reducing services to patients, providing services more efficiently, and squeezing the incomes of health professionals, drug companies, and other providers of goods and services. One likely consequence of managed care that deserves special scrutiny is the deterioration of professional norms. At its best, the patient–physician relationship is an integrative system characterized by reciprocal rights and responsibilities. Managed care tends to transform this relationship into an exchange system characterized by a market mentality similar to that found in the markets for most commodities. Similar changes are occurring in physicians' relationships with one another. Policymakers should be aware that medical care can suffer from too much competition, just as it suffered in the past from too little. Physicians and patients possess very different information; honesty and trust on both sides are extremely important; and patients often benefit from cooperation among physicians. Thus professional norms are necessary elements in the social control of medicine—along with market competition and government regulation.

The ascendancy of managed care has been accompanied by a stampede to consolidation of health care organizations through mergers, acquisitions, and long-term contractual ties. Like metal filings attracted to a magnet, physical and human assets and patient populations have been drawn to entrepreneurs who were quicker and more aggressive in exploiting the new managed care environment. If the consolidated organizations can achieve greater efficiency through realization of economies of scale, elimination of excess capacity, reductions in transactions costs, and improvements in the flow of information, society as a whole benefits. Some consolidations however, are motivated not so much by a search for efficiency as by a desire for market power—power that can force lower prices for everything the organization buys and higher prices for what it sells. This market power may be good for the organization's bottom line, but it is of questionable value to society. Economies of scale do not increase without limit; if they did, every industry would consist of one huge firm. Diseconomies of scale often lead eventually to breakups, spinoffs, contracting-out, and sales of parts of organizations to others.

It seems to me that the pace of consolidation in American health care is likely to slow or even reverse direction as excess capacity disappears, as the supply of managers who can function effectively under managed care increases, and as competition reveals that some organizations have grown too large to be efficient. The economies-of-scale question is more problematic in health care than in most industries because the efficient scale of organization varies enormously from one type of care to another. For instance, the scale required for an efficient perinatal service is orders of magnitude larger than the one required for efficient well-baby care because of differences in the importance of specialized equipment and personnel and differences in the predictability of the demand for services. Moreover, optimal scale is not fixed forever, but is likely to change as technology changes. In my judgment, managed care is here to stay. The challenge is to discover, through trial and (not too much) error what forms, types, and scales of organization can do the most effective job of managing care for the benefit of patients and society as a whole.

The organizational upheaval in medical care has been greatest in the United States, but many other countries have also modified long-standing institutional arrangements, mostly out of fear of rising expenditures, but also in response to pressures from patients for wider choice and better service. In countries with national health plans, reform typically has tried to decentralize decisionmaking and increase competition. Furthermore, all over the world there is talk—and some action— about putting the day-to-day practice of medicine on a more scientific footing. These efforts proceed under programs such as ''evidence-based medicine,'' ''outcomes research,'' and ''clinical guidelines.'' Particularly important, in my view, is the ''new technology assessment,'' which goes beyond the traditional concern over safety and efficacy to encompass measurement of quality of life, determination of patient preferences, and the evaluation of costs and benefits of medical technologies. Technological change, more than any other factor, is the driving force behind rising health care expenditures; every health care system must find some way of modifying its speed and direction.

Six new chapters in this volume, based on previously published papers, extend the framework and major themes of the original book, provide new analyses, and offer my current recommendations for reforming U.S. health care. The first of the new chapters, ''What Every Philosopher Should Know About Health Economics,'' is an expanded version of a talk delivered to the American Philosophical Society. I begin with the demise of the 1994 Clinton health plan and discuss the inability and/or unwillingness of policy makers and the public to make the difficult choices that are inevitable if the U.S. is to improve its approach to health care. These include: choosing priorities for the health care system, recognizing that universal coverage requires subsidization and compulsion, accepting the iron law of cost containment—''no pain, no gain''— and learning to cope with an aging society.

The second new chapter, on poverty and health, develops a series of questions which, if answered, would clarify the reasons for the strong correlation between health and socioeconomic status and point the way toward more efficient and just policies for the poor. Three chapters dealing with national health insurance follow. The first, written in 1976, examines the reasons for the popularity of national health insurance in most countries and its absence in the United States. The second, written fifteen years later, returns to this theme in the light of the experience of other countries with universal coverage and appraises the prospects for national health insurance in the United States. The third critiques American efforts to reform health care in the 1990s, with special attention to shortcomings in the arguments of both the proponents and opponents of reform.

The final chapter, which was my presidential address to the American Economic Association in 1996, traces the development of health economics in the United States, reports the results of a survey of health economists, economic theorists, and physicians about health economics and health policy, and considers the relationship between values and health policy. I believe that our values—our vision of the good society—inevitably play a role in our policy choices. Conversely, in the long run the policies we adopt can help to shape our values. A better understanding of this interplay between values and policies should have a prominent place on the agenda of health economists and policy analysts as we confront the problems of the 21st century.

What form will these problems take? Two of the most important will be how to cope with an aging society and how to adjust to scientific advances such as the genetics revolution. Most industrialized nations are sitting on a demographic time bomb: the number of elderly will increase sharply at a time when the number of workers will be stable or shrinking. The potential consumption of health care by the elderly is enormous, especially when one includes rehabilitation and assistance with daily living as well as treatment for acute and chronic illness. Nations will be hard-pressed to reconcile a desire to deliver services to the elderly within the constraints of competing claims on resources.

Scientific discoveries in genetics, the neurosciences, and other fields will open up many new opportunities for better diagnosis and treatment. Some of the breakthroughs may actually lower the cost of care, but others will, if implemented on a wide scale, lead to large increases in expenditures. Moreover, the problems of resource allocation will be exacerbated by concerns over privacy and autonomy. The bottom line is that both individuals and societies will have to make difficult choices. But the future need not be dismal. We know what the main problems are; what we need now is the political and professional leadership to deal with them in a timely, rational, and compassionate way.

VICTOR R. FUCHS
Stanford, California
May 1997

PREFACE TO THE
PAPERBACK EDITION (1982)

The favorable reception accorded *Who Shall Live?* by reviewers, academic colleagues, students in a wide variety of fields, health care practitioners and policy makers has far exceeded my expectations. I am, therefore, delighted to see this paperback edition and hope that it will enable an even wider audience to share my thoughts concerning the relationships among ''health, economics, and social choice.''

The comments I have received about the book, both publicly and in private communications, have not left me with a sense of having been misunderstood or with any need to use this opportunity to ''set the record straight.'' I would, however, like to indicate briefly how recent trends in health economics and health policy have changed or reinforced my views concerning the major themes of *Who Shall Live?*

The most central theme of the book—the inevitability of *choice* even with respect to something as precious as health—is much better understood in the 1980s than it was in the 1960s or the early 1970s. Today there are only a few who still argue that the nation should spend as much for medical care as is technically possible, regardless of costs and benefits. Acceptance of the relevance of economics to health care policy has grown so rapidly that for some audiences it is necessary to add a few words of warning against uncritical application of general economic principles with insufficient attention to the special characteristics of health and medical care.

Health is the outcome of a process that involves patients and health professionals working *together*; mutual trust and confidence contribute greatly to the effectiveness of that process. However desirable it might be in other markets, an arms-length, adversarial relationship between buyer and seller should not be the goal of health care policy. It is one thing for a healthy individual to choose among competing health plans, and another to expect a sick patient to shop among competing physicians and hospitals. Not only is cooperation between patient and physician often essential in the production of health, but cooperation among physicians is also valuable. Thus, the atomistic competition that economists set as the ideal market structure for producing and distributing most goods and services is far from ideal for health care.

A substantial portion of this book deals with the roles of medical and nonmedical factors in health. Writing at a time when most policy discussions called for more physicians and more hospitals, I thought it was crucial to emphasize the importance of individual behavior in health. This theme is widely accepted today. Indeed, so much publicity is now given to jogging, diet, and similar phenomena that I now want to warn against neglecting research that increases our understanding of health processes and behaviors. There is no doubt that we could improve our health by modifying our life styles, but it is also true that most of the great advances in health have come from discovering new and better ways of preventing or treating disease. In arguing that the marginal benefit of medical care is small relative to its cost, I have always tried to distinguish between the payoff from increasing the *quantity* of care and the benefits from raising the *quality* of care through scientific research. The latter is of crucial importance because only limited improvement in health can be purchased by increasing the number of physicians or hospital beds.

Support for research is now waning, and academic medical centers are themselves partly to blame because they have inadequately articulated the difference between fundamental scientific work and technological development. Some new technologies are real breakthroughs, but many others simply contribute to the escalation of health care costs. Expensive technology of uncertain value cuts into the funding of medical research directly by draining off health care dollars and indirectly by arousing suspicion that much of the research budget supports additional technological developments that will be put into practice with inadequate evaluation.

The leaders of academic medicine also need to articulate the difference between medical research and medical education. Discussion of research and education frequently proceeds as if the two activities were inextricably related. This may well be true with respect to *production*, but an important distinction can and should be made with respect to financing. Medical research confers large benefits on society as a whole. Unless subsidized, private individuals and organizations will not undertake the socially optimal amount of research because they cannot reap all the benefits. This is much less true of medical education because most of the benefits are realized (in the form of higher earnings) by those who receive the training. Thus, there is no obvious case for subsidization to achieve the socially optimal amount. If society wants to help poor students obtain access to medical education, it can do so through specifically focused loans and scholarships.

Another major theme of the book—the central importance of the physician in the cost of care—is reflected in the chapter title ''The Physician: The Captain of the Team.'' Today the situation is changed. A more appropriate title would be ''Physician: The Co-Captain of the Team.'' One of the most important developments in health care delivery during the past decade is the growth of *management* in hospitals, clinics, and other health care organizations. More than ever before, practicing physicians must share their power with professional managers. These managers take responsibility for funding large capital expenditures, deal with the ever more numerous armies of planners, regulators, and third-party reimbursers, and coordinate the diverse talents and interests of physicians, nurses, technologists, and other specialists. The sharing of power and control with managers does not come easily to most practicing physicians, and when it impinges on their ability to care for patients it becomes dangerous. But much of it is inevitable because the political and technological changes of recent decades are irreversible. The most important need now is to work out appropriate compromises that meet the legitimate interests of all concerned parties: health professionals, managers, patients, and society.

The book concludes with a series of policy recommendations that seem to me as appropriate today as when they were written. I would, however, like to use this opportunity to add four additional recommendations of a general nature, all of them involving the need for greater integration in approaches to health care.

1. *Integration of in-hospital and out-of-hospital care.* Most physicians already try to do a good job of integrating services for patients regardless of whether they are in or out of the hospital. But the structure of most health insurance policies creates a big problem. In too many cases private and public third-party coverage induces a misallocation of resources because in-hospital care is more generously covered than out-of-hospital care. This biases the choices physicians and patients make and often leads to inappropriate decisions on narrow financial grounds.

2. *Integration of the personal health service and public health service traditions.* As the late Walsh McDermott, M.D., so lucidly explained, these two traditions developed along virtually separate lines in the United States, each making notable contributions to the health of the American people. The personal health service tradition builds on a strong foundation of the natural sciences and a commitment to the needs of the individual patient. The public health service tradition draws heavily on the social and behavioral sciences and focuses on the health needs of populations. Today our most important health problems involve chronic disease; deaths from suicide, homicide, and accidents; mental illness; drug abuse; and genetic disorders. To deal with these problems effectively we need to integrate the skills and understandings of both traditions.

3. *Integration of physical and mental health services.* The artificial separation of the health problems of mind and body has persisted too long in American medicine. New discoveries in basic science confirm what many have known intuitively: there is often a close relation between physical and mental phenomena. Most health problems today have a significant emotional and behavioral component, and we need to integrate the physical and mental elements of medical education, medical practice, medical research, and medical financing in order to solve these problems.

4. *Integration of health and social services.* Most health care services today are delivered to patients who are in need of more than health care. They include the elderly, the emotionally disturbed, the physically and mentally handicapped, alcoholics and other drug abusers, and so on. Unless there is greater appreciation that these patients need an integration of health and social services, we will continue to pour billions into each with less than optimal effect.

The past decade has seen many notable advances in health: infant mortality has been cut by almost half; the death rate from heart disease is down 25 percent; great progress has been made in treating Hodgkins Disease, peptic ulcers, and other illnesses; and new surgical techniques have raised the quality of life for millions of patients. At the same time, new problems arise. The suicide rate among those ages fifteen to twenty-four has soared; each year hundreds of thousands of unwed teenagers have babies, many of whom are born below normal weight; the fragmentation of families places ever-increasing burdens on the health care system. Indeed, health care now consumes almost one-tenth of the nation's total output of goods and services, and resistance to further expansion grows ever stronger. *Who Shall Live?* does not offer easy solutions to these problems, but it does provide the conceptual framework and institutional background with which the reader can begin to forge his or her own answers.

VICTOR R. FUCHS
Stanford, California
October 1982

ACKNOWLEDGMENTS

Claire Gilchrist played a key role in the development of this expanded edition, and I am pleased to acknowledge her many editorial and secretarial contributions. I am also grateful to Chiang Yew Kee and Kim Tan for assistance in the publication process, to Lawrence J. Lau who introduced me to World Scientific Publishing, and to Deborah Kerwin-Peck for research and editorial assistance. Thanks are also due to the publications in which the papers in this volume originally appeared; the first page of each paper provides a specific citation.

Acknowledgments to the First Edition

My obligations to individuals and institutions who contributed to the publication of this book are numerous and only partially discharged by this brief expression of appreciation. The Center for Advanced Study in the Behavioral Sciences, where I was a fellow in 1972–73, provided an ideal setting for reflection and writing—stimulating colleagues, excellent support services, and freedom from other responsibilities. A grant from the Carnegie Corporation, arranged by Margaret Mahoney and administered by Avery Russell, partially financed my stay at the Center and made possible the valuable research assistance of Carol Breckner.

Helpful comments on portions of the manuscript were received from Walter Bortz, M.D., Lawrence H. Fuchs, Seth Kreimer, Bertha Laufer, Margaret Mahoney, Peter Rogatz, M.D., and Terrence Sandalow. Their criticisms did much to remove imperfections of substance and style; those that remain are my sole responsibility. The contributions of my wife, Beverly, have been, as always, many and varied—encouragement, a rigorous critique, and inspiration.

Although they were not involved in the writing of this book, several economists and physicians have helped me in recent years in my efforts to bridge the gap between economics and health. I am particularly grateful to my colleagues at the National Bureau of Economic Research, and to Morton Bogdonoff, M.D., Kurt Deuschle, M.D., Eli Ginzberg, and Richard Kessler, M.D. I would also like to thank Martin Kessler for several valuable editorial suggestions and Bill Green and Ruth Rozman for their conscientious editorial work.

Who Shall Live?

INTRODUCTION

Health and Economics

> The Theory of Economics does not furnish a body of settled conclusions immediately applicable to policy. It is a method rather than a doctrine, an apparatus of the mind, a technique of thinking which helps its possessor to draw correct conclusions.
>
> JOHN MAYNARD KEYNES
> Introduction to the
> *Cambridge Economic Handbooks*

The problems are all around us: a mother searching frantically for someone to see her sick child; a crippling disease that puts a family hopelessly in debt; a tenfold increase in deaths from emphysema * since 1955; a doubling of Blue Cross rates in just a few years. The list could be extended almost without limit.

If the problems are numerous and varied, so are the proposed solutions. National health insurance, health maintenance organizations, public utility regulation of hospitals, expansion of medical schools, stricter control of drugs—these are some of the panaceas that have been offered to meet the "crisis" in health care.

Amid the emotion-laden debates that have surrounded these topics, it is not easy for the concerned layman, government official, businessman, student, labor leader, or even health professional to define the problems, acquire the necessary facts, and understand the critical individual and social choices that must be made.

To assist in this process is the primary purpose of this book. In it I try to distill analyses and conclusions based on my research in health services over the past decade, my experience on a medical school faculty, first-

---

* Chronic obstructive disease of the lung.

hand observation of many innovative medical care organizations, and discussions with leading professionals in medicine, hospital administration, the drug industry, public health, and related fields. Most important, this book approaches the problems of health and medical care from a specific point of view—that of the economist.

The economic point of view is rooted in three fundamental observations about the world. The first is that resources are scarce in relation to human wants. It is hardly news that we cannot all have everything that we would like to have, but it is worth emphasizing that this basic human condition is not to be attributed to "the system," or to some conspiracy, but to the parsimony of nature in providing mankind with the resources needed to satisfy human wants. That inefficiency and waste exist in the economy cannot be denied. That some resources are underutilized is clear every time the unemployment figures are announced. That the resources devoted to war could be used to satisfy other wants is self-evident. The fundamental fact remains, however, that even if all these imperfections were eliminated, total output would still fall far short of the amount people would like to have. Resources would still be scarce in the sense that choices would still have to be made. Not only is this true now, but it will continue to be true in the foreseeable future. Some advances in technology (e.g., automated laboratories) make it possible to carry out current activities with fewer resources, but others open up new demands (e.g., for renal dialysis * or organ transplants) that put further strains on resources. Moreover, our *time,* the ultimate scarce resource, becomes more valuable the more productive we become.

The second observation is that resources have alternative uses. Society's human, natural, and man-made resources can, in most instances, be used to satisfy many different kinds of wants. If we want more physicians, we must be prepared to accept fewer scientists, or teachers, or judges. If we want more hospitals, we can get them only at the expense of more housing, or factories, or something else that could use the same land, capital, and labor.

Finally, economists note that people do indeed have different wants, and that there is significant variation in the relative importance that people attach to them. The oft-heard statement, "Health is the most important goal," does not accurately describe human behavior. Everyday in manifold ways (such as overeating or smoking) we make choices that af-

* A machine process that cleans the patient's blood of the waste chemicals that his non-functioning kidneys are unable to remove.

fect our health, and it is clear that we frequently place a higher value on satisfying other wants.

Given these three conditions, the basic economic problem is how to allocate scarce resources so as to best satisfy human wants. This point of view may be contrasted with two others that are frequently encountered. They are the *romantic* and the *monotechnic*. The romantic point of view fails to recognize the scarcity of resources relative to wants. The fact that we are constantly being confronted with the need to choose is attributed to capitalism, communism, advertising, the unions, war, unemployment, or any other convenient scapegoat. Because *some* of the barriers to greater output and want satisfaction are clearly man-made, the romantic is misled into confusing the real world with the Garden of Eden. Because it denies the *inevitability* of choice, the romantic point of view is impotent to deal with the basic economic problems that face every society. Occasionally, the romantic point of view is reinforced by authoritarian distinctions regarding what people "need" or "should have." Confronted with an obvious imbalance between people's desires and the available resources, the romantic-authoritarian response may be to categorize some desires as "unnecessary" or "inappropriate," thus protecting the illusion that no scarcity exists.

The monotechnic point of view, frequently found among physicians, engineers, and others trained in the application of a particular technology, is quite different. Its principal limitation is that it fails to recognize the multiplicity of human wants and the diversity of individual preferences. Every problem involving the use of scarce resources has its technological aspects, and the contribution of those skilled in that technology is essential to finding solutions. The solution that is optimal to the engineer or physician, however, may frequently not be optimal for society as a whole because it requires resources that society would rather use for other purposes. The desire of the engineer to build the best bridge or of the physician to practice in the best-equipped hospital is understandable. But to the extent that the monotechnic person fails to recognize the claims of competing wants or the divergence of his priorities from those of other people, his advice is likely to be a poor guide to social policy.

The basic plan of this book is straightforward. Thus, the first chapter presents from an economic point of view the nation's major health care problems: high and rapidly rising costs, inequality and difficulties of access, and large disparities in health levels within the United States and between the United States and other countries. The discussion of these problems, and the subsequent analysis of the choices we must make, set the stage for a few central themes that run throughout the book.

The first theme is that the connection between health and medical care is not nearly as direct or immediate as most discussions would have us believe. True, advances in medical science, particularly the development of antiinfectious drugs in the 1930s, '40s, and '50s, did much to reduce morbidity and mortality. Today, however, differences in health levels between the United States and other developed countries or among populations in the United States are not primarily related to differences in the quantity or quality of medical care. Rather, they are attributable to genetic and environmental factors and to personal behavior. Furthermore, except for the very poor, health in developed countries no longer correlates with per capita income. Indeed, higher income often seems to do as much harm as good to health, so that differences in diet, smoking, exercise, automobile driving and other manifestations of "life-style" have emerged as the major determinants of health. Chapter 2 develops this theme in some detail.

Although it is the patient rather than the physician who has the major influence on his health, the opposite is true regarding the cost of medical care. As we whall see in Chapter 3, it is the physician who, as "captain of the team," makes the key decisions (regarding hospitalization, surgery, prescriptions, tests, and X rays) that account for the bulk of medical care costs. Many of these decisions are not rigidly determined by "medical necessity," and, depending upon how medical care is paid for, utilization and costs can vary greatly. This theme is further elaborated in the chapters on hospitals (4), drugs (5), and medical care finance (6).

The relative unimportance of the physician in health and his great importance with respect to cost lead us naturally to a third theme—the folly of trying to meet the problem of access by training more M.D. specialists and subspecialists. The access problem involves mostly primary care * and emergency care—and could frequently be met with physicians' assistants, nurse clinicians, and other kinds of health professionals. The "doctor shortage" is far from universal, and in some specialties, such as surgery, there is actually a surplus. Furthermore, such surpluses, rather than reducing costs, actually raise them (see Chapter 3).

A fourth theme, concerning the payment for medical care (Chapter 6), is that there is no magic formula which can transfer the cost from individ-

---

* The care given by practitioners who agree to serve as the first point of contact for the patient who needs or thinks he needs health services. It typically deals with the more common and relatively uncomplicated types of health problems.

uals to government or business. If the American people want more medical care, they are going to have to pay for it through fees, insurance premiums, taxes, or, if the taxes are levied on business, higher prices. The choice of payment mechanism is not irrelevant, however, because of its implications for the poor, and its implications for the total cost of care.

The most central theme of the book is the necessity of choice at both the individual and social levels. We cannot have all the health or all the medical care that we would like to have. "Highest quality care for all" is "pie in the sky." We have to choose. Furthermore, while economics can help us to make choices more rationally and to use resources more efficiently, it cannot provide the ethics and the value judgments that must guide our decisions. In particular, economics cannot tell us how much equality or inequality we should have in our society (Chapters 1, 6, and the Conclusion).

A few words about what this book is *not* are also in order. Although I am a specialist in health economics, this book is not written for my fellow specialists. I have not attempted to fill in all the details or to argue exhaustively in support of every conclusion. I have tried very hard to get the main points right; indeed, to help the reader realize what the main points are. In a world that is becoming increasingly specialized, it is important to try to take a look at the "big picture," to reach an audience which, if not large, is certainly influential.

This is not an "angry" book; neither is it a defense of the status quo. Surely there is much in the American health care scene to criticize, much that ought to be changed. But if the change is to be for the better, it should be based on an understanding of why things are the way they are. Anger often gets in the way of understanding. As Gordon McLachlan, a leading British health care expert, has written, "One of the major policy requirements for most Western societies today is to eschew the drama for awhile, and examine critically with scientific techniques the dogmas and cliches with which the policy-making for medical care has been encumbered." [1]

This book is not a directory of villains. It is simply not true that you can always recognize the "bad guys" by their white coats. Most health care problems are complex, and, except for my desire to avoid being too technical, the complexities are not evaded. Few simple solutions are presented, because, in my view, few exist. Some health care problems defy "solution." At most one can hope for understanding, adjustment, amelioration.

Although I have tried to avoid polemics, I have not tried to conceal my

opinions or to present a balanced point of view on every issue. Other observers—indeed, other economists—may well reach conclusions different
from mine. Some of the data are certainly open to alternative interpreta-
tions. More important, value judgments undoubtedly differ. My greatest
hope is not that readers will uncritically accept all my conclusions, but
that this book will help them reach their own with a firmer command of
the facts and a clearer understanding of the relationships among health,
economics, and social choice.

CHAPTER 1

Problems and Choices

A rational man acting in the real world may
be defined as one who decides where he will
strike a balance between what he desires and
what can be done. It is only in imaginary
worlds that we can do whatever we wish.

WALTER LIPPMANN
The Public Philosophy

The Problems We Face

In recent years, almost every American family has become acutely aware
of the soaring costs of medical care, the difficulties of access to physicians, and the mounting health problems of our society. According to
many observers, the U.S. health care system is in "crisis." But a crisis is
a turning point, a decisive or crucial point in time. In medicine the crisis
is that point in the course of the disease at which the patient is on the
verge of either recovering or dying. No such decisive resolution is evident with respect to the problems of health and medical care. Our "sick
medical system," to use the headline of numerous magazine and newspaper editorials, is neither about to recover nor to pass away. Instead, the
basic problems persist and are likely to persist for some time to come.

What are these problems? Many of them are related to the *cost* of care.
Indeed, one close observer of the Washington scene has argued that "the
medical 'crisis' . . . is purely and simply a crisis of cost. The infla-
tionary rise in medical costs is the key concern of congressmen and consumers, a fundamental political and economic fact of life for both." [1]
Another category of problems concerns *access* to care; while a third
major set involves the determinants of *health levels*. Let us look briefly at
each of the problems in turn.

COST

In 1973 Americans spent an average of $450 per person for health care and related activities such as medical education and research. This was almost 8 percent of the GNP (the gross national product is the total value of all goods and services produced in the nation). Twenty years before, health care represented only 4.5 percent of the nation's output, and even as recently as 1962 the proportion was only 5.6 percent. Thus from 1963 to 1973 health expenditures rose at the rate of 10 percent annually while the rest of the economy (as reflected in the GNP) was growing at only 6 to 7 percent.

One often reads or hears that costs have become so high that the average family can no longer pay for health care and that some other way must be found to finance it. This is pure nonsense. The average family will always have to pay its share of the cost one way or the other. Payment may take many forms: fee-for-service, insurance premiums, or taxes. If the system is financed by taxes on business, then people pay indirectly, either through higher prices for the goods and services business produces or through lower wages. True, a highly progressive tax could result in some redistribution of the burden. But given the likely pattern of tax incidence, the only meaningful way to ease the cost burden on the average family is to moderate the increase in total expenditures.

Not only is *average* cost of health care high and growing at a rapid rate, but there is also the problem of *unusual* cost. It is clear that in any particular year a relatively small number of families make extensive use of health services, and if payment is on a fee-for-service basis, the cost to them is exceedingly high. Renal dialysis for one individual, for instance, may cost ten thousand dollars a year; some surgical procedures cost even more. But the remedy for this problem has been known for a long time—some form of insurance or prepayment. This will not help the *average*-cost problem—indeed, it would aggravate it if insurance were to induce additional utilization—but it does take care of those individuals who require unusually large amounts of care.

Note that these two cost problems have little to do with one another. If average costs were half their present levels or rising at half their present rate, some families would still experience mammoth medical care bills in any given year. Similarly, even if every family had complete protection against unusual costs through major-risk insurance, the problem of slowing the escalation of rising average costs would remain. They are separate problems and require separate solutions.

Why has average cost grown so rapidly, and what can be done about it? One useful approach is to realize that cost, measured by total expenditures, is equal to the *quantity* of care utilized multiplied by the *price* per "unit" of care. Utilization, measured by number of visits, prescriptions, tests, days in hospital, and the like, depends upon the *health condition* of the population as well as its *propensity to use health services* for any particular health condition. This propensity depends in part on the patient, who, in most instances, must initiate the care process and consent to its continuance. But it also depends on the physician who, because of his presumed superior knowledge, is empowered by law and custom with the authority to make decisions concerning utilization. It is the physician who sends the patient to the hospital and sends him home, who recommends surgery, who orders tests and X rays, and who prescribes drugs.

So much for utilization. What about price? The price of a given "unit" of medical care depends on the relative *productivity* (i.e., output per unit of input) of the labor and capital used to produce it and on the *prices paid* for this labor and capital. Productivity depends on such factors as the appropriateness of the scale and type of organization in question, on the amount of excess capacity, on technological advance, and on the effectiveness of incentives and training. Thus productivity is directly affected if a hospital is either too large or too small to be efficient, or if the community has more hospital bed than it needs, or if there are less expensive ways of performing laboratory tests.

The physician can have considerable influence on productivity because of his broad powers of decision making. For instance, the physician decides how many and what kinds of auxiliary personnel work with him in his practice. And committees of physicians make many of the critical decisions that affect productivity in the hospitals they are affiliated with. The patient can also affect productivity through his cooperation and general behavior. For instance, a patient who gives a physician a full and reliable medical history and who complies with the latter's instructions regarding drugs and diet can contribute substantially to the efficiency of the care he receives. Furthermore, although the prices paid for labor and capital used in health care are largely governed by forces at work in the economy at large, special circumstances within the health field, such as the unionization of hospital employees, can affect wages and thus costs.

Any explanation for the rise in the average cost of health care and any proposal for containing or lowering this cost can be analyzed within the accounting framework just described, for nothing affects cost that does not first affect the health of the population, the propensity of people to use health services, the productivity of the factors of production (labor and capital) used in medical care, or the prices paid for those factors. It should be stressed, however, that this is an *accounting* framework; it cannot provide a behavioral explanation of cost change. That can only come through an analysis of the actual behavior of patients, physicians, hospital administrators, government officals, and other decision makers.

It is not easy to say how much of the increase in cost in the past decade is due to the increased quantity of health care and how much to higher prices. Price should refer to some well-defined unit of service, but in fact the "content" of a physician's visit, or of a day in the hospital, keeps changing over time. The official price index for medical care, which is an average of changes in the price of a hospital day, a physician visit, and other elements of care and is published by the U.S. Bureau of Labor Statistics, shows an annual increase of 5 percent since 1962. This implies that there was also a 5 percent annual increase in *quantity* of these goods and services over the same period (for the sum of the two must equal the 10 percent annual increase in total medical expenditures cited at the beginning of this section). But because the official price index makes little allowance for changes in health care *quality* (i.e., the effects on health or the amenities associated with care) it may give a misleading picture of the true changes in *quantity*. To the extent that the quality of care has increased, the price index is overstated; if quality has decreased, it is understated.

Part of what we know to be an increase in quantity is due to the growth of population which has been about 1 percent annually since 1962. The balance must reflect either an increased propensity to use health services or adverse changes in the health condition of the population because of pollution, smoking, increased numbers of accidents, and the like.

The price of medical care has been growing more rapidly than the overall price index and at about the same rate as the price index for all services. This reflects higher prices for the inputs used in medical care, particularly the labor of physicians, nurses, and other personnel. It also reflects our inability to increase productivity in health care as rapidly as in the economy as a whole.

Most proposals for medical care reform seek to contain costs, but there are important differences in the strategies proposed for accomplishing this. These strategies, which will be discussed in more detail in subsequent chapters, are introduced briefly here.

The first strategy looks to *changes in supply* to drive down price and ultimately cost. According to this view, a substantial increase in the number of hospitals and physicians would force significant reductions in charges and fees, presumably either by stimulating increases in productivity or decreases in prices and wages.

A second strategy would reduce utilization by *improving the health* of the population. Advocates of this approach argue that more preventive medicine, health education, and environmental improvements could reduce the need for hospitals, physicians, and drugs.

A third approach would depend upon administrative *controls and planning* to contain costs. Such devices as hospital planning councils, utilization review committees, and drug formularies fall into this category, as do more direct interventions such as wage and price ceilings. Some controls are intended to reduce utilization, others to improve productivity, and still others to limit prices paid to the factors of production.

A fourth strategy attempts to induce *greater cost-consciousness* in consumers by modifying health insurance to include substantial deductibles (amounts the patient must pay before the insurance becomes effective) and coinsurance (partial payment by the patient after the insurance becomes effective). The goal here is to reduce the propensity to use health services for any given health condition, and also to increase the consumer's incentive to maintain his health.

Finally, there are those who look to the *physician to control costs;* changing the method of compensation, according to this strategy, would give him a strong incentive to do so. For instance, it is argued that payment on a capitation * basis, rather than fee-for-service, would reduce the number of unnecessary operations.

In order to evaluate these diverse strategies, one needs a good understanding of the determinants of health and of the workings of the health care market. My own view is that decentralized administrative controls and modification of patient behavior both have something to contribute, but I would put greatest emphasis on the physician. My reasons for emphasizing the physician as the key to controlling costs are developed in subsequent chapters.

ACCESS

The problems of access to health care fall into two main categories, which may be labeled "special" and "general." The special problems of access are those faced by particular groups in society—the poor, the ghetto dwellers, and the rural population. The general problem of access

* A system in which the physician receives a fixed amount per patient per year regardless of the amount of care actually delivered.

is one that is felt even by individuals and families who have enough income or insurance to pay for care and are not disadvantaged by reason of location or race. For them the problem is simply to get the kind of care they need when they need it.

The problems the poor face in getting access to medical care are similar to those they face in obtaining other goods and services. To be poor is, by definition, to have less of the good things produced by society; if they did not have less they would not be poor. There are many people, however, who argue that medical care is special, that access to care is a "right" and should not be dependent upon income. Opposed to this is the view that if one wishes to help the poor, the best way to do so is to give them more purchasing power and let *them* decide how they want to spend it. According to this view, it makes little sense to use hard-to-raise tax money to lift the poor up to some arbitrarily high standard of medical care while they have grievous deficiencies in housing, schooling, and other aspects of a good life. A more systematic look at this question is presented later in this chapter.

Poverty explains part of the access problem for the rural population, but not all of it. Even in rural areas with substantial purchasing power, the physician-population ratio is typically much lower than in the cities. This is true not only in the United States but in almost every country in the world. It is true in Israel, which has a very large supply of physicians because of immigration; it is true in Sweden, which is frequently said to have a model health care system; it is even true in the Soviet Union, where physicians are government employees and supposedly must practice wherever they are sent.

The reason for the access problem in rural areas is very clear: physicians prefer to practice in highly urbanized areas. They do so partly for professional reasons such as the desire to practice with colleagues, use up-to-date facilities, and concentrate on a specialty. They also generally prefer the educational, cultural, and recreational facilities available for themselves and their families in metropolitan areas.

What, if anything, to do about the rural access problem is less clear. Should physicians be forced to go to rural areas? Should they be bribed to go there with very high incomes financed by taxes on citydwellers? One popular proposal is to subsidize medical education on condition that the student promise to practice in a rural area. In the absence of any demonstration that health is worse in rural areas, however, I do not see any strong case for adopting special measures aimed solely at changing physicians' location decisions. If, however, such decisions were to be influenced by broader programs aimed at rural poverty, or at a wider dispersion of the population, that would be a different matter.

The access problem for blacks and some other minority groups is largely a question of poverty. Many members of minority groups with adequate incomes and insurance do not experience any unique problems with respect to health care. Where discrimination in housing is severe, however, and middle- and upper-income blacks are locked into low-income ghettos, they probably will experience access problems because the supply of services is geared to the low average level of income in the area. The best solution for this problem is to eliminate discrimination in housing. Another distinct problem arises when blacks (or Chicanos or Indians) prefer to be treated by other blacks (or Chicanos or Indians); this can only be solved by increasing the number of health professionals from these minority groups.

The *general* problem of access, which will receive considerable attention in this book—especially in Chapter 3, where we discuss the physician—is a complex phenomenon that in the broadest sense represents a failure of the medical care market to match supply and demand. While the term *general problem* implies that it is experienced by the population generally and not only by particular groups, it must not be thought that the problem is general in the sense of applying to all kinds of physicians. As already mentioned in the Introduction (and as Chapter 3 will make clear), there are actually substantial surpluses of some types of physician specialists, such as surgeons. The general problem of access exists mainly with respect to primary care, emergency care, home care, and care outside customary working hours. And so the solution, as we shall see in Chapter 3, does not lie in simply increasing the number of physicians.

HEALTH LEVELS

Concern about health levels in the United States primarily takes two forms. First, there is concern that health levels in this country are not as high as in many other developed nations. The principal evidence for this is found in comparisons of age-specific death rates and of life expectancies (life expectancy is a summary measure of these death rates). The excess of death rates in the United States over those elsewhere is, in some cases, striking. For instance, the death rate for males ages 45 to 54 is almost double the Swedish rate. Of every hundred males in the United States who turn 45, only ninety will see their fifty-fifth birthday. In Sweden, ninety-five will survive the decade. Granted, there are many dimensions of health besides mortality, but the lack of adequate measures precludes their use for comparisons among populations. In any case, there seems little reason to believe that examination of these other dimensions would reverse conclusions based on mortality. Most deaths, after all, are preceded by illness, either physical or mental.

Infant mortality is another frequently used index of health. This indicator usually falls as income rises, but the United States, which has the highest per capita income in the world, does not have the lowest infant death rate. Indeed, the rate in this country is one-third higher than in the Scandinavian countries and the Netherlands.

The other principal cause for concern regarding health levels is that they vary greatly among different groups in the United States. For instance, the disparity between whites and blacks is very great. Black infant mortality in this country is almost double the white rate, and black females ages 40–44 have two-and-one-half times the death rate of their white counterparts. Other minority groups (e.g., the Indians) also have very poor health levels, while still others, such as the Japanese and the Mormons, enjoy levels that are considerably above the national average.

The most important thing to realize about such differences in health levels is that they are usually *not* related in any important degree to differences in medical care. Over time the introduction of new medical technology has had a significant impact on health, but when we examine differences among populations at a given moment in time, other socioeconomic and cultural variables are now much more important than differences in the quantity or quality of medical care.

Medical advances beginning in the 1930s and extending through the late 1950s brought about significant improvements in health, especially through the control of infectious diseases. These advances have been widely diffused among and within all developed countries and even some of the less developed ones. For more than a decade, however, the impact of new medical discoveries on overall mortality has been slight; indeed, the death rate for U.S. males at most ages, except the very young and the very old, has actually been rising. The chief killers today are heart disease, cancer, and violent deaths from accidents, suicide, and homicide. The behavioral component in all these causes is very large, and until now medical care has not been very successful in altering behavior.

The preceding discussion of the problems of cost, access to medical care, and health levels indicates why there is so much concern about health care and so many proposals for changes in its organization and financing. In appraising such proposals it is useful to keep in mind the central economic problem of allocating scarce resources among competing needs. The promises of the planners and the panaceas of the politicians, then, must be seen against the reality of difficult choices.

The Choices We Must Make

An appreciation of the inevitability of choice is necessary before one can begin to make intelligent plans for health-care policy, but more than that is required. Some grasp of the variety of levels and kinds of choices we make is also essential. All of us, as individuals, are constantly confronted with choices that affect our health. In addition, some choices must be exercised collectively, through government.

HEALTH OR OTHER GOALS?

The most basic level of choice is between health and other goals. While social reformers tell us that "health is a right," the realization of that "right" is always less than complete because some of the resources that could be used for health are allocated to other purposes. This is true in all countries regardless of economic system, regardless of the way medical care is organized, and regardless of the level of affluence. It is true in the communist Soviet Union and in welfare-state Sweden, as well as in our own capitalist society. No country is as healthy as it could be; no country does as much for the sick as it is technically capable of doing.

The constraints imposed by resource limitations are manifest not only in the absence of amenities, delays in receipt of care, and minor inconveniences; they also result in loss of life. The grim fact is that no nation is wealthy enough to avoid all avoidable deaths. The truth of this proposition is seen most clearly in the case of accidental deaths. For instance, a few years ago an airplane crashed in West Virginia with great loss of life. Upon investigation it was found that the crash could have been avoided if the airport had been properly equipped with an electronic instrument-landing device. It was further found that the airport was fully aware of this deficiency and that a recommendation for installation of such equipment had been made several months before the crash—and turned down because it was decided that the cost was too high.

Traffic accidents take more than fifty thousand lives each year in the United States, and because so many of the victims are young or middle-aged adults,* the attendant economic loss is very high. As a first approximation, the relative economic cost of death can be estimated from the discounted future earnings of the deceased if he had lived. According to such calculations, the death of a man at twenty or thirty is far more costly than death at seventy. Many of these traffic deaths could be prevented, but some of the most effective techniques, such as the elimination of left turns, are extremely expensive to implement. The same is true of deaths from other causes—many of them are preventable if we want to devote resources to that end. The yield may be small, as in the case of a hyperbaric chamber † that costs several million dollars and probably saves a few lives each year, but the possibilities for such costly interventions are growing. Current examples include renal dialysis, organ transplants, and open-heart surgery. Within limits set by genetic factors, climate, and other natural forces, every nation chooses its own death rate by its evaluation of health compared with other goals.

But surely health is more important than anything else! Is it? Those who take this position are fond of contrasting our unmet health needs with the money that is "wasted" on cosmetics, cigarettes, pet foods, and the like. "Surely," it is argued, "we can afford better health if we can afford colored telephones." But putting the question in this form is misleading. For one thing, there are other goals, such as justice, beauty, and knowledge, which also clearly remain unfulfilled because of resource limitations. In theory, our society is committed to providing a speedy and fair trial to all persons accused of crimes. "Justice delayed is justice denied." In practice, we know that our judicial system is rife with delays and with pretrial settlements that produce convictions of innocent people and let guilty ones escape with minor punishment. We also know that part of the answer to getting a fairer and more effective judicial system is to devote more resources to it.

What about beauty, natural or manmade? How often do we read that a beautiful stand of trees could be saved if a proposed road were rerouted or some other (expensive) change made? How frequently do we learn that a beautiful new building design has been rejected in favor of a conventional one because of the cost factor? Knowledge also suffers. Anyone who has ever had to meet a budget for an educational or research en-

---

* The motor accident death rate reaches its peak in the late teens and early twenties.

† A specially constructed facility for raising the oxygen content of air in order to treat more effectively certain rare diseases.

terprise knows how resource limitations constrain the pursuit of knowledge.

What about more mundane creature comforts? We may give lip service to the idea that health comes first, but a casual inspection of our everyday behavior with respect to diet, drink, and exercise belies this claim. Most of us could be healthier than we are, but at some cost, either psychic or monetary. Not only is there competition for resources as conventionally measured (i.e., in terms of money), but we are also constantly confronted with choices involving the allocation of our time, energy, and attention. If we are honest with ourselves there can be little doubt that other goals often take precedence over health. If better health is our goal, we can achieve it, but only at some cost.

Stating the problem in this fashion helps to point up the difference between the economist's and the health professional's view of the "optimum" level of health. For the health professional, the "optimum" level is the highest level technically attainable, regardless of the cost of reaching it. The economist is preoccupied with the *social optimum,* however, which he defines as the point at which the value of an additional increment of health exactly equals the cost of the resources required to obtain that increment. For instance, the first few days of hospital stay after major surgery might be extremely valuable for preventing complications and assisting recovery, but at some point the value of each additional day decreases. As soon as the value of an additional day's stay falls below the cost of that day's care, according to the concept of social optimum, the patient should be discharged, even though a longer stay would be desirable if cost were of no concern. The cost reminds us, however, that those resources could be used to satisfy other goals.

The same method of balancing *marginal benefit* and *marginal cost* * is equally applicable in choosing the optimum number of tests and X rays, or in planning the size of a public health program, or in making decisions about auto-safety equipment. Indeed, the concept of margin is one of the most fundamental tools in economics. It applies to the behavior of consumers, investors, business firms, or any other participant in economic life. Most decisions involve choosing between a little more or a little less—in other words, comparing the marginal benefit with the marginal cost. The optimum level is where these are equal and the marginal cost is increasing faster (or decreasing slower) than the marginal benefit.

* Marginal (or incremental) benefits and costs are those resulting from small changes in inputs.

MEDICAL CARE OR OTHER HEALTH PROGRAMS?

But weighing individual and collective preferences for health against each and every other goal is only the first choice. There is also a range of choices within the health field itself. Assume that we are prepared to devote x amount of resources to health. How much, then, should go for medical care and how much for other programs affecting health, such as pollution control, fluoridation of water, accident prevention, and the like? There is no simple answer, partly because the question has rarely been explicitly asked. In principle, the solution is to be found by applying the economist's rule of "equality at the margin." This means relating the incremental yield of any particular program to the incremental cost of the program and then allocating resources so that the yield per dollar of additional input is the same in all programs.

Expenditures for any type of health-related activity, be it a hyperbaric chamber for a hospital or a rat-control program in the ghetto, presumably have some favorable consequences for health which can be evaluated. It is not easy to measure these consequences, but we could do a lot better than we are doing and thus contribute to more rational decision making.

Note that decisions about expanding or contracting particular programs should be based on their respective *marginal* benefits, not their *average* benefits. Thus, while a particular health program—say, screening women once a year for cervical cancer—may be particularly productive (that is, yield a high average benefit per dollar of cost), it does not necessarily follow that expanding that program twofold—for example, screening women twice a year—will be twice as productive. Some other program— say, an antismoking advertising campaign—might not show as high an average return as the screening program, yet the marginal return to *additional* expenditures might exceed that obtainable from additional cancer screening. In the following hypothetical numerical example, cancer screening has a higher average benefit than the antismoking campaign at every expenditure level, but the *incremental* yield from additional expenditures at any level above $40,000 is higher for the antismoking program. Thus if both programs were at the $40,000 level, it would be preferable to expand the second one rather than the first.

An objection frequently raised to such an approach is that "we can't put a price on a human life." One answer to this is that we implicitly put a price on lives whenever we (or our representatives) make decisions about the coverage of a health insurance policy, the installation of a traffic light, the extension of a food stamp program, or innumerable other

Hypothetical Illustration of Distinction between Average and Marginal Benefit

	EXPENDITURES	VALUE OF BENEFITS	AVERAGE BENEFIT PER DOLLAR OF EXPENDITURES	MARGINAL BENEFIT PER DOLLAR OF EXPENDITURES
Cancer Screening Program	$10,000	$ 50,000	$5.00	
				$3.00
	20,000	80,000	4.00	
				2.00
	30,000	100,000	3.33	
				2.00
	40,000	120,000	3.00	
				1.00
	50,000	130,000	2.60	
				.50
	60,000	135,000	2.25	
Antismoking Program	$10,000	$ 30,000	$3.00	
				$2.00
	20,000	50,000	2.50	
				2.00
	30,000	70,000	2.33	
				2.00
	40,000	90,000	2.25	
				1.50
	50,000	105,000	2.10	
				1.00
	60,000	115,000	1.92	

items. A second answer is that it may be possible to choose from among health programs *without* placing a dollar value on human life; it may be sufficient to compare the marginal yield of different programs in terms of lives saved in order to determine the allocation of resources that yields the more significant social benefits.

PHYSICIANS OR OTHER MEDICAL CARE PROVIDERS?

But that is not the whole story. Even if we could make intelligent choices between medical care and other health-related programs, we would still be faced with a significant range of decisions concerning the best way to provide medical care—that is, the best way to spend the medical care dollar. One of the most important of these decisions, which will be discussed in Chapter 3, concerns the respective roles of physicians and such other medical care providers as physician assistants, nurses, clinicians, midwives, and family-health workers. A related set of decisions concerns the optimal mix between human inputs (whether physicians or others) and physical capital inputs, such as hospitals, X-ray equipment, and computers.

In short, if we are concerned with the best way to produce medical care, we must be aware that the solution to the problem requires more than medical expertise. It requires consideration of the relative prices, of various medical care inputs, and of their contribution (again at the margin) to health. The argument that these inputs must be used in some technologically defined proportions is soundly refuted by the evidence from other countries, where many health systems successfully utilize doctors, nurses, hospital facilities, and other health inputs in proportions that differ strikingly from those used in the United States.

HOW MUCH EQUALITY? AND HOW TO ACHIEVE IT?

One of the major choices any society must make is how far to go in equalizing the access of individuals to goods and services. Insofar as this is a question of social choice, one cannot look to economics for an answer. What economic analysis can do is provide some insights concerning why the distribution of income at any given time is what it is, what policies would alter it and at what cost, and what are the economic consequences of different distributions.

Assuming that some income equalization is desired, how is this to be accomplished? Shall only certain goods and services (say, medical care) be distributed equally, or should incomes be made more equal, leaving individuals to decide how they wish to adjust their spending to take account of their higher (or lower) income?

For any given amount of redistribution the welfare of all households is presumably greatest if there is a general tax on the income of some households and grants of income to others, rather than a tax on particular forms of spending or a subsidy for particular types of consumption. Common sense tells us that if a household is offered a choice of either a hundred dollars in cash or a hundred dollars' worth of health care, it ought to prefer the cash, because it can use the entire sum to buy more health care or health insurance (if that is what it wants) or, as is usually the case, increase consumption of many other commodities as well. By the same reasoning, if a household is offered a choice between paying an additional hundred dollars in income tax or doing without a hundred dollars' worth of health care, it will opt for the general tax on income, and then cut back spending on the goods and services that are, in its opinion, most dispensable.

Despite the obvious logic of the foregoing, many nonpoor seem more willing to support a reduction in inequality in the consumption of particular commodities (medical care is a conspicuous example) than toward a general redistribution of income. In England, for instance, everyone is eligible to use the National Health Service, and the great majority of the population gets all of its care from this tax-financed source. At the same time, there is considerable inequality in other aspects of British life, including education and income distribution in general.

Support for the notion that medical care ought to be available to all, regardless of ability to pay, is growing in the United States. There is, however, also growing recognition of marked disparities in housing, legal services, and other important goods and services. Whether these disparities should be attacked piecemeal or through a general redistribution of income is one of the most difficult questions facing the body politic. The pros and cons of this issue as it affects medical care will be discussed in Chapter 6.

TODAY OR TOMORROW

One of the most important choices every individual and every society has to make is between using existing resources to satisfy current desires or applying them to capital-creating activities in anticipation of future needs. Economists call the former *consumption* and the latter *investment*.

This broad concept of investment should not be confused with the narrow use of the term in financial transactions—e.g., the purchase of stock. Broadly speaking, investment takes place when a tree is planted, when a student goes to school, when you brush your teeth, as well as when you build a house, a factory, or a hospital. Any activity that can be expected to confer future benefits is a form of investment. (To be sure, sometimes a single activity—such as education—will have elements of consumption—that is, provide current satisfaction—along with those of investment.)

Such investment can be in both physical or human capital.* Thus health is a form of capital: health is wealth. Investment in health takes many forms. Immunization, annual checkups, exercise, and many other activities have current costs but may yield health benefits in the future. Medical education and medical research, both involving expenditures of billions of dollars annually, are prime examples of investment in the health field that results in the diversion of resources (physicians and other personnel) from meeting current needs in order to reap future rewards.

How far should we go in providing for tomorrow at the expense of today? As with all economic decisions, price plays a role here, too. Specifically, in making decisions concerning health investments, we must somehow take into account the fact that people discount the future com-

* The development of the theory of human capital by Gary Becker, Jacob Mincer, T. W. Schultz, and others and its application in fields such as education and health is one of the great advances in economics in the past quarter-century.

pared with the present. Using the concept of the special kind of price called *rate of interest* or *rate of return* answers that need.

No investment in health is undertaken unless the investor believes it will yield a satisfactory rate of return. Health professionals frequently despair over the failure of some people to invest in their own health; such behavior, they assert, is irrational. But this need not be the case. If a person discounts the future at a high rate, as evidenced by a willingness to pay 20 or 30 percent annual interest for consumer loans or installment credit, it would not be rational for him to make an investment in health that had an implicit return of only 15 percent.

It is abundantly clear that people differ in their attitudes toward the future; that is, they have different *rates of time discount.** The reasons for these differences are not known. They may be related to perceptions about how certain the future is, and they may depend upon how strongly rooted is one's sense of the past. Young children, for instance, characteristically live primarily in the present; they lack both a historical perspective and a vision of the future. Thus it is often difficult to get children to undertake some unpleasant task or to refrain from some pleasureable activity for the sake of a beneficial consequence five or ten years away. Some adults, too, set very little store in the future compared with the present; they have a very high rate of time discount.

Most health-related activities—smoking, exercise, diet, periodic checkups and so forth—have consequences which are realized only after long periods of time. One possible reason for the high correlation between an individual's health and the length of his schooling (see Chapter 2) is that attending to one's health and attending school are both aspects of investment in human capital. Thus the same person who has accumulated a great deal of human capital in the form of schooling may, for the same reasons, have made (or had made for him) substantial investments in health.

YOUR LIFE OR MINE?

Suppose a small private plane crashes in an isolated forest area and no one knows whether the pilot is dead or alive. How much of society's resources will be devoted to searching for him? How much "should" be devoted to the search? If the pilot is a wealthy or prominent man, the search is likely to be longer and more thorough than if he is not. If he is

---

* *Rate of time discount* is a measure of how willing people are to incur present costs or defer present benefits in order to obtain some benefit in the future.

wealthy, his family's command over private resources will make the difference; if he is a prominent government official, it is likely that publicly owned resources will be utilized far more readily than if the pilot were unknown and poor.

We see in this simple example one of the basic dilemmas of modern society. On the one hand, we believe that all people should be treated as equals, especially in matters of life or death. Against this we have what Raymond Aron calls the imperative "to produce as much as possible through mastery of the forces of nature," [2] a venture requiring differentiation, hierarchy, and inevitably unequal treatment. The problem arises in all types of economic systems, and in all systems the response is likely to be similar.

If the family of a wealthy man wants to devote his (or their) wealth to searching for him, thereby increasing his probability of survival, is there any reason why the rest of society should object? (If the family used their command over resources for some frivolous consumption, would anyone else be better off?) Suppose, however, that instead of a plane crash the threat of death came from an ordinarily fatal disease? Would the same answers apply? The capacity of medical science to intervene near the point of death is growing rapidly. Such interventions are often extremely costly and have a low probability of long-term success—but sometimes they work. Whose life should be saved? The wealthy man's? The senator's? Society cannot escape this problem any more than it can avoid facing the other choices we have discussed.

A related dilemma concerns the allocation of resources, either for research or care, among different diseases and conditions. The potential for social conflict here is high because the relative importance of different diseases is perceived differentially by groups according to their income level, race, age, location, and other characteristics.

A particularly striking example of this problem is sickle-cell anemia, a disease which in the United States affects primarily blacks. Recently there has been a substantial increase in the amount of funds available for research on this as-yet-incurable disease, primarily as a result of the growing political strength of the black community.

Many other diseases have a particularly high incidence among specific groups. Thus cigarette smokers have a much greater stake in research or services for lung cancer than do nonsmokers. And in the case of occupation-related diseases, the interests of workers and employers directly affected are much greater than those of the general public.

Economics cannot provide final answers to these difficult problems of social priorities, but it can help decision makers think more rationally about them. In allocating funds for medical research, for instance, economic reasoning can tell the decision maker what kind of information he ought to have and how to arrange that information so as to find the probable relative value of various courses of action.

Contrary to the opinion of many medical researchers, the criterion of "scientific merit" is not sufficient to form the basis for a rational allocation of medical research funds. Certainly decision makers should consider the relative importance the scientific community attaches to particular problems. But other kinds of information—such as the number of persons affected by a particular disease, the economic cost of the attendant morbidity * and mortality, and the cost of delivering preventive or therapeutic services if research is successful—should also be considered. The last item is particularly important when funding applied as opposed to basic research, because the development of a "cure" that is enormously expensive to implement probably has a low return and creates many serious social problems as well. For example, if a cure for cancer were discovered tomorrow but cost $150,000 per case to implement, the resulting controversies over the method of financing and the selection of cases to be cured might be so great as to make one view the cure as a mixed blessing.

THE JUNGLE OR THE ZOO?

One of the central choices of our time, in health as in other areas, is finding the proper balance between individual (personal) and collective (social) responsibility. If too much weight is given to the former, we come close to recreating the "jungle"—with all the freedom and all the insecurity that the jungle implies. On the other hand, emphasizing social responsibility can increase security, but it may be the security of the "zoo"—purchased at the expense of freedom. Over the centuries man has wrestled with this choice, and in different times and different places the emphasis has shifted markedly.

Nineteenth-century Western society idealized individual responsibility. This was particularly true in England and the United States, where a system of political economy was developed based on the teachings of Locke, Smith, Mill, and other advocates of personal freedom. As this system was superimposed on a religious foundation which exalted hard work and thrift, the result was an unprecedented acceleration in the rate of growth

---

* *Morbidity* is the extent of an illness in the population.

of material output. Each man's energies were bent to enhancing his own welfare, secure in the knowledge that he and his family would enjoy the fruits of his efforts and in the conviction that he was obeying God's will.

That the system worked imperfectly goes without saying. That the outcome for some individuals was harsh and brutal has been recounted in innumerable novels, plays, histories, and sociological treatises. But when set against man's previous history, the material benefits and the accompanying relaxation of social, religious, and political rigidities were extraordinary.

By the beginning of this century, however, reactions to such uninhibited "progress" had arisen in most Western countries. Since then a variety of laws have been passed seeking to protect individuals from the most severe consequences of unbridled individualism. Laissez-faire is dead, and only a few mourn its passing. In fact, the attitude of many intellectuals and popular writers on political economy seems to have swung to the other extreme. In the 1920s R. H. Tawney, surveying the eighteenth- and nineteenth-century attitudes toward poverty, wrote that "the most curious feature in the whole discussion . . . was the resolute refusal to admit that society had any responsibility for the causes of distress." [3] Some future historian, in reviewing mid-twentieth-century social reform literature, may note an equally curious feature—a "resolute refusal" to admit that individuals have any responsibility for their own distress.

From the idealization of individual responsibility and the neglect of social responsibility we have gone, in some quarters, to the denial of individual responsibility and the idealization of social responsibility. The rejection of any sense of responsibility for one's fellow men is inhuman, but the denial of any individual responsibility is also dehumanizing.

Moreover, with respect to health such a view runs contrary to common sense. As Henry Sigerist, an ardent advocate of socialized medicine and other expressions of social responsibility, has observed: "The state can protect society very effectively against a great many dangers, but the cultivation of health, which requires a definite mode of living, remains, to a large extent, an individual matter." [4] Most of us know this is true from personal experience. As long as we believe that we have some control over our own choices, we will reject theories that assume that "society" is always the villain.

A great deal of what has been written recently about "the right to health" is very misleading. It suggests that society has a supply of "health" stored away which it can give to individuals and that it is only the niggardliness of the Administration or the ineptness of Congress or the selfishness of physicians that prevents this from happening. Such a view ignores the truth of Douglas Colman's observation that "positive health is not something that one human can hand to or require of another. Positive health can be achieved only through intelligent effort on the part of each individual. Absent that effort, health professionals can only insulate the individual from the more catastrophic results of his ignorance, self-indulgence, or lack of motivation." [5] The notion that we can spend our way to better health is a vast oversimplification. At present there is very little that medical care can do for a lung that has been overinflated by smoking, or for a liver that has been scarred by too much alcohol, or for a skull that has been crushed in a motor accident.

The assertion that *medical care* is (or should be) a "right" is more plausible. In a sense medical care is to health what schooling is to wisdom. No society can truthfully promise to make everyone wise, but society can make schooling freely available; it can even make it compulsory. Many countries have taken a similar position with respect to medical care, although the compulsory aspects are sharply limited. Our government could, if it wished to, come close to assuring access to medical care for all persons. But no government now or in the foreseeable future can assure health to every individual.

Because utilization of medical care is voluntary, the mere availability of a service does not guarantee its use. The discovery of polio vaccine was rightly hailed as a significant medical advance, but in recent years there has been a sharp drop in the proportion of children receiving such vaccinations. At present, probably one-third of the children between 1 and 4 years of age are not adequately protected. The problem is particularly acute in poverty areas of major cities, where as many as half the children probably are without full protection against polio. There are undoubtedly many difficulties facing poor families that make it more difficult for them to bring their children to be vaccinated, but the service itself is available in most cities.

Another example of a gap between availability and utilization comes from a study of dental services covered by group health insurance. The study reported that white-collar workers and their families used significantly more preventive services than their blue-collar counterparts even though the insurance policy provided full coverage for all participants. The only dental service used more frequently by blue-collar families was tooth extraction—a procedure which is usually a consequence of failure to use preventive services, such as repair of caries.

If people have a *right* to care, do they also have an *obligation* to use it?

This complex question will assume greater significance as the collective provision of care increases. In our zeal to raise health levels, however, we must be wary of impinging on other valuable "rights," including the right to be left alone. Strict control over a man's behavior might well result in increased life expectancy, but a well-run zoo is still a zoo and not a worthy model for mankind.

As we attempt to formulate responsible policy for health and medical care, we should strive for the balance advocated by Rabbi Hillel more than two thousand years ago when he said, "If I am not for myself, who will be for me, but if I am for myself alone, what am I?"

The preceding discussion of the choices that face our society helps to put the major problems of health and medical care in proper perspective. These problems, as perceived by the public, are high cost, poor access, and inadequate health levels. In order to attack them intelligently, we must recognize the scarcity of resources and the need to allocate them as efficiently as possible. We must recognize that we can't have everything. In short, we need to adopt an economic point of view.

The discussion of choices also reveals some of the limits of economics in dealing with the most fundamental questions of health and medical care. These questions are ultimately ones of value: What value do we put on saving a life? on reducing pain? on relieving anxiety? How do these values change when the life at stake is a relative's? a neighbor's? a stranger's?

Nearly all human behavior is guided by values. Given the values, together with information about the relationship between technological means and ends, about inputs and constraints (resources, time, money), economics shows how these values can be maximized. To the extent that individual behavior attempts to maximize values, economic theory also possesses significant power to predict behavior. If and when values change and these changes are not taken into account, however, economics loses a good deal of its predictive power. The most difficult part of the problem is that values may change partly as a result of the economic process itself.

According to one well-known definition, "economics is the science of means, not of ends": it can explain how market prices are determined, but not how basic values are formed; it can tell us the consequences of various alternatives, but it cannot make the choice for us. These limitations will be with us always, for economics can never replace morals or ethics.

CHAPTER 2

Who Shall Live?

Who shall live and who shall die, who shall
fulfill his days and who shall die before his
time. . . .
Yom Kippur (Day of Atonement)
prayer book

Good health and long life have traditionally been among the most prized
goals of mankind. In every age and in every land there have been significant efforts to postpone death, whether through sacred dance and song,
the imbibing of magic potions, or the application of the most modern
medical techniques.

Despite these efforts, for most of man's history life was short and uncertain. It depended primarily upon such basic economic conditions as
adequate supplies of food, water, and shelter. Medicine men and healers
of all kinds were abundant, but apart from the sympathy and psychological support that they may have provided, it is doubtful that they did
more good than harm. Historians of medicine now mostly agree that it
was not until well into the twentieth century that the average patient had
better than a fifty-fifty chance of being helped by the average physician.

Today, at least in developed countries, the situation is markedly different. First, there is a core of medical knowledge that contributes greatly
to life expectancy. This knowledge is widely diffused throughout the
United States, Europe, Japan, and Oceania and is even reducing mortality
in less developed countries, including some with very low standards of
living. That portion of medicine which is most dramatically effective,
such as vaccines and antiinfectious drugs, is relatively simple and inexpensive to administer. But once basic levels of medical sophistication,
personnel, and facilities become available, additional inputs of medical
care do not have much effect. In other words, the total contribution of

modern medical care to life expectancy is large, but over the considerable range of variation in the quantity of care observed in developed countries, the marginal contribution is small.

A second profound change is the disappearance of the traditional relationship between life expectancy and per capita income. As with medical care, a certain minimum level of income is important, but beyond that there is little correlation between mortality and income across and within industrialized countries.

These themes comprise the focus of this chapter, which also highlights the importance of "life-style" and personal behavior as major determinants of "who shall live."

The First Year of Life

The human infant is an exceptionally vulnerable creature. It comes into the world with a precarious hold on life; unassisted, it cannot live for more than a week. This extreme dependency on others persists much longer in humans than in any other species and is the major reason why human beings require an elaborate social structure.

Consideration of the complex support mechanisms required for human survival reveals the fallacies in the arguments of extreme libertarians and romantics. The former assume that man is autonomous, beholden to no one, answerable to no one, capable of rationally determining his own fate on the basis of contractual relationships with other autonomous souls. In fact, each of us owes our very life to others. Without the care given by family or friends, or provided by the church or state, we would not be alive to propound theories of human independence.

Rousseau and other romantics have viewed man as being born into a free and golden future only to be shackled by family and society. The truth is that throughout history most men have been born into a promise of early death. The more "simple" the environment, the more certain was it that the promise would be fulfilled. Even when the infant's mother survived childbirth (until this century the risk of maternal mortality was not small) and was willing to care for her child as best she could, prospects for its survival were not good.

Under primitive conditions it is not unusual for one out of every two newborns to die before the age of one; for many families the survival rate is much worse. Enrico Caruso, the great Italian tenor, was the eighteenth child born to his poor Neapolitan parents but the first to survive beyond infancy. According to one estimate, the infant mortality rate (the number of deaths in the first year of life per 1,000 live births) for Europe's *ruling families* was over 200 in the sixteenth and seventeenth centuries.[1] The rate for families of lesser means must have been appreciably higher, for, as indicated below, chances for survival improved markedly with increases in living standards.

By the nineteenth century, infant mortality for Europe's ruling families was down to 70. But in New York City the rate for the general population was still as high as 140 per 1,000 live births in 1900. With rising living standards the chances of infant survival began to improve markedly. Between 1900 and 1930 the infant mortality in the United States fell at an annual rate of 2.5 percent to 65 per 1,000, and similar declines were experienced by all other countries undergoing rapid economic development. Most of this decline was the result of a sharp reduction in deaths from what physicians call the "pneumonia-diarrhea" complex.* In New York City infant mortality from this cause fell from 75 in 1900 to about 17 in 1930.

It is important to realize that medical care played almost no role in this decline. While we do not know the precise causes, it is believed that rising living standards, the spread of literacy and education, and a substantial fall in the birth rate all played a part. Some writers also give credit to chlorination of the water supply and the pasteurization of milk, but there is considerable debate about the quantitative importance of these measures. The "pneumonia-diarrhea" complex is still a major killer of infants on some American Indian reservations, and one well-studied attempt to bring all the skills of medicine to bear on this problem was, on the whole, unsuccessful.[2]

The mid-1930s saw the introduction of sulfonamide, the first of the great antimicrobial drugs. During the fifteen years that followed, many other potent antiinfectious drugs were discovered, and the rate of decline in infant mortality improved substantially. Between 1935 and 1950 the infant death rate fell by 4.3 percent annually, an appreciable acceleration over the decline of preceding decades. During this period both medical advances and rising living standards contributed to the reduction in infant deaths.

By 1950, about 70 percent of all infant deaths were occurring in the

---

* A common cause of death among infants living in poor, unsanitary conditions is internal infection leading to diarrhea which so weakens the infant that it contracts fatal pneumonia.

first month after birth, compared to only 40 percent in 1900. Such "neo-natal" deaths, which are usually related to prematurity, congenital malformations, and problems associated with delivery, have proved less responsive to the growth of real income and to medical advances. It is not surprising, therefore, that beginning about 1950 there was a marked deterioration in the rate of decline of infant mortality. Between 1950 and 1965, the average annual decline was only 1.1 percent. During that period there was a great deal of talk about having reached some minimum level below which it would be very difficult to go.

Then, fairly suddenly, infant mortality began to drop again sharply, and since 1965 the rate of decline has been over 4 percent annually. By 1971 the U.S. rate had fallen to 19.2. The reasons for this marked improvement are not known. One possible explanation is that there was a substantial decrease in "unwanted" births after 1965 as a result of improved contraception and more liberal abortion laws. Indeed, the U.S. birth rate fell from 19.4 per 1,000 population in 1965 to 15.1 in 1973. The birth rate for births of fourth order or higher (i.e., those in which the mother has had at least three other children), which present a greater risk, fell by 50 percent. There can be little doubt that a "wanted" child will receive better care, both during pregnancy and after birth, than one that is "unwanted."

Furthermore, beginning in the late 1960s more was done to combat infant deaths by extending maternal and infant care services to families that had not previously been as well served. In some particular settings substantial reductions in infant deaths were achieved through the use of intensive-care units for premature babies, which have greatest risk. How important such additional medical care was in affecting the overall trend, however, is not known.

PREMATURITY

Numerous studies of infant mortality have shown that low-birth-weight babies (defined as under 5½ pounds) face considerably higher risk of death than those of normal weight. One comprehensive report issued by the federal government's National Center for Health Statistics states that "such infants have thirty times the risk of dying in the first four weeks of life compared with infants weighing more than 2500 grams [5½ pounds] at birth." [3] The correlation between low birth weight and post-neonatal deaths is much weaker, but according to one authority, "the premature infant not only has a poorer chance of surviving, . . . but if he does survive he has a higher risk of having a handicapping condition." [4]

We know surprisingly little about the specific reasons for short gestation (premature delivery) or low birth weight. The physical condition of the mother is undoubtedly a major factor, and this in turn is probably related to her diet, to whether she smokes or not, and to other environmental influences. Some of the variables found to be associated with low birth weight and infant mortality in general are income, schooling, race, and prenatal care.

INCOME

Traditionally, as income goes up, infant mortality goes down. In recent years, however, this relationship has become weaker for two primary reasons. First, the relationship was always much stronger for post-neonatal deaths (those occurring in the first year but after the first month) than for neonatal deaths. But today, as noted earlier, infant mortality in developed countries is concentrated in the first month.

A second reason is that once income rises to a level that assures adequate nutrition, housing, water, and waste disposal, further increases in income have much less significance for life expectancy. Most American families have passed that minimum level. A study published in 1972 and based on 1964–66 data showed appreciable declines in white infant death rates as family income rose from under $3,000 to the $5,000–7,000 range. Above that income level, however, there was no further decline with rising income.[5]

A third possible reason for a weakening of this relationship is a wider diffusion of medical care throughout the population. The extent of this diffusion and its effectiveness are, however, open to question. It is relevant to note that large differences in infant mortality among socioeconomic classes in England and Scotland persist despite the existence of free national health services available to all segments of the population.

SCHOOLING

Numerous health studies have shown that length of schooling is one of the most important correlates of health. This is true regardless of the measure of health (mortality, morbidity, or days lost from work) and regardless of whether the data are for individuals or population averages. Infant mortality also conforms to this pattern: in the United States, infants born to white mothers with eight years of schooling or less have almost double the mortality rate of those born to mothers with twelve or more years of schooling. (The correlation with length of father's schooling is also very strong.)

There is, of course, also a very strong correlation between schooling and income, making it difficult to estimate the separate effects of each. There does, however, seem to be some independent contribution to infant health both from schooling and from income. Among *adults* the relationship between schooling and health is much stronger, although, as we shall see in the next section, the effect of income is weak.

RACE

If one wanted a single simple index of the cumulative effects of hundreds of years of prejudice and oppression, the fact that in the United States black infant mortality is almost double the white rate would serve as well as any.

Some investigators believe that this difference can be explained mostly or entirely by a few socioeconomic variables; others report data that refute this view. It does seem clear that the excess of black over white infant death rates is greater than can be explained by *current* differences in income or schooling. As an illustration, *black* infant mortality in New York and California is two-thirds greater than *white* infant mortality in Arkansas and South Carolina, although income and schooling levels are comparable.

Low birth weight is the major factor in black infant mortality (as it is in white). Why so many black infants should be born weighing under 5½ pounds is not known. Diet, rest, and other aspects of care during pregnancy are probably important. It may also be true that the deprived conditions of many black families a generation ago are still taking their toll today. Scientists have shown with animal experiments that nutritional deprivation of females in infancy can affect their subsequent reproductive performance, even when they are provided with adequate diet as adults. Sir Dugald Baird, Regius Professor of Obstetrics and Gynecology at the University of Aberdeen, Scotland, has suggested that this mechanism may also be at work among humans. Finding that infant deaths from malformation of the central nervous system rose sharply in 1946 in first births to women in the semiskilled and unskilled occupational classes, he concluded that "the increase in the death rate could not be traced to any factor operating during the mother's pregnancy, but seemed to be related to the year in which the mother was born. For example, the rates were highest in women born between 1928 and 1936, the years during which the economic depression was at its worst." [6]

Although infant mortality for American blacks has declined over time, just as it has for American whites, the relative differential has not changed much. This is somewhat surprising because, given the diminishing importance of income on infant mortality as income rises, one might have expected the infant mortality gap to narrow even though relative income differentials have remained about the same. One possibility is that reported black infant death rates for earlier decades were understated because many deaths went unreported. Inequality of access to medical care is also frequently cited as a reason for the black-white differential in infant mortality. But this inequality is probably less now than in earlier decades, and, in any case, the role of medical care in determining the outcome of pregnancy is a subject of considerable controversy.

MEDICAL CARE

Medical care enthusiasts insist that every pregnant woman should consult an obstetrical specialist early in her pregnancy, should continue to visit him frequently, and should be delivered in a hospital with a full range of attending health personnel and elaborate facilities. Skeptics like to point out that in the Netherlands, where a substantial proportion of all births occur at home under the supervision of a midwife, the infant mortality rate is one of the lowest in the world. The Dutch example suggests that *how* medical care is used may be more important than *how much* is used.

The strongest evidence that medical care does have a significant effect on infant mortality appears in a study published by the Institute of Medicine of the National Academy of Sciences. All deliveries in New York City during 1968 were classified according to ethnic group, social and medical risk, and adequacy of medical care during pregnancy and delivery. The study found that within each ethnic-risk category, infant mortality was much lower for the children born to mothers who had adequate care. If the infant mortality rate of children born to mothers with *inadequate* care could have been reduced to the rate of the adequate-care groups, the overall rate for the city would have been 18.4 instead of 21.9 per 1,000 live births.[7] This method of calculation surely overstates the contribution of medical care by assuming that within a given ethnic-risk category *all* of the difference in infant mortality between groups getting different levels of care was in fact due to the care. Furthermore, even a reduction to 18.4 would have left infant mortality in New York City considerably above the rates recorded in Scandinavia and the Netherlands for that same year. Factors other than medical care are clearly of major significance.

Variation in infant mortality rates among various states in this country does not reflect any significant correlation between rate and the number of physicians per capita after account is taken of differences in income, schooling, and similar variables.[8] Such studies, however, deal only with average results. Medical care programs aimed at groups of particularly high risk—very young girls, women of low socioeconomic status, and the like—have in recent years been able to show substantial reductions in neonatal mortality. Therein may lie an important clue to the role of medical care. For very risky pregnancies, the quantity and quality of care available may be critical; for pregnancies that present little risk (that is, among well-educated, well-fed mothers, neither very young nor very old) the quantity and quality of care may be of minor importance, except insofar as poor care can be worse than none at all.

The possibility that medical care can do harm as well as good is a real and growing one. As the tools of medical intervention—drugs, surgery, radiotherapy, and the like—become more powerful, the risks of iatrogenic disease (ill health arising out of the medical care process itself) increase. For example, two decades ago it was standard procedure in the best hospitals to administer oxygen to low-birth-weight babies. It is now believed that this practice was responsible for considerable retrolental fibroplasia, which leads to blindness.

It is easy to assemble a catalog of horror stories about misdirected medical efforts, but this, too, can be misleading. It is obvious that as knowledge grows in medicine, some of the presently accepted therapies will be found to be useless or even harmful. It is also obvious that mistakes are made in every field and by every profession. What is required is some sense of balance so that the contribution of medical care is not oversold and so that both patient and provider realize the wisdom in the ancient warning to physicians, "Do no harm."

INTERNATIONAL COMPARISONS

What light, if any, do the preceding considerations throw on the large international differences in infant mortality that presently exist? If we compare developed countries with less developed ones, they explain a great deal. But if we confine our attention to differences among developed countries, they don't provide much help. The lowest rates, averaging about 13 per 1,000 in 1970, are found in the Netherlands, Scandinavia, Australia, New Zealand, and Japan, all countries having relatively high levels of income and schooling. Yet in the United States, which has even higher income and education levels, the rate in 1970 was almost 20 per 1,000. The rate for U.S. whites was 17.4; and for whites in

North Dakota, the most favorable state in the country, but certainly not the wealthiest, the rate was 14.

In comparison with *large* European countries, however, the United States does not fare so badly: in 1970 the infant mortality in Italy was 29.2, in West Germany 23.6, in the United Kingdom 18.3, and in France 15.1. Our neighbor, Canada, had almost exactly the same rate as we did, and highly industrialized Belgium and Luxembourg were slightly worse off.

It has been popular to use international comparisons in infant mortality as a stick with which to beat the American medical profession. Some of this criticism has been constructive. It has shattered the smug and incorrect assumption that "Americans have the best health in the world." It has also helped to dramatize gross disparities within this country. Perhaps most important, it has forced some leaders in medicine to begin focusing on health *outcomes* as the criteria of "quality," instead of preoccupying themselves with credentials, expensive equipment, and other ingredients of the *process* of care.

If one examines the data closely, however, the claim that the wide disparities between the U.S. infant mortality rate and rates elsewhere are primarily attributable to deficiencies in American medicine becomes unpersuasive. Many of these differences are of long standing. The U.S. rate was substantially higher than the rate in the Netherlands or New Zealand, for example, long before medical care could have made much difference either way. Even the presence of free national health services does not guarantee low rates, as the United Kingdom data indicate.

In the final analysis, we must recognize the critical importance of the mother—the care she takes of herself during pregnancy and the care she provides for the child after birth. Effective family planning—that is, the bearing of children when and in the number that the parents want—is surely also important in achieving low infant mortality. Just how religion, culture, the political, economic, and social structure, medical care, and other forces combine to affect the outcome of pregnancy remains to be determined.

INFANT HEALTH

Mere survival is not, of course, everything. We want to raise children who will be equipped mentally and physically to contribute to the world's work and to share in the pleasures life has to offer. Their capacity to do this as adults may be dramatically affected by what happens to them during the first year of life. As Dr. Walsh McDermott notes: "We are beginning to get a solid scientific base for the concept that mental capacity and the capability to be educated can be permanently impaired by early infancy." [9]

There is a widespread belief that reductions in infant and child mortality keep alive persons with "weak constitutions" or other health impairments, thus increasing the health problems and death rates of the population when they become adults. A contrary point of view, however, should be considered. It can be argued that the same forces, socioeconomic and medical, that reduce mortality among infants and children also strengthen the health of those who would have survived anyway, albeit marginally. Mortality can be viewed as one end of a distribution of health conditions, and reductions in mortality can be viewed as part of a more general process which shifts the entire distribution in the direction of better health.

A long-term British study of more than seventeen thousand births has shown that not only do low-birth-weight babies have less chance of surviving, but those that do survive are more likely to have other problems (behavior, learning ability, etc.) by the time they reach school age. Thus, the same measures that offer the most promise for lowering infant mortality (improved nutrition, reduction in cigarette smoking, better timing and spacing of births, and the like) will probably raise rather than lower the quality of life for those who survive.

One thing is clear. The decrease in U.S. infant mortality over the years has *not* resulted in higher death rates among children or adults. Nor does the lower infant mortality in Scandinavia mean that death rates there exceed those of the United States at subsequent ages. The next section provides a closer look at the factors associated with adult mortality.

Three Score and Ten

The days of our years are three score years and ten.

Psalms 90 : 10

According to the Bible, the normal life span for humans was 70 years. This was not an absolute upper limit: the psalmist did hold out the possibility of 80 years "by reason of strength." Neither was this life expectancy in the technical sense of the term (the average number of years lived by all persons born at a particular time). Indeed, life expectancy in the biblical era was probably less than 35 years. A more plausible interpretation is that this was the "expected" life span in the sense that people could not expect to live beyond that age, assuming they were among the fortunate ones who survived the perils of infancy, childhood, and young adulthood.

In this sense the estimate has remarkable force, even today. In the United States more than half of those who reach the age of 70 will die during the subsequent decade, and after 80 the death rate becomes very high indeed. The great increase in life expectancy that has occurred in developed countries over the past two hundred years has been the result primarily of reductions in death rates at early ages, not in the lengthening of the "normal" life span.

Life expectancy is now almost exactly 70 years in the United States, and slightly higher in some other countries. Comparison of life tables from various countries at various times suggests that as life expectancy rises from 35 to 70, about four-fifths of the increase is contributed by reductions in death rates under 70 and only one-fifth comes from reductions in death rates at age 70 or above.

We have already reviewed the significant reductions in infant mortality that have been achieved in this century. The fall in death rates for children over the age of 1 year has been even more impressive. For ages 1 through 4 the decline has been almost 5 percent annually; this means that on the average the death rate for this group has been halved every 15 years since 1900. For the 5-to-14-year-old group the annual decrease has been at about 3.5 percent, more rapid than the annual 3 percent decline in infant mortality over the same period.

The decrease in the child death rate has been particularly striking since the 1930s as the result of advances in medicine. One by one the dread diseases of childhood—pneumonia, influenza, diphtheria, typhoid fever, polio, and so on—have succumbed to immunization or powerful new drug therapies. The reduction in parental grief and fear brought about by rising living standards and medical advances surely stands as one of the greatest achievements of industrial society. Today, the risk of death in all the years between 1 and 20 combined is appreciably less than in the first year alone!

Although most Americans can now expect to reach the age of 70, about four in ten do not. An examination of the causes of death in adolescents and young adults (ages 15–24), in early middle age (35–44), and in late middle age (55–64) will give us a clearer understanding of the role economic and social factors play in early death and what medical care can and cannot do to prevent them.

YOUTH: AGES 15–24

Adolescents and young adults are on the whole extremely healthy. Their strength, energy, capacity to go without sleep, withstand the elements, and shake off minor infirmities are the envy of their elders. In the United States their chances of dying from "normal" diseases are very small indeed. Unfortunately, their overall probability of death is not that small, especially for males. Because the sex differential in mortality is so large in the United States, it is given an extended discussion later in this chapter. For the moment we shall concentrate on *male* deaths, highlighting the differences associated with age and color.*

Suppose we consider 100,000 American males age 15. The following figures show how many will die from selected causes and all causes before they reach the age of 25, assuming that the latest available death rates (1968) continue unchanged. †

Expected Number of Deaths per 100,000
from Ages 15 through 24

CAUSE OF DEATH	WHITE MALES	NONWHITE MALES
Motor accidents	807	661
Other accidents	310	545
Suicide	113	82
Neoplasms	103	82
Homicide	75	771
Influenza and pneumonia	29	58
Heart diseases	28	69
All causes	1,690	2,777

The most striking aspect of these data is the tremendous loss of life from accidents, especially motor accidents. Of every one hundred thousand American males age 15, about 1,100 will lose their lives in ac-

* The data are for whites and nonwhites; blacks account for about 95 percent of nonwhite male deaths at the ages discussed in this chapter.

† All the United States mortality statistics presented in the following pages are calculated from data in Department of Health, Education, and Welfare *Vital Statistics of the United States,* vol. 2, *Mortality,* Part A, Table 1–9: Death Rates for 69 Selected Causes, by 10-Year Age Groups, Color, and Sex (Washington, D.C.: Government Printing Office, 1968).

cidents before reaching 25; more than half of those deaths will involve automobiles. "Epidemic" is almost too weak a word to describe this situation; when polio was at its worst, the death rate from that disease among males ages 15 to 24 was less than one twentieth as high. To be sure, polio causes illness as well as death, but the disabilities and impairments resulting from auto accidents also far exceed the number killed.

Also striking is the fact that *homicide* is the leading cause of death among young black males; indeed, it continues to be a significant cause of death right up through middle age. Thus if you are a 15-year-old black American male, your chances of being a homicide victim sometime before you reach 55 are thirty out of a thousand—more than triple the risk of your dying from tuberculosis.

Among young white males, suicide claims almost as many victims as do neoplasms (cancer and related illnesses) and heart disease combined. When one considers that many auto deaths might well be classified as suicide, it is apparent that the self-destructiveness of young American males is a major health problem today. The suicide rate for young black males is lower than for whites, but has been increasing at a faster rate.

Accidents, suicide, homicide—deaths from violence in one form or another account for *three out of every four* male deaths in this age group. Twenty years ago, the overall death rate among this age group was 15 percent lower, and the rate for violent deaths was 40 percent lower! The increase since then can hardly be attributed to a deterioration in medical care. On the contrary, the treatment of trauma is an area of medicine that has seen particularly significant advances, and there are undoubtedly many victims of violence being saved today who would have died two decades ago.

Numerous theories have been advanced to explain the increase in violent deaths among the young—affluence, the Vietnam war, the decline in religious belief, overly permissive parents, and so on—but the only thing we can be certain of is the increase itself. The suspicion also exists that the self-destructiveness of the young is a symptom of more widespread problems in society at large.

Among all U.S. males, deaths from accidents, suicide, and homicide account for one in every ten. Moreover, the cost to society of these deaths is relatively much greater than those due to other causes because so many of them involve men who had many productive years ahead of them. One frequently used measure of the economic cost of premature death is based on the earnings a man would have realized had he lived, discounted to take account of the fact that a dollar in hand is worth more than the expectation of a dollar sometime in the future. When deaths are weighted in this way, we find that violent deaths accounted for about 25 percent of the economic cost of all male deaths in 1968, compared to only 17 percent of the cost in 1960.

THE PRIME OF LIFE: AGES 35–44

By the time a white male American reaches 35 years of age, his chances of dying in a motor accident are less than half of what they were when he was 20. As we can see from the following figures, however, deaths from violence continue to take a heavy toll, still accounting for almost three out of every ten deaths.

Expected Number of Deaths per 100,000
from Ages 35 through 44

CAUSE OF DEATH	WHITE MALES	NON-WHITE MALES
Heart diseases	999	1,831
Neoplasms	507	803
(lung cancer)	(146)	(285)
Motor accidents	351	596
Other accidents	321	787
Suicide	232	126
Cirrhosis of liver	188	557
Homicide	98	1,146
Influenza and pneumonia	79	422
All causes	3,458	9,203

Diseases of the heart become the number-one cause of death at about age 35 and continue to hold that position from then on. Between ages 35 and 45 approximately one white male out of every hundred dies of a heart attack or related disease. Among black males the figure is approximately two out of a hundred. Neoplasms, especially lung cancer, also become significant among American males at age 35. Cirrhosis of the liver, which is usually attributable to alcoholism, is another major cause of death, exceeding even lung cancer in number of fatal victims. The *total* impact of smoking and drinking on health is thus apparently very great: in addition to the toll from lung cancer and cirrhosis, there are such other effects as the contribution of cigarettes to heart disease and of alcohol to motor accidents.

The differential between non-whites and whites at ages 35–44 is very pronounced; however the rates for non-whites may contain some upward bias because of substantial underenumeration of black males of this age in the Census of Population. The numerator in the death rate ratio (the number of deaths) is more accurately measured than the denominator (the population).

LATE MIDDLE AGE: AGES 55–64

By age 55 the risks of death of American males increase appreciably, as can be seen in the following figures:

Expected Number of Deaths per 100,000
from Ages 55 through 64

CAUSE OF DEATH	WHITE MALES	NONWHITE MALES
Heart diseases	9,940	11,679
Neoplasms	4,697	6,484
(lung cancer)	(1,848)	(2,148)
Cerebrovascular disease	1,196	3,519
Cirrhosis of liver	645	677
Other accidents	508	945
Influenza and pneumonia	505	1,210
Motor accidents	382	628
Suicide	348	120
Homicide	62	508
All causes	21,902	32,607

The chances of dying between ages 55 and 64 are much greater than during the entire period between ages 15 and 55. The major reason is the sharp increase in the chances of succumbing to a heart attack. For white males the death rate from this cause is ten times what it is at ages 35–44, and it accounts for half of all deaths in this age group. The death rate from lung cancer is also more than ten times greater than at ages 35–44. In both cases, behavior *earlier in life* may have started the fatal process, the consequences of which are realized only after several decades.

One unusual difference between whites and nonwhites that is worth noting concerns their respective rates of suicide: the white rate is higher for all three age groups discussed here and the differential tends to increase with age. Such statistics seem to contradict the belief that low income and related problems are major causes of suicide; they suggest that an individual's perception of what constitutes low income may depend as much, or more, on expectations as on absolute dollar amounts.

COMPARISON WITH SWEDEN

Some insight into the health problems of American males can be obtained by comparing the white American death rates already presented with comparable rates for Swedish males, whose rates are among the most favorable in the world.*

Expected Number of Deaths per 100,000
Swedish Males at Various Ages

CAUSE OF DEATH	15–24	35–44	55–64
Heart diseases	22	369	5,293
Neoplasms	110	343	3,159
Cerebrovascular disease	6	76	950
Cirrhosis of liver	—	50	204
Other accidents	228	287	426
Influenza and pneumonia	25	30	310
Motor accidents	335	197	285
Suicide	140	427	520
Homicide	9	4	9
All causes	1,045	2,286	13,410

At ages 15–24, the U.S. rate is 62 percent higher than the Swedish rate; thus the differential between white American males and Swedish males is as large as that between U.S. nonwhites and whites. The major reason for the white American–Swedish differential is the high rate of violent deaths in the United States. Violent deaths show a differential of 83 percent, while the excess of white American over Swedish nonviolent deaths is only 16 percent. The motor accident death rate for white American males, for example, is about two-and-one-half times that for Swedish males.

In the 35–44 age group the pattern changes. The overall differential (white American–Swedish) is still 51 percent, but deaths from violence are only 10 percent greater in the United States. The differential at early middle age is because deaths from heart disease at this point are almost three times as likely in the United States as in Sweden. The excess of deaths from this cause alone accounts for well over half of the total excess in the white male American death rate in the age group. By ages

* The Swedish mortality statistics presented in the following pages are calculated from data in United Nations, *Demographic Yearbook 1967* (New York: United Nations, 1968), Tables 5 and 25.

55–64 the U.S.-Swedish differential is 63 percent, and the U.S. rate for heart diseases is still double the Swedish rate.

A reasonable inference from these comparisons is that the huge mortality difference between the two countries is not connected to the quantity or quality of medical care. At younger ages the difference is mostly attributable to violent deaths, and at middle age the excess is primarily due to heart disease, which is probably related to diet, exercise, smoking, and stress. Given our present state of knowledge, even the most lavish use of medical care probably would not bring the U.S. rate more than a small step closer to the Swedish rate. Of course, as our knowledge grows this situation could change. For instance, some progress is being made in sorting out genetic factors that increase one's likelihood of suffering a heart attack, research that could lead to early detection of susceptible persons and possibly to preventive measures that would reduce their risk. At present, however, the greatest potential for reducing coronary disease, cancer, and the other major killers still lies in altering personal behavior.

THE CORRELATION WITH SCHOOLING

One of the most striking findings of recent research on the socioeconomic determinants of health in the United States is the strong positive correlation between health and length of schooling. This result holds for several types of health indexes ranging from mortality rates to self-evaluation of health status and for comparisons of individuals or populations such as cities or states. It also holds after allowing for the effects of such other variables as income, intelligence, and parents' schooling.

This relationship *may* reflect a chain of causality that begins with good health and results in more schooling. In the most detailed investigation yet undertaken of this subject, however, Michael Grossman has shown that the reverse hypothesis—that more schooling leads to better health—stands up well under a number of critical tests.[10] One of Grossman's most interesting findings concerns the relationship between schooling and premature death. Suppose you were studying, as he was, a group of white men in their thirties and you wanted to predict which ones would die in the next ten years. According to his results, educational attainment would have more predictive power that any other socioeconomic variable—including income and intelligence, two variables that are usually highly correlated with schooling.

Of course, neither Grossman nor anyone else is certain *why* or *how* schooling affects health. It may result in more sensible living habits; it may contribute to more effective use of medical care; or it may help people absorb new information about health and medical care more rapidly.

One possibility is that the completion of formal schooling increases self-confidence and thus reduces the stress associated with many social and work situations. Among business executives, for instance, it would not be surprising if those who work their way up from blue-collar positions are more prone to heart disease and ulcers than those who enter the executive suite via graduate schools of business. Another possibility is that both schooling and health are aspects of investment in human capital. Differences among individuals and their families in willingness and ability to make such investments may help explain the observed relationship.

So far all research on the relationship between health and schooling has utilized retrospective statistical analysis and thus is lacking in the precision and definitiveness of controlled experiments. Such research has nevertheless suggested an important connection between an individual's behavior and his health. Additional support for this view emerges from a consideration of male–female differences in mortality, the subject of the following section.

The "Weaker" Sex

Judged by that harshest and in some sense most significant of all tests, the ability to survive, females are clearly much stronger than males. In all developed countries and at all ages the female death rate is appreciably below that of the male. This fact has significant economic and social consequences. For instance, by age 60, when female life expectancy is still 20 years, more than one out of five American females is a widow and another 10 percent are single or divorced with very little prospect of remarriage. An exploration of the extent of and variations in the sex differential in mortality rates at different ages and for different populations provides new insights into some current major health problems in the United States and their relation to economic and social factors.

THE AGE PATTERN

The excess of male over female deaths varies considerably with age. The differential is manifest even before birth, with the fetal death

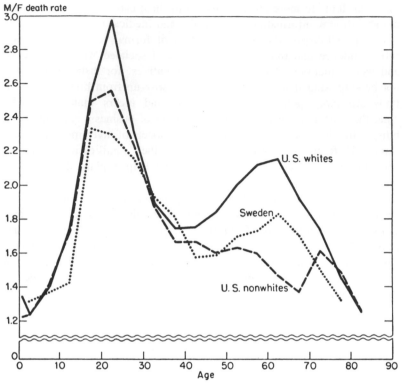

Figure I
Male-Female Death Rate Ratio, 1967–68

SOURCES: U. S. Public Health Service, *Vital Statistics of the United
States,* vol. 2, *Mortality* (Washington, D.C.: Government Printing
Office, 1967, 1968) and U. S. Public Health Service, *Statistical Abstract of Sweden* (Washington, D.C.: Government Printing Office,
1971).

rate of males running about 10 percent above the rate of females. Since
this differential emerges before the child's sex is known, there are clearly
some biological differences at work in addition to the cultural and social
factors that come into play after birth.

In the United States infant mortality among males is about one-third
higher than for females, and throughout childhood the excess is in the
range of one-third to one-half (see Figure I). At age 15 the differential
starts to rise sharply. Males between 15 and 24 have a death rate which is

almost triple that of females, largely because of the high rate of violent deaths among males that we previously described. Indeed, if we exclude violent deaths, the differential is only 40 percent—about the same range as for infants and children.

The differential begins to fall during the late 20s and continues to do so until about age 40, at which point the male death rate is about 75 percent above the female rate. Then it begins to rise again, so that by age 60 the probability of death for males is more than double that for females. At this age the high incidence of heart disease in males is the principal cause of the differential. The male death rate from heart diseases is more than triple the female rate, while the differential for all other causes is only about 50 percent.

In old age the differential declines again, but even at ages 80–84 the male death rate is 25 percent above the female rate. Thus, over the entire life span the average differential is more than 75 percent, with the smallest differences at very young and very old ages and the biggest differences in the early 20s and early 60s.

VARIATIONS IN THE PATTERN

Although the basic shape of the age pattern is similar for most populations, there are some significant differences within the United States and between the United States and other countries that are worthy of attention. At young ages the differential of one-third to one-half is fairly constant for all developed countries and for different parts of the United States, suggesting that some inherent biological difference is the primary explanation. After age 15, however, the size of the differential varies considerably, both within the United States and among developed countries. This variation is probably related to an interaction between biological and socioeconomic factors.

As Figure 1 indicates, the male/female mortality ratio in Sweden for young adults is appreciably lower than for U.S. whites. Again, at ages 45–65 the ratio is considerably lower in Sweden. In both cases the high ratio for U.S. whites is attributable to relatively high death rates for males, while female rates approach those found in Sweden. As noted previously, among young males the excess deaths in the United States over Sweden are primarily the result of accidents, and in the 45–65 age group the excess is primarily due to heart disease. Although attempts are frequently made to link the lower mortality rates in Sweden to differences in medical care systems, it seems unlikely that these differences are selective for males and females or that they play a significant role in the lower incidence of accidents and heart disease in Swedish men.

Among U.S. whites the largest sex differentials in mortality are in small southern towns; the smallest are in the suburbs of large northern cities. At young ages, before sex-linked behavioral patterns have had an opportunity to emerge, there are no significant regional differences. For instance, under age 15 the excess of male deaths is 37 percent in the nonmetropolitan counties of the South Atlantic and 36 percent in the metropolitan counties (without central city) of the Middle Atlantic.* At ages 15–64, however, the differentials are 137 percent and 82 percent, respectively. As in the case of the United States–Sweden comparison, it is extremely unlikely that these differences in male/female ratios can be attributed to medical care, income, or the like. The most promising hypothesis is that sex-role differentiation in work and consumption varies sufficiently from one population to another to have significant implications regarding mortality.

The above data are consistent with the view that as female life-styles become more like those of males, differentials in mortality narrow. One study that foreshadows such a trend examined unexpected deaths from heart attacks. In the decade 1949–59 the ratio of male to female deaths of this type was 12 to 1, but in the period 1967–71 the ratio was only 4 to 1. In the recent period a majority of the females who died of heart disease were heavy smokers, while only 10 percent had not smoked at all.[11]

MARITAL STATUS

One particularly interesting aspect of sex-related mortality is its relationship to marital status. In all developed countries the unmarried have significantly higher death rates than the married, and this differential is much greater for males than for females: on the average, unmarried males ages 45–54 in developed countries have *double* the death rate of their married counterparts. For females the marital status differential is only 30 percent.

One possible explanation for this is that "life" is produced more efficiently in a husband-wife household and that it is the female who plays the more important role in the process. Thus females who are single, widowed, or divorced can cope almost as well as married women,

---

* The South Atlantic census division consists of Delaware, Maryland, Virginia, District of Columbia, West Virginia, North Carolina, South Carolina, Georgia, and Florida. The Middle Atlantic division consists of New York, New Jersey, and Pennsylvania.

whereas males without spouses seem to be at a much greater disadvantage. One study, moreover, has found a positive effect of the wife's schooling on the husband's health after allowing for many other related variables such as husband's schooling, I.Q., and income.[12]

To be sure, the thread of causality need not run entirely from marital status to health. The marriage market may be selective with respect to health, tending to leave those with poor life expectancy unmarried. This relationship varies considerably from one country to another, however. In the United States about 13 percent of males ages 45–54 are unmarried, and their death rate is 123 percent higher than that of like-aged married males. In the same age group in England and Wales a smaller fraction (11 percent) are unmarried, but their death rate is only 53 percent above the rate for married males. Just as the male-female mortality ratio is higher in the United States than in nearly all other developed countries, so is the unmarried male–married male ratio higher. There is something about life in the United States that is hard on men, particularly on unmarried men. In the United States the probability of death in middle age for an unmarried man is about five times that for a married women! In England the comparable ratio is only about 2.75.

Among unmarried males in the United States (and in most other developed countries) divorced men have the highest death rate and widowers the next highest, while single men come closest to the married rate. Why should the rates for widowed and divorced men be so much higher than for single men? It could be adverse selection (i.e., the sick and the unstable are the ones who do not remarry). However, the earnings of widowed and divorced men are just as high as the earnings of single men, which tends to refute this hypothesis. Another possible explanation is a decreased desire to live after the loss of a wife. When we examine the mortality ratios of divorced to single males and of widowed to single males by cause of death, we find the highest ratios recorded for suicide, motor accidents, cirrhosis of the liver, homicide, and lung cancer—all causes where a self-destructive behavioral component is very significant. At the other end of the scale, the widowed and divorced rates come closest to the single in the categories of vascular lesions, diabetes, leukemia and aleukemia, and cancer of the digestive organs—all diseases in which identified behavioral decisions play a smaller role.

One does not ordinarily look to poets for insights into health care, but Edna St. Vincent Millay surely expressed a profound truth when she wrote:

Love cannot fill the thickened lung with breath,
Nor clear the blood, nor set the fractured bone;
Yet many a man is making friends with death
Even as I speak, for lack of love alone.[13]

A Tale of Two States

In the western United States there are two contiguous states that enjoy
about the same levels of income and medical care and are alike in many
other respects, but their levels of health differ enormously. The inhabitants
of Utah are among the healthiest individuals in the United States, while
the residents of Nevada are at the opposite end of the spectrum. Comparing death rates of white residents in the two states, for example, we find
that infant mortality is about 40 percent higher in Nevada. And lest the
reader think that the higher rate in Nevada is attributable to the "sinful"
atmosphere of Reno and Las Vegas, we should note that infant mortality
in the rest of the state is almost exactly the same as it is in these two cities. Rather, as was argued earlier in this chapter, infant death rates depend critically upon the physical and emotional condition of the mother.

The excess mortality in Nevada drops appreciably for children because,
as shall be argued below, differences in life-style account for differences
in death rates, and these do not fully emerge until the adult years. As the
following figures indicate, the differential for adult men and women is in
the range of 40 to 50 percent until old age, at which point the differential
naturally decreases.

Excess of Death Rates in Nevada
compared with Utah, Average for 1959–61 and 1966–68

AGE GROUP	MALES	FEMALES
<1	42%	35%
1–19	16%	26%
20–39	44%	42%
30–39	37%	42%
40–49	54%	69%
50–59	38%	28%
60–69	26%	17%
70–79	20%	6%

The two states are very much alike with respect to income, schooling, degree of urbanization, climate, and many other variables that are frequently thought to be the cause of variations in mortality. (In fact, average family income is actually higher in Nevada than in Utah.) The numbers of physicians and of hospital beds per capita are also similar in the two states.

What, then, explains these huge differences in death rates? The answer almost surely lies in the different life-styles of the residents of the two states. Utah is inhabited primarily by Mormons, whose influence is strong throughout the state. Devout Mormons do not use tobacco or alcohol and in general lead stable, quiet lives. Nevada, on the other hand, is a state with high rates of cigarette and alcohol consumption and very high indexes of marital and geographical instability. The contrast with Utah in these respects is extraordinary.

In 1970, 63 percent of Utah's residents 20 years of age and over had been born in the state; in Nevada the comparable figure was only 10 percent; for persons 35–64 the figures were 64 percent in Utah and 8 percent in Nevada. Not only were more than nine out of ten Nevadans of middle age born elsewhere, but more than 60 percent were not even born in the West.

The contrast in stability is also evident in the response to the 1970 census question about changes in residence. In Nevada only 36 percent of persons 5 years of age and over were then living in the same residence as they had been in 1965; in Utah the comparable figure was 54 percent.

The differences in marital status between the two states are also significant in view of the association between marital status and mortality discussed in the previous section. More than 20 percent of Nevada's males ages 35–64 are single, widowed, divorced, or not living with their spouses. Of those who are married with spouse present, more than one-third had been previously widowed or divorced. In Utah the comparable figures are only half as large.

The impact of alcohol and tobacco can be readily seen in the following comparison of death rates from cirrhosis of the liver and malignant neoplasms of the respiratory system. For both sexes the excess of death rates from these causes in Nevada is very large.

The populations of these two states are, to a considerable extent, self-selected extremes from the continuum of life-styles found in the United States. Nevadans, as has been shown, are predominantly recent immigrants from other areas, many of whom were attracted by the state's

*Excess of Death Rates in Nevada
compared with Utah for Cirrhosis of the Liver
and Malignant Neoplasms of the Respiratory System,
Average for 1966–68*

AGE	MALES	FEMALES
30–39	590%	443%
40–49	111%	296%
50–59	206%	205%
60–69	117%	227%

permissive mores. The inhabitants of Utah, on the other hand, are evidently willing to remain in a more restricted society. Persons born in Utah who do not find these restrictions acceptable tend to move out of the state.

Summary

This dramatic illustration of large health differentials that are unrelated to income or availability of medical care helps to highlight the central themes of this chapter—namely:

1. From the middle of the eighteenth century to the middle of the twentieth century rising real incomes resulted in unprecedented improvements in health in the United States and other developing countries.

2. During most of this period medical care (as distinct from public health measures) played an insignificant role in health, but, beginning in the mid-1930s, major therapeutic discoveries made significant contributions independently of the rise in real income.

3. As a result of the changing nature of health problems, rising income is no longer significantly associated with better health, except in the case of infant mortality (primarily post-neonatal mortality)—and even here the relationship is weaker than it used to be.

4. As a result of the wide diffusion of effective medical care, its marginal contribution to health is again small (over the observed range of variation). There is no reason to believe that the major health problems of the average American would be significantly alleviated by increases in the number of hospitals or physicians. This conclusion might be altered, however, as the result of new scientific discoveries. Alternatively, the *marginal* contribution of medical care might become even smaller as a result of such advances.

5. The greatest current potential for improving the health of the American

people is to be found in what they do and don't do to and for themselves. Individual decisions about diet, exercise, and smoking are of critical importance, and collective decisions affecting pollution and other aspects of the environment are also relevant.

These conclusions notwithstanding, the demand for medical care is
very great and growing rapidly. As René Dubos has acutely observed,
"To ward off disease or recover health, men as a rule find it easier to
depend on the healers than to attempt the more difficult task of living
wisely." [14]

The next three chapters focus specifically on medical care: physicians,
hospitals, and drugs. As discussed in Chapter 1, problems concerning the
cost of care and access to care are high on the agenda of the American
people. The following chapters provide the background for understanding
these problems and for analyzing them from the economic point of view.

CHAPTER 3

The Physician: The Captain of the Team

[The physician's] position in society, the task assigned to him and the rules of conduct imposed upon him changed in every period. They were determined primarily by the social and economic structure of society and by the technical and scientific means available to medicine at the time.

HENRY SIGERIST
Medicine and Human Welfare

More than 4½ million men and women from some two hundred occupations are employed in the delivery of health services in the United States. One type of health professional—the physician—plays a unique role. Although physicians account for only 8 percent of health service employment, their actions and decisions are of critical importance to the entire system. The term "health team" is sometimes only a figure of speech, but the "captaincy" by the physician is beyond doubt. It is impossible to understand the problems of medical care without understanding the physician. And it is impossible to make significant changes in the medical field without changing physician behavior.

The preeminent position of the physician in medical care is rooted in law, custom, and his more extended training. Historically, he *was* the health team. At the beginning of this century, for instance, two out of every three persons employed in the health field were physicians; today the proportion is one out of every twelve. This huge change in the manpower mix is profoundly altering the role of the physician, although medical education and medical practice have all too often failed to adapt to the new circumstances. With the growth of more complex technologies, the changing nature of health problems, and the commitment to serve the total population, a true team effort is required for the successful delivery of health care.

The dominant role of the physician is particularly important with respect to the problem of the *cost* of care. This is not primarily because physicians' fees are too high, though they are in many instances, but because physicians control the total process of care. Typically, this process begins when a patient seeks help. From then on the initiative passes to the physician, whose decisions significantly influence the quantity, type, and cost of service utilized. For instance, the physician, and only the physician, can prescribe drugs. On average, one prescription is written for every outpatient visit; frequently the visit is undertaken primarily to obtain the prescription. The cost of drugs is often as great as the physician's fee, but closer attention by the physician to the choice of drug and brand of drug could significantly reduce that cost.

There are many other decisions that lie solely within the discretion of the physician. He may, for example, order tests or X rays. He may recommend surgery. He may tell the patient to enter the hospital. It is true that the patient is not compelled to follow the physician's advice, but it is equally true that the patient could not obtain the drugs, tests, or hospital admission without the concurrence of the physician. He is the gatekeeper to the production of medical care.

The actual delivery of care is frequently in the hands of other health professionals—pharmacists, nurses, technicians, and the like—but they take their instructions from the physician and report back to him. For instance, while the pharmacist who fills the prescription is usually an independent businessman and may even be more knowledgeable about drugs than the physician, he is legally obliged to fill the prescription exactly as written. In many states he cannot so much as substitute one brand of the same drug for another, even though such substitution could result in substantial savings for the patient.

Or consider the role of the physician in the hospital. Typically, he is not an employee of the institution, but a member of the "voluntary" staff and is referred to as an "attending" physician. Although not an employee, he has considerable, if not primary, influence over what happens in the hospital. It is he who will decide who enters, what is done to and for the patient while he is there, and how long he stays. It is the physician who, to a large extent, controls the activities of such hospital employees as nurses and technicians, who report to him and follow his directions even though he usually occupies no formal position in the hospital chain of command. Not only do physicians influence the day-to-day activities of the hospital, but they play a major role in determining what capital equipment will be purchased and what long-run policies will be followed.

There are, to be sure, changes taking place within the hospital-physician relationship. A significant new development in the United States is the growth of full-time medical staffs. Some hospitals now have senior physicians acting as chiefs of the various services on a salaried basis. There also has been an increase in salaried house staff, particularly interns and residents. These developments modify the role and influence of the "attending" physicians who are not employees of the hospital, but note that the new full-time men are also physicians. As Dr. Paul Elwood has so well put it, "Hospitals don't have patients; doctors have patients and hospitals have doctors." From the point of view of the hospital administrator, running a hospital is like trying to drive a car when the passengers have control of the wheel and the accelerator. The most the administrator can do is occasionally jam on the brakes.

In many discussions about physicians, primary attention is given to their high fees. "He only saw me for ten minutes and charged $25" is a typical complaint. It is true that physicians' fees have risen more than twice as fast as other consumer prices since the end of World War II and that their incomes have almost doubled in the last decade, but physicians' fees and income are only a small part of the cost problem.

Of every $100 spent for health in the United States only a bit over $20 goes for physicians' services, compared to more than $40 for hospital care and another $10 for drugs. After deducting legitimate expenses for rent, personnel, and supplies, physicians' income represents at most about 15 percent of total health expenditures. This income is admittedly very high, averaging close to $50,000 in 1973. The typical physician makes at least $10,000 more per year than do other highly trained professionals, and his earnings are more than double those of the average college professor.

Part of physicians' high income can be explained by longer and more expensive training and longer hours of work. Most economists believe that part also represents a "monopoly" return to physicians resulting from restrictions on entry to the profession and other barriers to competition. Let us assume that some way could be found to drive down physicians' fees and income to a "competitive" level—that is, to a level commensurate with the training, ability, and effort of the average physician. Such a reduction, even if it cut income by 20 percent while holding

utilization constant, would reduce total health costs by only 3 percent.*
Clearly the potential saving here is small.

On the other hand, consider the physician's influence on other elements
of cost. Expenditures for hospital care and out-of-hospital prescription
drugs account for about 50 percent of total health outlays. As we have
seen, physician decisions have significant influence on these costs: the
volume of surgery, the number of hospital admissions, the length of stay
in the hospital, the number and type of prescriptions—all are subject to
physician control.

Moreover, there is frequently a wide range of choices open to the
physician; it must not be imagined that medical science rigidly determines
the appropriate course of treatment. Comparisons within this country and
between this country and others reveal wide differences in the use of
surgery, drugs, and hospitalization, with significant implications for cost
but little apparent effect on health outcomes. For instance, a comparison
of surgical procedures performed in an East Coast suburb by physicians
practicing under the customary fee-for-service system with the procedures
performed by surgeons in a prepaid group practice on the West Coast
revealed that 25 percent of the operations for which patients were hospitalized in the East were done on an ambulatory basis in the West, with
resulting savings of several hundred dollars per case.[1] No adverse health
effects were noted for the nonhospitalized patients; indeed, there may
well be more risk when a patient is unnecessarily hospitalized.

Differences in modes of treatment are frequently attributable to institutional differences rather than to differences in the intelligence or competence of the physicians involved. For instance, one of the reasons why
more operations are not performed on an ambulatory basis in the East is
that sometimes the medical insurance will only pay if the patient is hospitalized, or will pay more for the same procedure if performed on a hospitalized patient.

In the West Coast health plan described above, where patients pay a
single annual fee to cover hospitalization, physicians' services, and prescription drugs, the average length of hospital stay for patients with uncomplicated myocardial infarction (heart attack) is ten days compared
with a national average of about three weeks. With hospital costs running
over $100 per day, the shorter stay represents a saving of over $1,000 per
patient for a frequently encountered medical condition. Even more strik-

* Income of physicians (15% of total) × 20% cut = 3% reduction in total.

ing are reports from England indicating no difference in health outcomes between heart attack patients who were hospitalized and those who were treated at home.[2]

The elimination of unnecessary surgery, hospital admissions, tests, prescriptions, and the like is the surest, swiftest, safest way of stopping the runaway inflation of health care cost. This goal could be pursued by government regulation or by trying to make the patient more cost-conscious through deductibles and coinsurance. The route that offers the most promise, however, is through informed modification of physician behavior. To accomplish that it is necessary to understand the incentives and constraints that motivate physicians.

A common mistake is to think that the behavior of physicians can be understood only in terms of their desire to maximize income. It is true that physicians' incomes far surpass those of other standard occupations. Most physicians, however, also respond to other kinds of incentives. One significant factor is peer approval. In this respect physicians are very much like writers, artists, athletes, scientists, and performers, all of whom place considerable value on being well regarded by their colleagues. Such high regard can, of course, indirectly yield financial value as well, but it is not unusual for the physician to sacrifice financial reward in order to maintain peer approval. Patient approval is another significant factor that motivates physicians—again, not only because it results in a busier practice and hence more income, but also because of the psychological rewards derived from the dependency relationship frequently established between patient and physician.

Another motivating force in physician behavior is "instinct of workmanship." During their medical school and residency training, physicians are "imprinted" with what they understand to be "best medical practice," to which they try to conform throughout their careers. This can be a mixed blessing because it is closely related to what I have called the "technological imperative"—namely, the desire of the physician to do everything that he has been trained to do, regardless of the benefit-cost ratio.

Other significant influences on physician behavior are the demands of his family and his own life-style preferences. The physician's decision regarding where to locate his practice, for instance, is significantly influenced by the frequent desire to be near cultural, educational, and recreational facilities. Similarly, the preference of most physicians for specialization is partly motivated by a desire to avoid the night calls, house visits, and other demands that disrupt the life of the general practitioner.

Social scientists have tended to criticize the great power that physicians wield in the health care process. Many economists believe that the root of the problem is in licensure laws and other legislation that restrict competition. The case for compulsory licensure (requiring licenses to practice a profession) presumably rests on the proposition that the consumer is a poor judge of the quality of medical care and therefore needs guidance concerning the qualifications of those proposing to sell such care. Assuming this to be true, *voluntary certification* could provide guidance just as well—indeed, probably better. Under a certification system several grades or categories could be established and periodic recertification required. This would be more practicable—and less threatening—than periodic relicensure because a change in certification would not completely destroy the physicians right to practice. Patients would be free to choose practitioners at whatever level of expertise they wanted, including uncertified practitioners. John Stuart Mill was an early advocate of this position in his famous *Essay on Liberty*. He wrote, "Degrees or other public certificates of scientific or professional acquirements should be given to all who present themselves for examination and stand the test; but such certificates should confer no advantage over competitors other than the weight which may be attached to their testimony by public opinion."

The principal objections to voluntary certification are that some patients might receive bad treatment at the hands of unqualified practitions and that such a system might result in an expansion of unnecessary care. Obvious advantages, on the other hand, are greater availability of care and lower prices. For certain health care needs, practitioners with lesser qualifications than physicians presently have would be adequate—and possibly preferable to a system (like the current one) that results in some sick persons receiving no care or being treated by laymen without any medical training (such as family members, neighbors, or friends).

A reasonable compromise between the existing restrictive system and complete laissez-faire would be *institutional licensure,* which would restrict care to institutions and organizations that met licensure standards while permitting them considerable freedom and flexibility in the use of personnel. (This approach is discussed in more detail at the end of this chapter.)

Sociologists have been at least as critical of physicians as have economists. Professor Eliott Friedson, for instance, has written, "Health services are organized around professional authority and their basic structure is constituted by the dominance of a single profession over a variety of other subordinate occupations," and goes on to assert that "professional dominance is the analytic key to the present inadequacy of health services." [3] One can sympathize with the thrust of such criticisms, but some nagging questions remain. Why have these laws and customs developed? Why are they present in so many countries with diverse political and economic systems? Are there aspects of the production and delivery of medical care that make these arrangements desirable or, lacking better solutions, the least undesirable one?

Some suggestion of an affirmative answer to the last question can be found in the work of economic theorist Kenneth Arrow. He argues that the *uncertainty* surrounding medical care—that is, uncertainty regarding the need for and the consequences of care—precludes an optimal solution through market competition and gives rise to the various laws and customs that provide the physician with his unique power.[4] A related point is that the consumer-provider relationship can significantly affect the effectiveness of medical care. Thus, the arm's-length bargaining position between buyer and seller that is normal and desirable in most markets may actually interfere with the efficient delivery of health services. If I badly need an automobile, I am not likely to reveal to the car dealer the urgency of my demand because it will hurt my chances of a good deal. Furthermore, the utility of the automobile once I purchase it will be unaffected by such bargaining strategy. In medicine, however, lack of candor in giving a history to a physician can significantly reduce the value of the service being purchased. Similarly, the patient's *trust* in the physician often contributes to the cure.

An appreciation of the intimate nature of the relationship between patient and physician and of the desire to be able to fix *responsibility* should make us wary of proposals for radical changes in medical practice. On the other hand, some changes are already taking place, and others should take place.

In evaluating these changes, it is useful to understand the historical forces currently modifying the physician's task. Prior to World War II, the typical American physician was a self-employed general practitioner working alone and delivering a wide variety of services, from maternity to pediatric to geriatric, on a fee-for-service basis. He practiced on a small scale presumably because there were no substantial economies to be achieved in large-scale organization. (For similar reasons the traditional practice was also characterized by a low capital-labor ratio.) The physician usually had strong roots in a small town or a well-defined neighborhood of a large city and was substantially involved in the problems of his community. He often took a broad view of the doctor's role with respect to health as distinct from medicine. He recognized the connections between environment and health and felt some sense of responsibility for initiating beneficial changes.

This form of practice is not unknown today, but it can no longer be regarded as typical. At present most physicians are specialists in a single branch of medicine, confining their attention to a particular age group, disease, or part of the body. Moreover, fee-for-service practitioners working by themselves are now outnumbered by physicians who practice in groups, who are salaried employees of hospitals, or who otherwise depart from the traditional mode.

These developments are partly in response to changes in medical science. Recent years have seen the development of new diagnostic and therapeutic techniques that require large capital investment and skilled teams of personnel. Improvements in transportation, communication, and information storage and retrieval also have profound implications for the production process in medical care.

Significant changes are also occurring on the side of demand. First, the rapid development of insurance and other types of prepayment has tended to reduce the constraining influence of cost on patients. Second, there has been increasing pressure to distribute medical care more equally regardless of patients' ability to pay. Also, as noted in Chapter 2, there have been major changes in the relative importance of different kinds of health problems. A mode of practice efficiently geared to the detection and treatment of acute infectious diseases may no longer be satisfactory for dealing with the chronic diseases, emotional illness, and other problems that now plague the American people. Finally, it is worth noting that today's physician must deal with a much-better-educated public. At one time physicians were part of an educational elite treating mostly uneducated patients. In 1900 there were five times as many physicians as there were faculty members of colleges and universities. Only in the early 1950s did the number of college teachers catch up with the number of physicians. Now the ratio is more than two to one the other way.

The creation of a health care system that will provide adequate access at reasonable cost requires taking a realistic view of what patients want and need and what physicians actually do. In particular, it requires rejecting the romantic notion that every patient-physician contact is a matter of life or death and recognizing the importance of the *caring* function in medical care.

Caring and Curing

Fully 80 percent of illness is functional, and
can be effectively treated by any talented
healer who displays warmth, interest and
compassion regardless of whether he has fin-
ished grammar school. Another 10 percent of
illness is wholly incurable. That leaves only
10 percent in which scientific medicine—at
considerable cost—has any value at all.

Letter from a physician to
Medical Economics

One of the central themes of Chapter 2 was that the marginal contribution
of medical care to health in developed countries is very small. While this
conclusion emerged from gross analyses of differences in health across
large populations, it is confirmed by those who have intimate knowledge
of medicine and health in clinical settings. Medical intervention has a significant effect on outcome in only a small fraction of the cases seen by
the average physician. Most illnesses are self-limiting: they will run their
course and disappear. The common cold is a familiar example. Many
others are chronic: given the present limits of medical knowledge, they
are incurable. Arthritis is an all-too-familiar example in this category.

Even this limited capacity of a physician to make a decisive difference
is mostly the result of medical advances of the last fifty years. Prior to
that time a patient had as much chance of being harmed as helped by the
treatments of the day. Describing pre-twentieth-century physicians, Dr.
Walsh McDermott writes that "these rather haphazardly trained and educated men and women provided great human comfort, but in retrospect it
is clear that they had virtually no power to alter the course of a disease in
a predictable and decisive fashion." [5]

Yet the practice of medicine goes back thousands of years, and the
demand for the services of doctors and healers of all types has always
been strong. How can we understand this, if their remedies were so often
irrelevant or harmful? This question is of more than historical interest
because the answer may help explain the current situation as well.

In my view it is critical to appreciate that the physician has always fulfilled a "caring" as well as a "curing" function. People who are troubled, who are in pain, who are disabled, want to see someone, to talk to
someone, to share their troubles with someone. As much as a "cure,"
they want sympathy, reassurance, encouragement. They want explanations: "Why did this happen?" "How long will it last?" They want jus-
tifications: "Should I stay home from work?" "Should I have any more
children?" Above all, they want someone who *cares*.

Doctors, among others, have traditionally fulfilled this function, and it
would be a great mistake to believe that it is not still of importance today.
Indeed, with the decline of religious belief, the breakup of families, the
increase in mobility and anonymity in our urban culture, it may well be
that the demand for "caring" is greater than ever before. To quote Dr.
McDermott again: "Without question an appreciable portion of what the
public voices as the medical services they need and should have, is not
really this decisive portion of our medicine at all, but practices that have
survived from a day when [physicians] could not act decisively." [6]

Different kinds of physicians encounter the "demand for caring" in
different ways. Pediatricians, for instance, know that calming nervous
mothers is often more time-consuming than treating their children. Obstetricians must deal with expectant fathers as well as their pregnant spouses. Relieving anxiety is a large part of almost every physician's stock-in-
trade. This "noncuring" role of the physician takes many strange forms.
In Israel, for example, new immigrants make particularly heavy use of
the nationally supported health services. Upon examination it was found
that this was not because their medical needs were so much greater than
those of the rest of the population, but because using the health service
was a means of identifying with this new society, of feeling more a part
of the new culture.

"Caring" is particularly important at the close of life, when a "cure"
is impossible. Each year some 2 million people die in the United States,
in most cases after suffering illness, pain, loss of normal functions, lone-
liness, and fear. Family, friends, and clergy provide some care, but increasingly this difficult task is being delegated to physicians and other
health personnel, especially since more than half of all deaths occur in
hospitals or nursing homes.

Although the discussion so far has emphasized the distinction between
"caring" and "curing," increasing evidence regarding the connection
between psychological states and physical pathology makes it clear that

the former can have a significant effect on the latter. In particular, "caring" can be excellent preventive medicine for a patient who has just lost a loved one, say, or suffered some other psychological trauma.

A prominent characteristic of the United States medical care market is that fees are invariably based on the care rendered, not on the cure effected. The almost total divorce of fees and charges from health outcomes makes sense if, as suggested here, it is care that is typically being bought (and sold) and if there is only infrequently a significant relation between care and outcome.

Once we have acknowledged the importance of the "caring" function in the total spectrum of physician activity, several critical questions arise. First, what determines the demand for "caring"? It is obvious that this demand varies greatly among individuals and groups, for levels of anxiety, the need for reassurance about one's health, and the need for sympathy are not constants of human nature. It is also obvious that some part of this demand is satisfied outside the medical care industry in various degrees within different cultures, socioeconomic groups, and "life-styles," although the decline of traditional families and religions in most developed countries has surely expanded the role of health professionals. Still, it is not clear whether such demand arises completely exogenous to medical care or is in part behavior that is learned by patients from physicians.

Another set of questions concerns the ability and willingness of physicians to supply "caring." How well does medical training, which has become increasingly more technical and scientific, prepare physicians for this role? Has the increase in opportunities to help patients by strictly medical means made physicians more intolerant of and dissatisfied with their "caring" function? Should the criteria for admission to medical school take into account the need for this kind of work? One possible solution may be to establish a variety of "hotlines," "drop-in centers," and multiservice organizations manned by volunteers and dedicated paraprofessionals expert in "caring" by virtue of temperament and/or training. Such a service is probably most effective when provided by someone who "cares" by choice rather than by necessity.

Finally, there are a number of questions that society must face concerning the financing of "caring." How much should this service cost? Who should pay for it? If "caring" is to be provided by physicians with long years of training, it would be very costly—unless the higher price for their time were offset by greater efficiency. What, if any, is the government's obligation in providing "caring," and what are the obligations of individuals and families? When people talk of health care being a "right," or of a "shortage" of care, do they also have "caring" in mind?

Some of these questions will be discussed in Chapter 6, on paying for medical care, and others in the Conclusion. The implications of this subject for the problem of access are considered in the next section.

"I Can't Get a Doctor"

Each physician treateth one part and not more. And everywhere is full of physicians; for some profess themselves physicians of the eyes, and others of the head, others of the teeth, and others of the parts about the belly, and others of obscure sicknesses.

HERODOTUS
(describing Egypt 2,400 years ago)

"I can't get a doctor." So runs the complaint, so often, and in so many places from so many people, one would think that physicians are a vanishing species along with the whooping crane and the California condor. For those who in recent years have experienced great difficulty and delay in securing medical care, it must come as a surprise to learn that the ratio of physicians to population in the United States is higher now than at any time since before World War I. There is actually a higher proportion of physicians in the population of the United States than in Australia, Denmark, England, Japan, the Netherlands, Norway, or Sweden. It may also surprise some to learn that the average annual number of physician-visits per capita, 4.6, is about the same as it was twenty-five years ago and greater than in the pre–World War II period.

Why, then, is *access* perceived as one of the major problems of health care? There are several reasons, some related to changing expectations and demands, and some to the changing nature of medical practice.

First, it should be noted that complaints about access to medical care have their parallel in complaints about the schools, the courts, mass transportation, and so on. Similarly, in affluent suburbs there is an access problem regarding plumbers, electricians, domestic servants, and repairmen of all types. In short, ours is an age of "great expectations" and little patience—which is not an argument for complacent acceptance of current shortcomings, regarding medical care or anything else, but simply a plea to place these shortcomings into proper perspective.

One contributing factor is the growing ability of the poor to *pay* for care, either in cash, or via private insurance, or through publicly funded programs. A paying patient is likely to apply a different standard than one receiving "free" care. Thus part of the access problem is related to the fact that care is being distributed more equally than ever before; among groups (particularly the poor) who now have better access than formerly there are those who tend to forget how bad things once were or are simply unaware of the enormous problems their parents faced. Moreover, even though access for them may be better, it may still leave much to be desired. On the other hand, among groups (particularly the wealthy) who have suffered a deterioration in access there are those who remember all too well when physicians would come running at the call of a promptly paying patient.

Probably the most important reason for current complaints about access, however, is the growth of specialty practice within medicine, which has made it more difficult to gain access to primary care, access to emergency care, access to the medical system itself. A related phenomenon is the change in control of the *terms* of access. In earlier times a patient could decide pretty much when and where his doctor visit would take place: frequently this was at home, and just as often as not it would be at night or on a weekend. Today's specialist sees his patients only at certain specified hours, usually in his office or in the hospital.

The growth of specialization has also contributed to the phenomenon of patients making greater distinctions among physicians. Mr. Jones complains that he has to wait six weeks to be operated on by Dr. X, and doesn't bother to mention that Drs. Y or Z, who have passed their boards in the same specialty, would be happy to take his case tomorrow. (See the next section, on the "surgeon surplus.")

Another difficulty often cited is in finding a physician who will take continuing responsibility for the whole patient. A generation ago more than half of all active physicians were general practitioners; now only one out of seven is in general practice. Specialists in internal medicine have tended to fill the need for "first-contact" general care, but many younger internists prefer to limit their practice to a subspecialty, such as cardiology, hematology, or endocrinology.

What the typical patient wants us easy, quick, reliable access to a source of care seven days a week, twenty-four hours a day. Moreover, he wants this source to know him, have all his records, care about him, take continuing responsibility for him, and guide him through the labyrinth of whatever specialty care may be necessary. Such access is indeed rare. Instead, the medical care industry offers him a multitude of highly trained specialists, each of whom can provide better care than was previously available—but only within his specialty and only during office hours.

In my view the patient's demand for access cannot be met for the total population by personnel now known as physicians—that is, highly skilled specialists with ten to twelve years of training beyond high school. Such personnel are not only too expensive, but also frequently illsuited to meet the typical demands of most first-contact situations.

An efficient, effective solution to the access problem requires the deployment of properly trained, properly supervised nurse clinicians, physician's assistants, pediatric assistants, family health workers, and other health professionals. The exact form of organization can vary. One farseeing physician, Dr. Sidney Garfield, one of the pioneers of the Kaiser Health Plan, advocates the organization of care around four centers of activity: (1) A triage (screening) center for the worried well; (2) a health-maintenance center for immunization and other care of the well; (3) a center for the chronically ill; and (4) an acute care center. Only in the last would the bulk of patient contact be with physicians. In the others, physicians would help to design and monitor diagnostic and therapeutic protocols and would be available for consultation, but most of the patient contact would be with other health professionals.[7] One reason why it is currently so difficult to get care in time of need is because physicians' offices and hospitals are full of people who are not acutely ill. The four-tiered organization of health services would thus facilitate access for all— those who were acutely ill as well as those who are not.

No discussion of the problem of access would be complete without reference to geographic disparities in the availability of physicians. It is perfectly clear that physicians prefer to locate in urban areas. The number of physicians per capita is three times as high in metropolitan counties as in nonmetropolitan counties in the United States. The average physician in nonmetropolitan counties sees about one-third more patients per week, but that still leaves a disparity of more than two to one. The relative shortage of physicians in rural areas is not peculiar to the United States; it is true of almost every country. It is not a function of the national physician/population ratio, or of the method of financing health care, or of the type of economy. The basic reason for geographic inequality is the same in every country: the reluctance of physicians to live and practice in remote areas. Of course, medical care is not the only service that is relatively scarcer in rural areas. Cultural, educational, and recreational facilities are usually scarce as well—which, as we have already mentioned, is a principal reason why physicians prefer urban locations.

Comparisons of the health levels of inhabitants of rural and urban areas do not suggest that the former are significantly worse off on balance. Living in low-density areas undoubtedly has offsetting advantages: fresh air, beautiful scenery, privacy. Rural death rates tend to be slightly higher than urban rates for infants, children, and young adults, but after age 45 the differential is in favor of rural areas. Thus if American country dwellers suffer from their lower physician/population ratio, it is primarily in terms of convenience, not of health.

Geographical inequality is often cited as a reason for increasing the total number of physicians in the country. Presumably, the resultant excess in the number of physicians in certain areas would induce some to move to areas with lower physician/population ratios. But if we test this theory by examining the four regions of the United States (Northeast, North Central, South, and West) and comparing each region's overall physician/population ratio with the degree of internal geographic inequality, the argument is dramatically refuted. The two regions with the highest physician/population ratios—the Northeast and the West—also exhibit the greatest relative inequality among their states. Within the North Central region and the South, with much lower physician/population ratios, there is much *less* intraregional inequality.

Certainly this is not to suggest that an increase in the total number of physicians in the United States would not result in some absolute increase in rural areas as well. But there is no reason to believe that if the total supply were much larger than now, the *relative* disparity between urban and rural areas would be any less. Moreover, increasing the number of physicians as they are now being trained would involve a significant waste of resources, for some specialties, such as surgery, are already in oversupply.

The "Surgeon Surplus"

The "doctor shortage" has become a stock phrase in almost every speech and article about American medical care. As suggested in the preceding section, this is an accurate characterization for some types of care. For some medical services, particularly house calls and emergency care, the quantity demanded at the going price is greater than the quantity supplied. But there are other kinds of medical services where the opposite situation prevails. For most types of surgery, the quantity physicians would like to supply at the going price is far greater than the quantity demanded. In the opinion of most experts, within both medicine and economics, there is indeed a "surgeon surplus."

The existence and extent of this surplus have been discussed from a number of different points of view. At the clinical level, experienced surgeons have known for a long time that there is not enough "business" to keep everyone as active as they would like to be. Back in 1965 Dr. William P. Longmire wrote, "In each community in our country there are a few surgeons who are doing all or more than they humanly can do. Many, though, are working at a pace far below their capacity and this is a tremendous waste of highly skilled talent." [8] In his inaugural address as president of the American College of Surgeons in 1972, Dr. Longmire went so far as to propose limiting the number of surgical training residencies in order to bring about a better balance between supply and demand.

Professor John Bunker, a leading anesthesiologist, in 1970 compared the situations in the United States and England and found that there were twice as many surgeons per capita in this country and twice as much surgery being performed here. Some procedures, particularly those for which indications are frequently in doubt (such as tonsillectomy), were found to be three or four times as prevalent here.

A comprehensive, detailed study of general surgeons in one suburban community in the New York metropolitan area revealed that the surgical workload of the typical surgeon was only about *one-third* of what experts deemed a reasonably full schedule. Furthermore, the uneven distribution of work was quite marked. The busiest man in the community was very busy, doing more than four times as much surgery as the average surgeon. One-fourth of the surgeons were doing 50 percent of the surgery; their average work load was triple that of their colleagues.

This study also revealed that a large part of the surgical work load in the community consisted of relatively simple procedures. For instance, more than half the operations were less complex than a simple herniorrhaphy. The repair of hernia, which is one of the most common general surgical procedures, is a task which is often assigned to surgical residents in their first year of training. [9]

There is no reason to believe that the findings from this study are atypical of the general situation. Calculations based on the total number of surgeons and the total volume of operations in New York State revealed about the same average work loads, and similar calculations for the United States produced results that were only slightly higher.

By contrast, in organized health care settings where the number of surgeons employed is geared to patient requirements, the average work load is much higher. In one prepaid group practice the average surgeon was found to be performing more than twice as much surgery as those in the suburban private practice setting previously discussed. Moreover, the work load was very evenly distributed among all the surgeons in the group. A large fee-for-service multispeciality clinic in which all physicians are on salary reports an even higher average work load—more than three times the national average. In this clinic extensive use of assistants in the operating room helps to maintain the high level of productivity. The most important factor accounting for surgical productivity in any setting, however, is limiting the number of surgeons relative to the work to be done.

One might think that a surgeon without enough surgery to do would spend the rest of his time in other kinds of medical work, such as general practice. With the surgeons in the New York suburb mentioned above, however, this was not the case; rather they were enjoying a great deal of leisure. On the job they appeared to be very busy, but when account was taken of long weekends, days off, afternoons off, and the like, it was found that they were at work only an average of thirty-four hours per week.[10] This was based on a generous definition of "at work" to include all the hours from the time the surgeon first appeared at hospital or office until he went home. Thus time for lunch and personal business were included in "at work."

Do surgeons with such small work loads find it difficult to make a living? In this case not at all, for fee levels were high enough to insure that even those with small practices made a comfortable living, and the surgeons with the heaviest work loads had very high incomes because the level of fees was generally about the same for all surgeons in the community. If fees were set as they are in the Netherlands—by establishing a reasonable income level and a reasonable work load for surgeons and then dividing the former figure by the latter—the result would be a sharp reduction in cost to the consumer. For instance, suppose a gross income of $ 60,000 per year from in-hospital surgery were considered appropriate for a general surgeon. (His total gross would include income from his office practice.) The equivalent of four hundred herniorrhaphies, requiring about ten hours per week in the operating room, is a reasonable annual work load. Therefore, under the system described above the fee for a herniorraphy would be $150, which is less than half the fee now charged in most major American markets.

Why doesn't competition among all these surgeons drive down fees and eventually force some to turn to other kinds of work? The answer to this is not clear, although one reason seems to be that lowering fees might provoke one's colleagues to deny a surgeon hospital privileges or seek to damage his reputation. Also, many surgeons believe, perhaps rightly, that demand would not increase appreciably in response to a price cut, so they might wind up making less rather than more money. There is one kind of price cutting that this situation does encourage, however, and that is fee splitting. In this practice, which is considered unethical, the surgeon kicks back part of the patient's fee to the physician who referred the patient to him for surgery. Even in the absence of fee splitting, surgeons usually make strenuous efforts to cultivate the goodwill of internists, general practitioners, and other physicians who are in a position to refer patients.

The existence of a "surgeon surplus" is fairly common knowledge within the profession. Why then are so many new surgeons being turned out every year? (Between 1950 and 1970, for example, the number of surgical residencies offered in the United States increased by over 100 percent!) One reason is that those responsible for the creation of new surgical residencies are not the same people who have to contend with excess supply after training has been completed.

The push for residencies comes from the surgical chiefs in hospitals, who are frequently full-time salaried physicians not involved in private practice and who like having a great many young physicians receiving training under them because it enhances their own position and provides them with abundant assistance in their clinical and research tasks. In addition, at least until recently, hospital administrators wanted a great many residents around because they were useful in providing medical care in the emergency room, on the wards, and the like. In other words, residents were a cheap source of skilled labor.

Because hospitals frequently use residents for duties only distantly related to their training needs, and because the supply of surgeons tends to exceed the demand for surgery, many surgical residency programs can only provide the resident with sufficient operating experience by prolonging the training period. Thus the training program is often drawn out to five or even six years, partly because there is not enough clinical "material" to go around.[11] A recent study of a surgeon-training program in a supposedly busy municipal hospital in New York City revealed that the surgical residents were actually doing very little surgery until their fifth year of training because of a shortage of cases requiring surgery.[12]

According to some critics, the existence of "excess capacity" among surgeons results in considerable "unnecessary" surgery. This is a highly controversial point, since it is frequently difficult to state with absolute certainty whether any operation is justified or not. It does seem to be true that physicians practicing in prepaid health plans are less likely to recommend surgery than those practicing fee-for-service. It also has been reported that making a second medical opinion mandatory before proceeding with surgery tends to reduce the number of operations.[13]

Defenders of traditional medical practice assert that only a small fraction of surgeons are "greedy" and likely to perform unnecessary surgery. This may well be true—but, the surgical work loads of these surgeons may be larger than average, and thus the proportion of unnecessary operations might be higher than the proportion of greedy surgeons. And since the average patient comes under the care of many different surgeons during his lifetime, the chances of undergoing an unnecessary operation may not be small even if the fraction of surgeons who are greedy is small.

In fairness to physicians it should be noted that some unnecessary surgery is probably the result of patient pressure rather than surgical greed. Parents of children with recurrent sore throats and similar problems frequently insist on tonsillectomies, and the high volume of hysterectomies among American women may say something about the women as well as their physicians.

Also in fairness to surgeons it should not be thought that every procedure and service ordered by internists and other physicians is of unquestionable value. There are vast numbers of cases where opinions concerning the proper course of treatment differ substantially, and the charge of "unnecessary" could be leveled against certain tests, X rays, visits, and injections with as much justification as against certain operations.

Even if it led to no unnecessary surgery at all, however, the surgeon surplus would still pose problems: it raises the overall cost of medical care, it prolongs the period of training, and it results in some surgeons losing valuable skills because they operate so infrequently. From both the economic and health points of view, a more rational approach to training and utilizing surgical manpower—and medical specialists in general—is badly needed.

Meeting the Challenge

The challenge facing American medicine is to devise a system of medical care that provides ready access at reasonable cost. In my view such a system would make extensive use of "physician extenders" practicing within licensed institutions. These physician extenders—variously known as physicians' assistants, nurse clinicians, pediatric assistants, nurse practitioners, and the like—would have considerably shorter training than physicians and would function in organized settings under physicians' guidance and supervision, performing many of the tasks now reserved by law and tradition for physicians. It has been repeatedly shown that today's physician, with his intensive training in specialty and subspecialty care, is too expensive and sometimes poorly suited to provide the primary, preventive, and emergency care which lie at the heart of the present access problem. Thus the availability of large numbers of physician extenders offers the promise of simultaneously lowering the cost of care, improving access, and possibly even raising health levels.

Some physician extenders are already at work in a variety of settings. Controlled studies of the care they deliver compared with conventional care by physicians have shown no diminution in quality and frequently enhanced patient satisfaction. In pediatric care, for instance, nurse practitioners were found to be more thorough in their examinations and in their communication with mothers than pediatricians who are frequently bored with the routine aspects of well-baby care. In a study of services for chronically ill patients, nurse practitioners working in consultation with physicians achieved health outcomes and patient satisfaction at least as high as when physicians had complete responsibility. Many physician extenders can relate more closely to patients and their problems, communicate better with them, and afford to spend more time with individual patients.

The number of training programs for physician extenders has grown at an extremely rapid rate. It is now possible to note several different types that will be coming into the health field. Some who are generalists are expected to work in rural settings with considerable independence except for consultation with physicians. Others will work more closely with primary-care physicians as assistants and assume less independent responsibility. Still others will receive specialized training and work with specialized physicians, such as orthopedic surgeons or urologists.

Numerous questions inevitably arise concerning the licensing of such personnel and their compensation. In the opinion of many experts it is of critical importance that the government avoid creating another spectrum of licensed health professionals practicing in a solo, fee-for-service mode. The power to issue licenses rests with individual states, some of which now license as many as two dozen separate health occupations. Such licensure ostensibly protects the public interest, but an increasing number of observers have begun to question whether it in fact serves that purpose.

A license to practice a health profession is usually granted early in a person's career; renewal is practically automatic regardless of subsequent changes in competence. Revocation or suspension of one's license is extremely rare; the percentage so affected is much smaller than the probable incidence of drug addiction, alcoholism, criminal behavior, or insanity in the numbers licensed.

According to the 1973 report of the Federal Commission on Medical Malpractice, only fifteen states permit a physician's license to be challenged on the ground of professional incompetence, and most state medical practice acts have no adequate provision for disciplining those practitoners who are in fact found to be incompetent.[14]

Because holding an individual license is now essential to practice, regulatory agencies and courts are extremely loath to revoke a physician's license, even when there are strong grounds for doing so. In one California case a physician was charged with gross incompetence in 1966, but the final court order suspending his license for ninety days and thereafter restricting his privileges was not issued until 1972. Other physicians have been allowed to continue to practice even after having been found guilty of fraud or comparable criminal acts.

The requirement of licensure often prevents persons who may be well qualified from providing needed services because they lack the degrees or other formal requirements for a license. Work experience and on-the-job training, which often help ambitious, able men and women move up the occupational ladder in other industries, does not facilitate upward mobility in the health field.

One suggested remedy is the substitution of institutional licensure for the licensing of individuals. Under such a system medical care institutions—hospitals, clinics, physicians' groups, etc.—would be licensed by the state and would then be free to hire and use personnel as each saw fit. As two leading advocates of institutional licensing have written:

> The state institutional licensing agency would require that the health institution use only objective criteria relating to the safe and competent performance in the

particular position. . . . The list of legally relevant factors [that institutions would consider in hiring and utilizing personnel] would no longer be limited to the status of being licensed, which is often of little or no value in assigning employees to particular positions, but would include criteria of formal education, job experience, in-service training and other relevant factors.[15]

This approach offers numerous advantages to both consumers and providers. It would permit a much more efficient deployment of health care personnel as well as provide greater opportunity for upward job mobility. And it would no doubt foster the development of a more rational health manpower mix. In most industries there is a continuum of personnel with respect to skills and earnings, with the heaviest concentration in the middle ranges. The health care field, by contrast, is characterized by a bimodal distribution in which very few persons' incomes fall between the arithmetic mean and twice the mean (see Figure 2).[16]

Institutional licensure would also help simplify and rationalize the state's control of medical care. At present there are within each state many health licensing agencies (usually one per occupation), and many are dominated by representatives of the occupations they are supposed to control. Institutional licensure would require but a single state medical

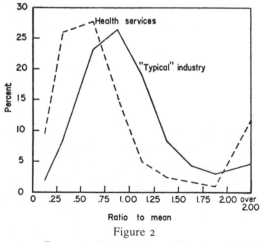

Figure 2

Percentage Frequency Distributions of Earnings Relative to the Mean, Health Services, and the "Typical" Industry, 1959

SOURCE: Victor R. Fuchs, Elizabeth Rand, and Bonnie Garrett, "The Distribution of Earnings in Health and Other Industries," *Journal of Human Resources* 5, no. 3 (Summer 1970).

licensing agency that could and should be dominated by public representatives.

What would be the fate of the physician under such a system? Would he still be "captain of the team"? Certainly in most cases he would be, by virtue of his more advanced training and knowledge. Indeed, the demands on him to play a true leadership role would be greater than they are under the present system of fragmented care. Some physicians would undoubtedly continue to function as highly specialized technicians in particular aspects of medicine or surgery. Many others, however, would not be directly or continuously involved in the personal delivery of care to patients, but would instead assume overall responsibility for the health of the population served. In such a role they would have to be a source of leadership, guidance, inspiration, and control for the entire health care team. Someone other than a physician might conceivably take this leadership role, although the need for expert knowledge and for someone whose authority is readily accepted by patients and health professionals alike make physicians the logical choice in most instances.

Would physicians accept such a role? Some might resist for fear of suffering reduction in income. But as was pointed out earlier in this chapter, the principal economic savings are to be achieved by changing the way physicians practice, not by reducing their compensation. Besides representing to physicians a financial threat, real or imagined, the changes suggested here imply modifying the physician's role. This shift is the inevitable result of technological, economic, political, and social forces which should not be blindly resisted. Physicians, Henry Sigerist noted, "look back to a task that has gone irrevocably; trained as highly specialized and efficient scientists, they are unprepared to grapple with problems that are primarily social and economic. They have built for themselves a legendary, sentimental and romantic history of their profession to which they cling desperately, and which determines their actions." [17]

Many of the present generation of physicians, trained for a more traditional practice, will undoubtedly view the changes recommended here as tending to diminish the compassion and humanity that they associate with the practice of medicine. The next generation, however, trained in new ways for new responsibilities, may prove to be more compassionate, more humane, and more devoted than the old.

CHAPTER 4

The Hospital:
The House of Hope

> The hospital has evolved from a House of
> Despair avoided by all but the impoverished
> sick to a House of Hope to which all roads
> lead in time of crisis—be it somatic, psychic
> or social in origin.
>
> JOHN H. KNOWLES, M.D.
> "The Medical Center and the
> Community Health Center," in
> Social Policy for Health Care

The American hospital is large, impersonal, and dominated by elaborate technology. The American hospital is small, inefficient, underequipped, and understaffed. The American hospital exists primarily to further the professional and economic interests of physicians. The American hospital exists to serve the community. The American hospital is crowded to the point of inefficiency and even danger, and serious delays are encountered in obtaining admission. The American hospital is often half-empty, and many of its patients should be at home or in extended-care facilities. The American hospital is the noblest expression of the philanthropic impulse. The American hospital is a business run to show a profit for its owners.

Will the "real" American hospital please stand up? Which of these many contradictory characterizations of United States hospitals is correct? To some extent, all of them are. No other country has such a heterogeneous collection of institutions comprising its hospital "system." In no other country is it as difficult to generalize about hospitals or to analyze their strengths and shortcomings. If it is important to recognize that American hospitals come in all shapes and sizes, it is equally important to realize that they are undergoing substantial change. This chapter is intended to provide both a still portrait of hospitals as they exist today and a motion picture of the changes that are under way.

The original function of hospitals was to provide the poor with a place to die. The ability of these hospitals to improve health outcomes was sharply limited by the paucity of medical knowledge, as discussed in Chapter 2. Until this century, wealthy individuals who were sick could usually find more comfort, cleanliness, and service in their own homes than in hospitals.

With the development of modern medicine the function of the hospital changed, and it became "the doctor's workshop." The image of the hospital changed from being a place to die to the place where good, effective medical cures could be obtained. Today numerous illnesses can be much more effectively diagnosed and treated in the hospital; for some procedures, such as major surgery, hospitalization is essential.

Now another change is in process. Some hospitals are beginning to function as "health care centers" for the community. The changing nature of health problems and of medical practice, the changing relationship between physicians and hospitals, and the explosive growth in numbers of health personnel other than physicians are all factors in this reorientation. According to many observers, hospitals should now be putting more emphasis on preventive medicine, health education, ambulatory care, home care, rehabilitation services, and responsibility for patients in other institutions (such as extended-care facilities). For the most part these are still matters for discussion rather than actual implementation, but they point to significant changes that lie ahead.

The Central Problem–High Cost

While many kinds of criticisms have been levied against American hospitals, the central problem at present is the high and rapidly rising *cost* of care. In 1973 the operating expenditures of U.S. hospitals plus the cost of new hospital construction amounted to approximately $40 billion, representing more than 40 percent of that year's total national health expenditures. In other words, Americans were spending almost $200 per person for this one aspect of medical care. Not only are costs high, but they have been rising at an extremely rapid rate—more than 10 percent annually over the past decade. It is the escalation in hospital costs that is threatening to blow our medical care system sky high; it is hospital costs that must be curbed if we are ever to bring the system under control.

The high cost of hospital care is attributable in large part to overutilization, inefficiency, and excess capacity resulting from the way current operations and capital investment are financed. Only a small fraction of the cost of hospital care is paid for directly by patients; the bulk comes from so-called third parties, of which the government is the most important, picking up over half the total bill. Private insurance pays about one-third, and the balance is accounted for by private philanthropy. Until recently, the third-party payers made very little effort to question the size of hospital bills. Matters such as weighing the necessity of admission and determining the appropriate length of stay were, and to a large extent still are, left to the professional judgment of the physician and are not to be questioned by "financial intermediaries." The rate of reimbursement for each hospital is determined primarily by *its* costs. Thus, high-cost hospitals are rewarded with higher reimbursement. Capital for construction of new hospitals or expansion of old ones comes primarily from government or philanthropy and does not necessarily flow to communities or institutions that demonstrate efficiency in providing for effective demand. This system is changing, but very slowly.

The deficiencies of the traditional financing system are compounded by the fact that most key decisions are made by physicians who typically have no financial stake in keeping down hospital costs. Indeed, their own self-interest is frequently served by decisions which raise the cost of care. As J. Douglas Colman, the late head of New York's Blue Cross, maintained:

We must remember that most elements of hospital and medical care costs are generated or based on professional medical judgement. The judgements include the decision to order various diagnostic or therapeutic procedures for patients, and the larger decision as to the types of facilities and services needed by an institution for proper patient care. For the most part, these professional judgements are rendered outside of any organizational structure that fixes accountability for the economic consequences of these judgements.[1]

Before taking a more detailed look at the cost problem and what can be done about it, a brief overview of the economics of the hospital industry will be useful.

Hospitals Today

In the United States there are just over seven thousand hospitals containing more than 1½ million beds. They employ more than 2½ million persons, admit more than 33 million patients annually for inpatient care, and provide over 200 million outpatient visits per year. Hospitals differ in many ways: by type of ownership, type of patient, number of beds, and so on. Probably the most important distinction is between the so-called short-term community hospitals and all others. Community hospitals have only a little over one-half of all hospital beds, but they account for 92 percent of all admissions and 78 percent of all hospital expenses. The "all others" category includes hospitals operated by the federal government, such as Veterans Administration hospitals; psychiatric hospitals, typically operated by states or counties; tuberculosis hospitals (rapidly disappearing); and other hospitals for long-term care.

The most distinctive feature of the community hospital is short average length of stay—the typical patient stays for less than eight days. In psychiatric hospitals, by contrast, the average length of stay is about eight months, and even this represents a considerable shortening from twenty years ago, when the average was about two years.

Because most admissions, personnel, and expenses are concentrated in community hospitals, they have received the most attention from researchers and policy makers. The discussion below follows that precedent, with particular emphasis on differences in the size, ownership, and location of community hospitals.

HOSPITAL SIZE

Hospital size is typically measured in terms of number of beds, and efficiency in terms of expenditures per case or expenditures per patient-day. It is difficult to make precise determinations of the effect of size on efficiency because hospitals that differ in size frequently differ also with respect to location, kind of patient admitted, services provided, extent of teaching responsibilities, and other characteristics that affect expenditures. As the result of a number of studies that have attempted to take account of these variables, however, a broad consensus is emerging. According to most health economists, substantial economies of scale (increasing efficiency) are associated with larger hospital size, at least until about 200 beds; some investigators believe that further gains are possible up to about 500 beds. A few prefer hospitals as large as 1,000 beds, although there are others who argue that this size is too big to be truly efficient.

One of the most interesting studies of the effect of size on costs, by John Carr and Paul Feldstein, found that this relationship varied with the number of services and facilities offered by the hospital. The authors concluded that "small hospitals with high service capability should not generally be built because they are likely to be of uneconomic size. Large hospitals having low service capability are also likely to be uneconomic, since there are few or no additional economies associated with increased size." [2] In other words, if hospitals are not going to provide a large number of complex services, they needn't be very large to be efficient; but if they are to provide a large number of services, it is very inefficient for them to be small. A hospital of 200 beds can efficiently provide most of the basic services needed for routine short-term care—radiology, laboratory, nursing, and the like. Should that hospital grow to 600 beds and still provide only the same basic services, some inefficiencies are likely to develop because of increasing difficulties of administrative control. What is likely to happen, however, is that more specialized services will emerge in the 600-bed unit, services which couldn't possibly have been provided at a reasonable cost when the hospital had only 200 beds.

Persons with direct experience in running hospitals tend to confirm the results of such econometric studies. The president of one major corporation that owns and operates a large chain of for-profit hospitals personally told me that his company would rather not build or operate one that had fewer than 200 beds, but they would be equally apprehensive about a hospital with more than 500 beds.

Given these views about hospital size, it is of interest and concern to note that many American hospitals are too small and some are probably too large. Despite the reservations of many experts about the ability of small hospitals to deliver efficient, high-quality care, *most* "community" (nonfederal, short-term general) hospitals have fewer than 200 beds. In fact, almost 40 percent of the hospital *beds* in the United States are in such "small" hospitals. Another 40 percent of the beds are in "medium-size" hospitals (those with from 200 to 500 beds), and 20 percent are in "large" hospitals (over 500 beds).

Statistics published by the American Hospital Association reveal some important differences among hospitals of different size, especially between small hospitals and those with over 200 beds.* For instance, oc-

* The statistics used in the following discussion are from *Hospitals: Journal of the American Hospital Association,* Guide Issue, part 2 (1972).

cupancy rates average only about 70 percent of capacity in small hospitals, while they are over 80 percent in the medium-size and large hospitals. Some excess capacity in the hospital system is desirable in order to meet peak and emergency demands, but an average occupancy rate of 70 percent is too low.*

The relationship among occupancy rate, size of hospital, and size of community served is a complex one. In theory, the size of the community should be the major influence. A small community needs relatively more excess capacity in order to provide the same degree of protection against random fluctuations in the demand for hospital care. Many small hospitals in fact serve communities with small populations, but many do not. In fact, well over one thousand small hospitals are located in metropolitan areas, where low occupancy rates represent a significant waste because the excess capacity cannot be justified in terms of community needs. Furthermore, improvements in transportation and communication diminish the need for small hospitals even in some areas of low population density.

Judging by average length of stay, the more seriously ill tend to get treated in the larger hospitals: the 1971 average-stay figures were 7.2 days for small hospitals, 8.1 days for medium-size hospitals, and 9.8 days for large ones. Some of the difference in average stay, however, may be due to the presence of teaching programs in larger hospitals or to inefficiencies that develop in large, complex institutions. Curiously, the small hospitals do not account for a disproportionate number of maternity cases, one of the simpler types of hospital admissions. In 1971, one out of ten admissions in small hospitals was for childbirth; in the others the ratio was one out of eight.

The number of hospital personnel per patient varies directly with hospital size. The 1971 ratios were 2.7, 3.0, and 3.4, respectively. Such differences are probably attributable to the tendency for larger hospitals to have sicker patients and more research and teaching responsibilities. Only 3 percent of the small hospitals have residency programs, compared with half of the medium-size ones and 90 percent of the large hospitals.

One of the most striking differences among hospitals is in the amount of capital investment. Assets per bed for hospitals with over 200 beds are about 40 percent greater than in the small hospitals. The relationship with size is much weaker among larger hospitals; the asset/bed ratio for those with over 500 beds is only 4 percent greater than those in the 200–500–bed category.

---

* Hospital administrators consider the optimum occupancy rate to be about 85 percent.

Differences in capital investment are reflected clearly in the data on availability of facilities and services by size of hospital. For instance, nearly all hospitals with over 200 beds have postoperative recovery rooms, but one-third of the small hospitals do not. And two-thirds of the small hospitals don't have intensive-care units. The percentages in small hospitals of other facilities and services that tend to be standard in medium-size and large hospitals are as follows: full-time registered pharmacist, 43 percent; diagnostic radioisotopic facility, 22 percent; histopathology lab, 29 percent; blood bank, 53 percent; inhalation therapy, 48 percent; and physical therapy department, 53 percent.

Of some forty-two facilities and services listed by the American Hospital Association, the mean percentage available in small hospitals is 19 percent. In hospitals in the 200–500–bed range the mean is 46 percent, and in those with over 500 beds it is 64 percent. Facilities and services that are much more frequently available in large than in medium-size hospitals are open-heart surgery, cobalt therapy, renal dialysis, occupational therapy, and numerous psychiatric services.

It is certainly not my intention in this discussion to suggest that these expensive facilities should be available in more hospitals. Indeed, there is considerable evidence that some of them, such as open-heart-surgery units, have proliferated far beyond the limits dictated by medical need or financial prudence.[3] A facility that is seldom used is not only wasteful of resources, but cannot deliver the same quality of care as one that is in regular use. The above statistics nevertheless serve to highlight the fact that hospitals differ greatly in the range of services they can provide. What is desperately needed is some sort of *systematic* approach to meeting the hospital care needs of a region, avoiding unnecessary duplication and insuring that patients are appropriately placed to receive the necessary services. There are probably some services that no hospital should be without, and institutions that are too small to provide them efficiently ought to be phased out of operation. Beyond that, all the hospitals in a given area should be functionally integrated so that there can be an easy flow of patients and physicians from one facility to another depending upon medical requirements and available space.

No one should imagine that such a rational system is easily put into effect. As indicated in Chapter 3, the typical hospital is dominated by the physicians who practice in it. A physician who has the privilege (that is the word used) of admitting patients to a hospital has a competitive advantage over physicians who have no such privilege. The admitting privilege may be obtained by having gone through a prestigious medical school and postgraduate training program, through family or other personal connections, by demonstrations of skill, by agreeing to provide free time for teaching or the care of charity patients, and in other ways. The practice of limiting admitting privileges to certain physicians is commonly defended as a necessary means of controlling the quality of care in the institution. This is probably a valid claim, but the system also limits competition and contributes to the fragmentation of the hospital system. It can also contribute to unnecessary utilization to the extent that physicians can be pressured to fill beds under pain of losing their admitting privileges when demand for hospital care is low.

Hospital trustees are also often a source of difficulty. Many hold their positions because of past or prospective financial contributions, and they are emotionally attached to "their" hospitals. At present philanthropy accounts for only a very small part of total hospital expenditures, but the philanthropists or their descendents continue to have a disproportionate degree of influence in hospital affairs. The notion of merging with a better-managed hospital, or of going out of business altogether, is not easily accepted by those with a large emotional stake in a particular hospital.

Institutional change is never easy, for any industry. The present system of hospital financing does not provide physicians or hospital trustees with enough incentives to undertake socially desirable reorganizations, nor does it impose punishments for failure to do so.

TYPE OF OWNERSHIP

Community hospitals are typically private nonprofit organizations. Many were founded by religious groups; others were established as a result of communitywide efforts or the benefactions of a few secular philanthropists. About one-fourth of the beds are in hospitals owned and operated by state or local governments, and 6 percent are in "proprietary" hospitals, that is, hospitals privately owned and run for profit.

The influence of type of ownership on the effectiveness, efficiency, and equity of care provided has always been a matter of considerable debate. Most people in the health field are strongly opposed to hospitals run for profit, primarily on the grounds that it is "wrong to make a profit out of illness," while ignoring the fact that this is precisely what physicians, pharmacists, and others do. Specific criticisms of for-profit hospitals are that they do not provide care for those who cannot pay, that they do not engage in teaching or research, and that they selectively admit the less seriously ill, thus "skimming the market." Certainly not every hospital need be engaged in teaching and research, however, nor is there any good reason for every hospital to have the personnel and facilities to deliver tertiary care * to very sick patients with complicated conditions.

As economists have begun paying more attention to the hospital field, the private non-profit institutions have come in for substantial criticism. They are, it is asserted, inefficient and lacking in adequate incentives; they carry on inappropriate research and teaching; they are too expansion-oriented; and they engage in wasteful rivalry rather than in effective price competition. State and local hospitals, on the other hand, which often exist primarily to serve the poor or those who cannot obtain admission elsewhere, are frequently accused of being inefficient, hamstrung by red tape, and insensitive to patient needs.

No definitive studies of the effects of type of ownership on hospital performance are available, although American Hospital Association data permit a few broad descriptive generalizations. Proprietary hospitals tend to be small. Their average size is 74 beds compared with 182 for private nonprofit institutions. More than 80 percent of the for-profit beds are in small hospitals; the balance, with the exception of one 507-bed hospital, are in the 200–500–bed category. There are also many small state and local government hospitals—half their beds are in the under–200–bed category. There are, however, many large ones as well: one-fourth of the state and local government beds are in hospitals larger than 500 beds.

Many of the small proprietary hospitals are located in rural areas where there isn't enough community support to start a nonprofit one. Others are located in large cities or surrounding suburbs, and were typically started by groups of physicians who lacked admitting privileges at existing non-profit hospitals. In recent years several large corporations have constructed chains of for-profit hospitals purely as commercial ventures.

The contention that the for-profit hospitals offer relatively limited facilities and services has only limited validity if one takes account of hospital size. At any given size there does not seem to be a marked difference in availability of services by type of ownership, except for psychiatric services and various kinds of outpatient services.

In each size class the occupancy rates are lower in state and local government hospitals than in either of the other types. One reasonable inference is that the public institutions are not the preferred ones in most communities. Indeed, the popular image of the public hospital is often one of limited staff and poor service to patients. The poor-service image may be

* Care rendered by specialists to patients who have been referred by other physicians, usually for complicated and serious health problems.

justified, but it cannot be blamed on any difference in number of personnel. The AHA data reveal that for any given hospital size the number of personnel per patient is as high in the state and local government hospitals as in the private nonprofit ones. Personnel mix, however, is apparently different in the public hospitals: average earnings tend to be lower in them, for any given hospital size, than in private nonprofit hospitals. Average earnings tend to be highest in the for-profit hospitals. The difference in earnings suggests that the nonprofit hospitals, especially the publicly owned ones, may be erring in the direction of employing too many relatively low-skill personnel instead of striving for greater efficiency with fewer but better-qualified employees.

REGIONAL DIFFERENCES

The U.S. hospital industry reveals striking regional differences that are worthy of close attention. If we understood the reasons for these differences and their consequences, we would be in a much better position to formulate rational and responsible policies for health care. The average hospital size in the West (119 beds) is much smaller than in the rest of the country—probably because of the lower population densities in the West—while average size in the Northeast (217 beds) is the largest of any region.* In keeping with the size differential, occupancy rates tend to be lowest in the West (70 percent) and highest in the Northeast (82 percent). The for-profit hospitals are relatively more important in the West (representing 12 percent of all beds) and are also somewhat important in the South (10 percent). They are much less important in the Northeast (5 percent) and almost nonexistent in the North Central region. There is also a significant regional difference in the relative importance of state and local government hospitals: they are most common in the South, accounting for 35 percent of all hospital beds there, and least common in the Northeast, where they account for 13 percent.

Probably the most striking regional difference is with respect to length of stay. In the Northeast the average patient stay is 9.2 days; in the West it is only 6.7 days. A small part of this differential—about 0.1 day—can be attributed to the difference in age composition of the population: the Northeast has a slightly older population (in 1970 10.6 percent of its population was 65 or over, as compared with 8.9 percent in the West), and older people everywhere tend to have longer stays. The differential of 2.5 days per patient, however, is far greater than can be explained by dif-

* This discussion of regions is based on the Bureau of the Census classification of Northeast, North Central, South, and West.

ferences in age alone. At given ages and for given diagnoses, stays are significantly shorter in the West. Nor can this be explained by greater pressure for beds in that region; as has been mentioned, occupancy rates are actually lowest in the West.

In recent years hospital expenditures per capita in the Northeast have averaged 50 percent higher than in the South and 30 percent higher than in the West. The Northeast-West differential can be explained entirely by the difference in length of stay. The admission rate and expenditures per patient-day are actually slightly higher in the West than in the Northeast. The South also has significantly shorter lengths of stay than the Northeast, but this is offset in part by a higher admission rate. The major reason for the large Northeast-South cost differential is labor cost. Payroll per patient-day in the Northeast is 40 percent higher than in the South, mostly because average earnings are much higher.

TEACHING HOSPITALS

Approximately fifteen hundred hospitals in the United States are known as "teaching" hospitals, and of this number approximately nine hundred are affiliated with a medical school. These are the great medical centers which pride themselves on being able to provide the most advanced diagnostic and therapeutic services which comprise the so-called tertiary care. Most of them in fact do a superb job in teaching young physicians how to deliver that type of care. In these centers there is also considerable emphasis on research—extending the frontiers of medical practice.

Because only a small and selected fraction of persons needing or seeking health care actually enter a university-affiliated hospital, however, students there often receive a distorted view of what the health problems of the population actually are and what medicine can or should do about them. As Dr. John H. Knowles has written, "Our teaching hospitals are called health centers today when, in reality, they enjoy a limited and exclusive function as the citadels of acute curative, scientific and technical medicine." [4] John Millis, in his incisive study of medical education, notes that about three-fourths of the country's interns and residents are in university-affiliated hospitals, but that "the university has never acknowledged any responsibility for them." He calls this the "strangest anomaly in medical education" and "finds it difficult to see any rationality in this arrangement." [5] Moreover, some six hundred "teaching" hospitals that provide training for the other 25 percent of interns and residents have no university affiliation at all.

In the opinion of most experts, internship and residency training has more influence over physicians' subsequent careers than does their medical school education. The nature and quality of these programs, therefore, should be a source of considerable concern. According to some critics, the present training programs do not give future physicians a balanced view of what health care is all about because their contacts are primarily with the hospitalized patient. Interns and residents develop disdain for the ambulatory patient, for the patient with only a minor illness, for the patient with emotional and psychological problems. The young physician develops the view that the hospital is *the* place to practice medicine, a "repair shop" view of medical care that tends to crowd out the ideals of preserving and enhancing health in the community.

All too frequently hospitals have viewed interns and residents as a cheap source of labor for the delivery of care in emergency rooms and for the coverage of patients of the attending physicians. Now that salaries for interns and residents have increased appreciably, some hospitals will reexamine the desirability of maintaining such so-called teaching programs, and some will probably drop this activity.

From the resident's point of view there is a real conflict between his desire to extend his knowledge and experience and the immediate needs of patients. I personally know of one resident who left a hospital at the midpoint of a two-year residency because he found to his dismay that the hospital was primarily interested in patient care, not in teaching. A further complication has arisen because of the disappearance of charity patients, the so-called teaching material. It is obviously desirable to have young physicians learn in actual care settings, and therefore teaching institutions will have to work out appropriate procedures so that all patients admitted can become part of the educational experience.

While there is some danger that patient needs tend to be subordinated to the research and teaching interests of the medical staff, the opposite type of problem has also arisen, particularly in large cities. I have in mind the attempts to divert medical schools from their primary responsibilities of the transmission and discovery of knowledge—teaching and research—to the delivery of services. Politicians frequently attempt to buy medical care for the poor at bargain prices by using the titles that a medical school can provide in order to hire physicians for less than they would have to pay in a strictly service setting. There can be no question that the provision of some patient care, and particularly a wide variety of services, is desirable for a medical school. But this is principally because it helps the schools to fulfill properly their primary functions of teaching and research. If government insists on emphasizing current delivery of services, however, future medical care will be imperiled.

DIRECTIONS OF CHANGE

Although we still have a long way to go, considerable progress has been made in bringing the average hospital size closer to the desirable range. Over the past twenty years the average number of beds per hospital has increased by 50 percent. The average size of for-profit hospitals, which were and are the smallest, has more than doubled. There has also been a constant upward trend in the number of hospital employees per patient, which has grown at about 2.5 percent annually for over twenty years and shows no sign of leveling off. Growth of staff is partly attributable to shortening of hours (at one time nurses worked twelve-hour days, so only two shifts were necessary) and partly to the growing complexity of hospital care. Curiously, this growth has been accompanied by increasing patient complaints about lack of service and attention. If such complaints are justified, one may well ask what all the additional staff are doing. Part of the answer must be that they are staffing and servicing the vastly more elaborate equipment now found in hospitals. The amount of capital investment per patient has been rising even more rapidly than the number of employees, and, unlike many other industries in which physical capital tends to diminish labor requirements, most new developments in medicine have tended to increase them.

Another significant trend has been the growth in importance of outpatient care. From 1962 to 1971 the number of outpatient visits more than doubled, while the number of inpatient admissions increased by only 25 percent. The surge in outpatient visits is related to the problem of access discussed in the preceding chapter. Many families no longer have a "family doctor," someone to whom they instinctively turn in time of trouble. The hospital, despite its impersonal character, is at least *there*, a known quantity where care is always accessible, albeit after a long wait. In many communities the hospital emergency room is becoming the principal source of primary care, although inpatients are still the main source of gross revenue for community hospitals, yielding about 90 percent of the total. The relative contribution of outpatient care to *net revenue*, however, is frequently significant because it tends to be more profitable than inpatient care.

The hospital industry has been expanding at an enormous rate. Employment in 1971 was twice that in 1955; in many cities one out of every twenty-five employed persons now works in a hospital. Hospital employees traditionally have not been organized, but unions have made considerable progress in hospitals in recent years, and average earnings have increased faster than the national average. These and related changes will be discussed in more detail in the next section on hospital costs.

Why Are Hospital Costs So High?

The reasons that hospital care costs so much today are complex and hard to pin down. Part of the problem is the matter of definitions: exactly what, for instance, comprises "costs"? Much of the popular discussion has focused on the cost of individual cases, noting especially how easily some patients can incur bills of five or ten thousand dollars or even more. Insofar as recent technological advances have created opportunities for treating previously untreatable conditions, high bills like these are often for procedures, such as organ transplants, that weren't possible ten or twenty years ago. As noted in Chapter 1, while the possibility of incurring such high bills is a good argument for carrying health insurance—indeed, perhaps carrying such insurance should be compulsory—it does not pose as serious a problem for analysis or policy formation as one would gather from the attention lavished on it by the popular press.

Another target the press singles out in its coverage of health care problems is high average cost per patient-day. Newspaper headlines warn that the average cost of semiprivate hospital accommodations now exceeds a hundred dollars a day and is projected to soar to two hundred dollars a day by 1980. Such emphasis on cost per day is often misplaced. Suppose, for instance, that it were possible to appreciably shorten the average length of stay. This might be highly desirable both in terms of economics and health, even though it resulted in an increase in cost per patient-day. Or suppose it were possible to reduce the number of hospital admissions by providing more ambulatory care and home nursing services. The result might be an increase in cost per patient-day for those who were admitted (because a higher percentage would be seriously ill) but a substantial decrease in total hospital costs. Every individual has a stake in keeping the *total* as low as possible, consistent with health needs, because these costs are eventually borne by every individual—in insurance premiums and taxes if not in direct personal expenditures.

While cost per patient-day has indeed been rising rapidly, more important is the fact that total expenditures in community hospitals are now triple what they were in 1965 and more than four times the 1960 level. Some of this increase in hospital expenditures is inevitable, given that wages and prices have been increasing in the economy as a whole. The hospital industry could hardly escape paying such increases for necessary goods and services, including labor services. But if that were all that were happening the increase in hospital expenditures per capita might have been about 4 percent annually. The fact that expenditures were actually increasing at more than triple that rate is what requires special explanation.

The explanation can proceed at two levels. First, at the purely mechanical or *accounting* level it is possible statistically to break down hospital expenditures into their various components—admissions, length of stay, personnel per patient, etc. Second, one can attempt a *behavioral analysis* of patients, physicians, and others whose decisions in the aggregate determine hospital expenditures. In either case, it is also possible—and indeed, it is important—to examine rising costs over different time periods, for while hospital expenditures per capita have been rising somewhat faster than expenditures for all services ever since World War II, the differential widened enormously after 1965. Much of the hospital cost "crisis" dates from that time.

From 1950 until 1965 per capita expenditures of community hospitals grew fairly steadily at a rate of about 8 percent annually, while the figure for all services in the U.S. economy for the same period was only 5 percent annually. In the early years a good part of this differential was attributable to sharp increases in the number of personnel per patient and to wage increases that exceeded those in the general economy. This may have been a true "catching up" period for hospital employees, who prior to World War II typically worked very long hours at very low wages. The period of most rapid growth in both personnel per patient and earnings per employee was from 1950 to 1955.

Around 1960 *non*labor expenditures such as for equipment and supplies started to grow more rapidly than labor expenditures, and the average length of stay, which had been falling, started to increase. It seems to me that these changes were associated with the character of medical advances.[6] In the early post–World War II years these advances mostly took the form of new drugs that were highly effective against infectious diseases and were relatively inexpensive to administer. After 1960 many of the advances involved complex diagnostic and therapeutic procedures that were expensive and frequently resulted in longer patient stays. Between

1960 and 1965 nonlabor expenditures per admission in constant dollars grew at 7 percent annually, compared with an annual rate of only 3 percent over the 1950–1955 period.

After 1965 hospital expenditures started to explode. Between 1965 and 1971 per capita expenditures grew at approximately 14 percent annually—a rate that amounts to a doubling every five years! Service expenditures in the economy as a whole during this period grew at only 7 percent annually.

It is possible, in an accounting sense, to pinpoint the principal elements in this runaway hospital inflation. First, it should be emphasized that it was *not* due to an unusual increase in the number of patients. Patient-days per capita grew at about the same rate after 1965 as before. Second, expenditures for labor and especially for nonlabor inputs per patient-day grew exceptionally rapidly. The number of personnel per patient after 1965 jumped by 3.4 percent annually, compared with a 1.7 percent annual rate from 1960 to 1965. Earnings per employee after 1965 soared at 8 percent annually. By contrast, earnings for all workers in the private nonagricultural economy grew at less than 5 percent annually during these same years. The sharp increase in nonlabor expenditures went mostly for new and more elaborate equipment and for supplies, including more disposables and prepared-prepackaged food.

Turning to a behavioral explanation of these same phenomena, a rich variety of hypotheses present themselves. One of the most compelling is that 1966 marked the introduction of Medicare and Medicaid, two large federal health insurance programs that made available huge amounts of new money for hospital care. The resulting large increase in demand for services was relatively insensitive to higher prices, because reimbursement was geared to cost. According to Professor Herbert Klarman, a leading authority on the economics of hospitals, the volume of services reimbursed on a cost basis jumped 75 percent as a result of the establishment of Medicare and Medicaid.[7]

This created an unprecedented opportunity for physicians and hospital administrators to do what they always want to do—improve the quality of care as they see it. This means more equipment, more personnel, more tests, more X rays, and so on. It did not, as noted above, result in an abnormal increase in the number of people getting care, but the intensity of care increased appreciably. The big unknown in the equation is: what effect, if any, has this had on health? Were physicians and hospital administrators truly serving the social interest, or were they merely fulfilling their own "technological imperative"? Was there a divergence between their interests and those of the community, or did they improperly diagnose the community's health needs and the consequences of the decisions they were making?

One reasonable interpretation is that the physician who pressed for more equipment and staff in *his* hospital was doing what he regarded as best for *his* patient, since the patient would get some benefit while the costs would be passed on to a third party (i.e., the federal government). The collective effect of these individual decisions, however, was what many regard as an unwarranted increase in the cost of hospital care. Unfortunately, this large increase in resources devoted to hospital care does not seem to have produced improvement in the health of the population. Whether in the absence of this increase there would have been deterioration in health is a matter for further conjecture and study.

A case study by Professor Bernard Friedman of the treatment of breast cancer in six Boston hospitals provides a possible illustration of the process described above. In 1965, prior to the introduction of Medicare and Medicaid, about 20 percent of the cases were treated with both surgery and radiation; the other 80 percent of cases received only one or the other treatment, at least initially. In 1967 more than 40 percent of (apparently similar) cases received initial treatment of both surgery and radiation. Friedman is not certain that the change in treatment was due to Medicare. He notes that women under age 65 also experienced changes in treatment, but speculates that this may be partly the result of a Medicare-induced change in the "standard" of care. It would be nice to be able to say that the additional care had a positive impact on survival, but Friedman reports that the percentage of patients who died within three years of initial treatment was essentially the same before and after Medicare.[8]

How To Keep Hospital Costs from Going Higher

Rufus Rorem, who did pioneering studies of health economics nearly fifty years ago, said that one of the most widely read articles he ever wrote was entitled "Why Hospital Costs Have Risen." The demand for reprints was enormous. Encouraged by this success he then wrote an article entitled "How to Keep Hospital Costs From Rising." Judging from a complete lack of requests, this piece was a total failure.

Rorem's experience is indicative of an attitude that was and perhaps still is all too common in the health field. Shrouded in the mantle of "nonprofit" and convinced of the worthiness of all their endeavors, hospital administrations have been primarily concerned with justifying high costs rather than considering whether the resources siphoned into the hospital field might not be better used in other directions, including other dimensions of health care. Moreover, even when administrators attempt to take a broader view, their freedom to act is sharply limited by the hospital's physicians on the one hand and the board of trustees on the other.

An approach to the control of hospital expenditures can profitably begin with a simple definition:

Expenditures = Admissions × Length of stay × Cost per patient-day

There is no way to affect hospital expenditures except by altering one or more of these variables.

Admissions

Hospital admissions per capita in the United States have been rising fairly steadily ever since 1950 at a bit over 1 percent annually. At present one out of every seven Americans enters a community hospital as an inpatient each year, while in 1950 only one in every nine did. If the present trend continues, by the end of the century the rate will be one out of every five. Inasmuch as it is doubtful that there is more morbidity in the population now than there used to be, it is not clear why admission rates have been rising.

One school of thought holds that the rate of admissions responds to bed availability: if we insist on installing more hospital beds, they will tend to get filled. This proposition, dubbed "Roemer's law," after Dr. Milton Roemer of UCLA, who first suggested it in 1959, has received considerable support in recent econometric studies.

The notion that supply can create its own demand in this market should not come as too much of a surprise. The decision to admit or discharge patients is largely in the hands of the physician. Such decisions are supposedly made on scientific grounds, but medical science is not exact and there are many cases where a plausible argument can be made either way. In such instances the availability or lack of availability of a bed can have a significant influence on the decision.

Many physicians have a built-in bias in favor of hospitalization. As mentioned previously, their training is heavily oriented toward the hospitalized patient. When in doubt they feel more comfortable if the patient is in the hospital. It is more convenient for the physician, there is more control and supervision of the patient's condition, it is easier to carry on diagnostic work, and emergency care is more readily available if needed.

One obvious way, therefore, to hold down hospital admissions is to sharply limit the expansion in the number of hospital beds. Such limitation can be sought through government regulation, by curtailing federal funding for new construction, or, as discussed below, by changing hospital reimbursement plans so as to eliminate the guarantee that the hospital will always be able to meet its bills.

From the patient's point of view hospital admission frequently seems attractive even when not medically necessary because his insurance will pay for procedures done for him as an inpatient but not as an outpatient. Another strategy, therefore, is to modify health insurance plans so that they do not encourage such inappropriate use of facilities. Adding outpatient coverage would tend to eliminate some hospital admissions, but it may also result in an increase in total health expenditures. A great deal depends on incentives offered physicians. Prepaid group practices such as the Kaiser health plans have demonstrated that it is possible to reduce substantially hospital admission rates without drastically increasing outpatient visits or jeopardizing patient health. Such plans have recorded admission rates one-third to one-half lower than those for comparable populations with conventional insurance coverage. A significant amount of the difference is related to the lower rates of in-hospital surgery among members of prepaid plans.

Some observers believe that the key factor in such plans is the financial incentive given to physicians to hold down hospital utilization; in some of the Kaiser plans the physicians benefit when hospital costs fall below projected levels. Others believe that the key is to be found in the limited availability of hospital beds. Because the number of beds per capita is often half of what is considered a "normal" ratio, Kaiser physicians are forced to reconsider the appropriate decision for a large number of marginal conditions.

Still others believe that the lower admissions under such plans can be attributed to the free or nearly free care available to outpatients, which results in much less pressure from patients for hospitalization. As has been stated, however, it does not appear that the reduced use of hospitals under such plans is accomplished by an unusual increase in outpatient care. My own view is that the capitation method of payment is the critical variable in changing physician behavior: when physicians know that there is only so much money available and that extra spending in the hospital has implications for the rest of the plan, they tend to use hospitals much more judiciously.

Length of Stay

Once a patient is admitted to the hospital there can be considerable variation in the length of stay, with significant implications for hospital expenditures. An important determinant is the efficiency with which the staff carries out the necessary diagnostic and therapeutic procedures. Are there delays in conducting tests and taking X rays? Do these have to be repeated because of errors? Are operating rooms available when needed? Do patients linger longer than necessary simply because their physicians are away or have forgotten to discharge them? Adverse side effects of drugs, tests, and surgery also frequently increase the length of stay. One study of hospitalization for neurosurgery found that postoperative infection, which occurred in 17 percent of the cases, extended the average stay (twenty-five days) by an additional eighteen days.[9]

The length of stay that physicians deem appropriate for various medical conditions often has a weak scientific basis. The few studies that have been done suggest that considerable variation is possible without discernible health effects. In England, for instance, a controlled study of patients who had been operated on for hernia could find no significant differences between patients who were discharged one day after surgery and comparable patients who were discharged after six days.[10]

Dr. Paul T. Lahti, a surgeon who is a vigorous advocate of early hospital discharge after surgery, contends that such procedure is actually better for the patient's health. Lahti has reported that of 611 consecutive patients on whom he performed a variety of general surgical procedures—including herniorrhaphies, appendectomies, and cholecystectomies (surgical excision of the gall bladder)—only 21 percent stayed in the hospital four days or more. The largest percentage went home on the first postoperative day.[11] Most physicians who perform the same type of surgery as Dr. Lahti keep their patients in the hospital about four or five days longer.

Length of stay for nonsurgical cases is also frequently arbitrary and lacking in scientific basis. A prospective controlled study of 138 randomly selected patients with uncomplicated but definite myocardial infarction tested the proposition that patients discharged after two weeks of hospital stay can do as well as those discharged after three weeks. For six months after discharge (as far as the study went) there appeared to be no additional benefit to the patients who received the three-week stay.[12]

A critical factor to consider before discharging a patient from the hospital before complete recovery is the nature and amount of care available on the outside. Sometimes all that is needed is an occasional visit by a nurse, or someone to provide a hot meal, or a conveniently located outpatient facility. Sometimes a simpler, less expensive type of institution, such as an extended-care facility, is indicated.

Even when such facilities are available, however, there may be institutional barriers that prolong hospitalization unnecessarily. Dr. Sidney Lee cites the example of a hospital that was planning to expand, because of pressure on capacity, even though an attached extended-care facility was half-empty. It was discovered that physicians were reluctant to transfer patients from the hospital to the attached facility because they had to complete a lengthy form and because the third party did not cover physician services in the facility. Simplification of the form and a change in the third-party coverage provisions put an end to plans for hospital expansion and resulted in significant savings in total health care costs. [13]

A legitimate concern of physicians who might otherwise be willing to consider earlier discharge is whether they can get their patients promptly readmitted in an emergency. Arrangements for such contingencies are certainly feasible, but in the absence of more concrete incentives for administrator, physician, and patient, early discharge is not likely to come into being.

One irony of hospital economics is that longer stays help to keep down the average cost per patient-day. This happens for two reasons. First, patients who stay on after the acute phase of their illness make fewer demands on staff and equipment. Second, it is easier to maintain a high occupancy rate when there is a less rapid turnover in patients. Thus short stays make life more difficult for hospital administrators and their staffs. Most administrators want to keep their occupancy rates up, and when too many beds become unoccupied, they try to put pressure on the physicians to fill them. One way is to suggest to each of the various service chiefs (for medicine, surgery, pediatrics, etc.) that unless he keeps the beds assigned to his service reasonably full they will be reassigned to another service. The result is a tendency to admit more freely and especially to have longer stays.

Attempts at controlling length of stay have been made both through internal review in the hospital and by third-party payers. In many areas of the country, for example, the Blue Cross plan keeps records on the average length of stay in each hospital for each diagnosis and exerts some pressure on hospitals and on physicians by asking them to justify unusually long stays. Of course, if hospitals were reimbursed in part on the number of cases treated rather than only the number of days of care rendered this would provide a stronger and more direct incentive for shorter stays.

Cost per Patient-Day

Given hospital admission rates and average lengths of stay, the only way to control expenditures—as the equation on page 96 indicates—is by reducing the cost per patient-day. About 60 percent of this cost now goes for labor and about 40 percent for nonlabor inputs. This total cost may exceed the socially optimal level in a given hospital for three reasons. First, given the fact that resources are needed for other pressing social needs, the hospital may be providing "too much" service or care. Second, it may be providing its services inefficiently, that is, using too many resources. And finally, it may be paying too high a price for the goods and services (including labor) that it buys. In most areas of the economy we rely on management's hope of profit and fear of loss to avoid such errors. With respect to hospitals it might be possible to introduce similar incentives by instituting new methods of reimbursement.

INCENTIVE REIMBURSEMENT

Reimbursement of hospitals in the aggregate clearly must bear some relationship to costs. If not, the hospital system would dissolve for failure to command the resources necessary to stay in business. But it does not follow that the reimbursement formula must permit each and every hospital to stay in business, nor does it follow that each service maintained by a hospital should have *its* full cost reimbursed regardless of its social utility.

One proposal for monitoring hospital costs would require each hospital to justify its annual budget to third-party payers or to a regulatory agency. Such a line-by-line policing of hospital decisions, where the judgment of the reviewer is presumably substituted for that of the hospital administration, would probably be difficult and expensive to administer and over time would tend to become very inflexible.

An alternative approach that I have advocated [14] provides considerable incentive for efficient management, permits great flexibility, and is administratively much more simple. The starting point of this approach is average cost (ideally both cost per case and cost per patient-day would be used) for all community hospitals. Statistical analysis would be used to determine the effect on cost of location, services offered, and various other hospital characteristics. The reimbursement rate for each hospital would then be established as a function of the average cost of all hospitals combined adjusted for the characteristics of the particular hospital. Thus hospitals located in higher wage areas, or those offering more services, would get above-average reimbursement; those in low-wage areas or offering fewer services would get less.

While statistical analysis could be used as a starting point to determine adjustments for different services, there is no reason why the third-party reimburser could not raise (or lower) the adjustment factor for particular services that it wished to encourage (or discourage). For instance, analysis might show that, other things being equal, the presence of an open-heart surgery facility adds two dollars to the patient-day cost of an average hospital. If the third party deemed this a poor use of resources, it could lower the adjustment factor to one dollar per patient-day. Hospitals so affected would thus have considerable incentive to eliminate this service, especially if it were infrequently used. On the other hand, if the third party desired to encourage hospitals to have certain services, say intensive-care units, it could raise the adjustment factor for this service. In contrast to reimbursement schemes where a central bureaucracy makes all the decisions, this system leaves a good deal of discretion to individual hospitals. Thus the judgment, experience, knowledge of local needs, and creative intelligence of physicians and administrators throughout the country would be allowed considerable scope.

One big advantage of this approach is that no hospital administration could be certain in advance that all its costs would be met. Thus an administration would be under constant pressure to keep costs in check while still meeting patient and physician demands for care. In describing this plan to hospital administrators I have always received the same reaction: each one is convinced that his hospital would get less reimbursement under this plan than it now gets. This is curious, since the plan, including the adjustments, calls for reimbursing in the aggregate the full cost of the system. The fact that each administrator fears the effect of such a plan on his hospital speaks volumes about the potential for eliminating waste and inefficiency.

This system, which appears to put hospital administrators under greater pressure, would, paradoxically, strengthen their position vis-à-vis the physicians. Under direct cost reimbursement an administrator finds it difficult to refuse requests for more equipment or staff regardless of his opinion of their cost effectiveness: a service chief can always tell him that when costs rise, so will his rate of reimbursement. But if there were a real possibility that the hospital would not be able to meet its bills, the administrator's "no" would carry a great deal more conviction and authority.

One disadvantage of such a system is that the hospital administration might be tempted to skimp on the services and care provided to patients. Some "skimping" is obviously what is wanted, but protection against unwarranted risks to patient health or safety would have to depend on the vigilance of physicians, accreditation bodies, third-party purchasers, and the patient himself.

COMPETITION OR REGULATION?

I am much in favor of trying to introduce more competitive behavior into the hospital field through the reimbursement mechanism, but I doubt that the industry can be safely left to a pure free-market approach. The essence of a free competitive market is that (1) there are many well-informed buyers and sellers no one of whom is large enough to influence price unilaterally; (2) buyers and sellers act independently (i.e., there is no collusion); and (3) there is free entry for other buyers and sellers not currently in the market. Many hospital markets depart substantially from these ideal competitive conditions, sometimes inevitably.

In most towns and even moderate-size cities the market is too small to support enough hospitals to fulfill the requirements of free competition. As was pointed out previously, there are significant economies of scale in hospitals up to a size of at least 200 or 300 beds. Since a community needs no more than 4 beds per 1,000 population (and probably less), a city of 60,000 would be most efficiently served by a single well-run hospital. It would thus be uneconomical to require numerous competitive hospitals except in large, densely populated markets. These constraints are even more imperative when specialty care is considered. It is doubtful that a population even as large as 1 million justifies enough independent maternity, open-heart surgery, and organ-transplant services to provide really competitive conditions. The fact that these services proliferate contrary to what economies of scale would indicate is the result of other problems, such as the absence of appropriate incentives and constraints for physicians and hospital administrators.

In such a condition of "natural monopoly" the traditional American response has been to introduce public utility regulation (e.g., electric utility, telephone, transportation). The results, however, have frequently been unsatisfactory, partly because the regulators often tend to serve the regulated rather than the public and partly because it is inherently difficult to set standards of performance without competitive yardsticks. Many other countries rely on government ownership and control, but the United States experience with government hospitals has not, on balance, been favorable. Another possible solution is the development of what J. K. Galbraith has termed "countervailing power" and what the economics textbooks describe as "bilateral monopoly." If, for instance, all the consumers in a one-hospital town were organized into a single body for purposes of bargaining with the hospital, at least some of the disadvantages of monopoly would be lessened.

The typical "solution" in the hospital field has been to emphasize the "nonprofit" character of community hospitals and to assume that because of it they will not abuse their monopoly power. This "solution" is open to the criticisms that the absence of a profit (loss) incentive too easily leads to waste, inefficiency, and unnecessary duplication and that perhaps the hospitals are run for the benefit of the physicians.

Even when there are numerous hospitals in the same market, society may benefit if they refrain from maintaining arm's-length competitive postures with one another. The free exchange of information, cooperative efforts to meet crisis situations, and reciprocal backup arrangements may help to reduce costs and increase patient satisfaction. Unfortunately, the intimacy and trust developed through such activities may spread in less desirable directions such as price fixing, exclusion of would-be rivals, and other practices restricting competition. For two hundred years economists have been impressed with the wisdom of Adam Smith's observation in *The Wealth of Nations* that "people of the same trade seldom meet together, even for merriment and diversion, but the conversation ends in a conspiracy against the public, or in some contrivance to raise prices."

Although some deviation from a purely competitive solution seems inevitable, regulation of hospitals by state public utility commissions would, in my opinion, be a disaster. In the first place, our experience with other industries has taught us that regulation is frequently introduced at the behest of the regulated as a device for achieving legal cartelization and restricting competition. Hospitals would certainly be no exception to this rule. The leading proponent of state public utility regulation approach is the American Hospital Association. Second, experience has shown that regulation rarely works to lower prices and frequently results in inefficiency and undesirable costs. Finally, regulation would tend to inhibit technological and organizational innovation.[15]

Public utility commissions, even if well managed by well-motivated men and women, would inevitably concentrate on setting per diem prices (based on cost) rather than on looking at the total cost of care to the com-

munity. The person who is in the best position to exert intelligent re-
straints on hospital costs is the physician. He knows better than anyone
which patients need not be admitted, which ones could go home a day
earlier, which tests are really superfluous. The physician is also best situ-
ated to appraise the excess capacity now appearing in many hospital care
markets. When one considers that perhaps one out of every five patients
now in a hospital need not be there, the possibility of really serious overcapacity cannot be lightly dismissed. As a first step toward getting a grip
on hospital costs, a five-year moratorium should be declared (allowing
very few exceptions) on all hospital construction and expansion. During
this period the financing system should be modified so as to provide incentives to physicians and hospital administrators and trustees to balance
costs against potential benefits. With hospital costs under control, more
funds would be available for ambulatory care, preventive medicine, treatment of emotional problems, medical research, and other needs that are
currently being squeezed out of the picture by our resource-devouring
hospital system.

CHAPTER 5

Drugs: The Key to Modern Medicine

> Powerful drugs are a mixed blessing. Active chemicals inevitably carry with them the capacity for both good and harm.
>
> LOUIS LASAGNA, M.D.
> "Research Regulation and Development of New Pharmaceuticals: Past, Present and Future," *The American Journal of the Medical Sciences*

Drugs are the key to modern medicine. Surgery, radiotherapy, and diagnostic tests are all important, but the ability of health care providers to alter health outcomes—Dr. Walsh McDermott's "decisive technology"—depends primarily on drugs. Six dollars are spent on hospitals and physicians for every dollar spent on drugs, but without drugs the effectiveness of hospitals and physicians would be enormously diminished.

The great power of drugs is a development of the twentieth century—many would say of the past forty years. Our age has been given many names—atomic, electronic, space, and the like—but measured by impact on people's lives it might just as well be called the "drug age."

Until this century the physician could with confidence give a smallpox vaccination, administer quinine for malaria, prescribe opium and morphine for the relief of pain, and not much more. As Dr. Allen Norton has noted, "The decades around 1900 were a time of famous diagnosticians. The cynic could reasonably say that this was not surprising. There was no other way in which an able doctor could express himself because there were so few remedies for any diseases." [1]

A quarter-century later the situation was not much different. Some advances had been made in surgery, but the death rates from tuberculosis, influenza and pneumonia, and other infectious diseases were still extremely high. With the introduction and wide use of sulfonamide and penicillin, however, the death rate in the United States from influenza and pneumonia fell by more than 8 percent annually from 1935 to 1950. (The annual rate of decline from 1900 to 1935 had been only 2 percent.) In the case of tuberculosis, while some progress had been made since the turn of the century, the rate of decline in the death rate accelerated appreciably after the adoption of penicillin, streptomycin, and PAS (para-aminosalicylic acid) in the late 1940s and of isoniazid in the early 1950s. New drugs and vaccines developed since the 1920s have also been strikingly effective against typhoid, whooping cough, poliomyelitis, measles, diphtheria, and tetanus; more recently great advances have been made in hormonal drugs, antihypertension drugs, antihistamines, anticoagulants, antipsychotic drugs, and antidepressants.

The great scientific advances of this century have been matched by a rapid growth in the size of the drug industry. In 1899, the year that marked the introduction of aspirin, the U.S. drug industry had a value added by manufacture * of just over $50 million. By 1929 this figure had increased sixfold, and the industry's most rapid expansion was yet to come. Between 1939 and 1958, a period when many of today's most effective drugs were introduced and widely diffused for the first time, the industry's value added multiplied eightfold, while that of manufacturing as a whole increased by less than six times. By 1970 the value added of the drug industry was over $5 *billion* dollars, making it one of the largest manufacturing industries in the country. (Only the motor vehicle, aircraft, iron and steel, industrial chemicals, and communications equipment industries have appreciably larger value added.)

Given its economic importance, its rapid rate of growth, and the unique contribution of some of its output to human welfare, it should be no surprise that the drug industry has begun to receive a great deal of attention from lawmakers, the press, and some academic researchers. The topics that have provoked greatest interest are drug safety, overuse and abuse of drugs, drug prices, drug industry profits, drug advertising, and drug research. Discussion of these topics and the policy issues that surround them follows a description of the drug industry.

---

* The *value added by manufacture* for a given industry is defined as the value of its shipments minus the cost of materials and supplies purchased from other industries.

Drug Manufacturing

About one thousand U.S. firms are engaged in the manufacture of drugs. Most of these firms are small, limiting their attention either to manufacturing a few specialized products, or to serving local areas, or to repackaging drugs bought in bulk from other producers. About one hundred firms, members of the Pharmaceutical Manufacturers Association, account for most of the industry's production, including about 95 percent of prescription drug sales. Prescription drugs are much more important than nonprescription ("over-the-counter") drugs from both the medical and economic points of view, and their relative importance has been increasing. Several U.S. drug firms are worldwide in scope, with from one-fourth to one-half of their production and sales taking place outside the United States. Conversely, about 10 to 15 percent of domestic drug consumption is produced by American subsidiaries of foreign companies.

Academic economists, in appraising the drug or any industry, typically attach paramount importance to its structure, by which they mean the size distribution of firms. Do a few large firms account for most of the industry's sales, or are there many effective competitors? Economic theory suggests (and historical experience confirms) that if the former is true, collusion among the dominant firms to fix prices and the practice of other kinds of restrictive and monopolistic behavior are more likely to occur. Explicit collusion (secret meetings and agreements to fix prices) is much easier to manage when only a handful of firms are involved, as is implicit collusion (setting one's prices in line with major competitors' prices in order to keep profits at satisfactorily high levels).

A commonly used index of "concentration" (a term denoting the size distribution of firms) is the proportion of industry output accounted for by the four largest (or eight largest) firms. For the U.S. drug industry this index is not exceptionally high. The four largest firms account for about 25 percent of all output, the eight largest for less than 50 percent— somewhat lower than typical figures for other U.S. chemical or manufacturing industries, and much lower than the indexes for the American automobile, aircraft, iron and steel, and many other industries.

There is, however, something special about drug manufacturing which makes the concentration index for the industry less relevant than usual. The output of most drug firms is specialized, with no possibility of substituting drugs in one category for those in another. Major product categories like antihistamines, antiinfectives, tranquilizers, cardiovascular preparations, and gastrointestinal preparations cannot compete with one another for sales the way that Chryslers compete with Chevrolets or even the way phonograph records compete with tapes. Thus to get a true picture of the drug industry's competitive structure one must calculate separate concentration indexes by product category. And these are typically quite high. In most instances the top four firms account for 50 to 60 percent of sales. Contributing to this lack of competition within drug product categories is the fact that production techniques for different types of drug products often differ considerably. Thus even the potential ability of drug firms to compete across product categories is sometimes limited—when not actually barred by patents—by lack of process "know-how" and of specialized production facilities.

Although the concentration indexes for drug product categories are at high levels, over time there is considerable turnover among category leaders. Of the top five firms in any category in a given year, there is a good chance that two or three will not be among the top five a decade later. Such turnovers, however, are usually the result of new-product development, and are rarely due to price competition.

PRICE POLICIES

In most industries, and especially in competitive ones, prices tend to fall when costs of production fall and to rise when costs rise. The prices of most prescription drugs, however, tend to remain constant for very long periods of time. Such price inflexibility, even when there have been large changes in demand and/or costs of production, suggests a remarkable freedom from competitive pressures.

While list prices tend to remain fixed for long periods, the price charged by a drug manufacturer often varies greatly depending upon the customer. Differences have been reported of as much as 500 percent between the price charged drug retailers (i.e., pharmacies) and the price charged hospitals, or between the domestic and the export price. Such differences, unless justified by equivalent differences in cost (and frequently they are not), are evidence of price discrimination. Such conduct suggests that drug manufacturers possess and use monopoly power, just as the ability of physicians to charge different fees to different patients has been taken as evidence of the weakness of competition in that market.[2]

Why do drug companies practice price discrimination? Because maximum profits are realized by cutting prices where sales are likely to be responsive to such cuts and by maintaining them in all other markets. The price discriminator makes more this way than if he charged a uniform price or one that simply varied with differences in cost. In markets where there is effective price competition, however, such a policy cannot succeed.

Drug manufacturers charge lower prices to hospitals and to the buyer on the export markets because the range of possible substitutes open to both is greater than that available to either retailers or domestic buyers in general. Hospitals, for example, are in a position to negotiate with several potential suppliers; moreover, they can conduct tests to determine whether quality standards are being met. The individual drug retailer, on the other hand, must stock whatever his customers require—and what the customers require is usually determined by the physician. Export markets are more competitive than domestic markets because there is more possibility of substitution from foreign producers.

Drug industry spokesmen resent the charge that they are not competitive. From their point of view, competition is keen, but is manifest in the development of new and better drug products. Such competition, they argue, serves the consumer better than would simple price competition on existing drugs. Drug research and development is a long and expensive process, with many years usually intervening between the initiation of research and the successful marketing of a new drug product. The hope of securing a monopoly position and the profits that go with it provides the incentive for firms to undertake that process.

PRODUCT DIFFERENTIATION

One of the outstanding characteristics of the drug industry is its emphasis on product differentiation. Much of the research effort, and nearly all of the marketing effort of major firms is devoted to developing drugs that, no matter how closely they resemble other drugs, are perceived as distinctive and superior. The distinctiveness and superiority of each brand is emphasized by heavy advertising and promotional efforts that, in the case of prescription drugs, attempt to persuade physicians to prescribe that brand rather than another manufacturer's version. By making minor modifications in the chemical formula of a drug, each manufacturer can truthfully claim that his product is "different," even though its mode of action and its effects are similar to other companies' drugs.

Distinctiveness is also sought by developing new dosage forms of existing drugs—capsules instead of tablets, an inhalant instead of a liquid, etc.—and by combining existing drugs into new products. In the 1950s such attempts at minor differentiation reached their peak. Less than 10 percent of the new drug products marketed during that decade were new chemical entities; most were combination products, new dosage forms, or simply duplications.

Every such attempt at product differentiation has some possible good consequences as well as bad ones. Physicians can prescribe reputable brand names with reasonable confidence in the uniformity and quality of the product. New dosage forms and combination products may serve the needs of some patients better than existing products. Minor molecular manipulation may result in a significant therapeutic advance: according to Dr. J. J. Burns, vice-president for research of Hoffman, LaRoche (a major drug manufacturer), "The steroids, sulfonamides, antihistamines and semi-synthetic penicillins, to cite a few types, are replete with examples of major bio-medical advancements resulting from allegedly minor molecular manipulation." [3]

On the other side of the ledger, excessive differentiation of basically similar drugs obviously results in increased prices for the consumer. Differentiation is usually accompanied by high expenditures for advertising and other sales efforts, much of it concentrated on establishing the drug's distinctiveness to a degree far beyond that which could be justified by a scientific comparison of the products in question. Another reason different versions of the same drug result in higher costs is because pharmacies must carry a larger inventory of products than is really necessary.

The advertising techniques used to promote the sale of *non*prescription drugs, as might be expected, are similar to those which are used to market cigarettes, beer, and cosmetics. What is more surprising, and disturbing, is the flashy prescription-drug advertising that appears in medical journals and is directed at physicians—professionals who presumably should not be so easily influenced by pictures of pretty girls or chic typography. In addition to advertising, U.S. drug firms employ over twenty thousand "detail" men, whose primary job is to visit physicians and push their company's products.

In defense of these practices the drug companies contend, with some justification, that information about new drugs must be delivered to the physician somehow, and that there is no cost-free way of doing this under any economic or political system. This is correct. Critics of the drug industry, however, seriously question whether it is necessary to spend, as do the drug companies collectively, an average of as much as $4,000 annually on every practicing physician in the United States in order to "provide him with the information he needs."

Not all competition among drug companies, then, takes the form of developing new drugs. Some is simply old-fashioned competition in marketing, but with the emphasis on persuasion, not price. Consider, for example, the methods of one of the country's fastest-growing drug companies as described in a 1971 *Fortune* article. Started as a one-man operation in 1950, by 1962 this firm was boasting annual sales of close to $2 million. With the help of high-pressure selling tactics, sales have since grown to over $50 million annually, while the company's founder has accumulated a personal fortune of over $150 million. The company, the *Fortune* article reports, "spends virtually nothing on basic research, it owns no patents on drugs it manufactures, and it has no products with exclusive therapeutic properties." Its salesmen, however, "make twice as many calls on doctors as salesmen from 50 leading pharmaceutical companies." [4]

Aggressive salesmanship clearly has a place in the American free-enterprise system. Neither expressions of moral outrage against the drug industry nor the passing of a flock of new laws is likely to alter the situation. The only person who can make prescribing more rational is the physician, because he is the only one who writes prescriptions. If he had a financial stake in keeping down the cost of the drugs he prescribes, as he would under a comprehensive capitation prepayment plan, he might be motivated to examine more closely drug prices and alternative products—and he undoubtedly would also be less susceptible to persuasive detail men and high-pressure advertising.

Keeping abreast of drugs is not an easy task for the physician. It is obviously difficult for a busy practitioner to be familiar with the properties, prices, and potential dangers of more than a small fraction of the eight thousand drug products listed in the *Physician's Desk Reference* (a commercial publication distributed free to physicians). One physician in five tries to keep up to date by subscribing to the *Medical Letter,* a nonprofit newsletter published biweekly. In highly readable language this four-page publication reviews new drugs and new experience with old drugs, provides advice about drug interactions and other adverse effects, and also supplies the physician with price information that could result in great savings for the patient. One item in the May 11, 1973 issue, for instance, discussed the use and cost of oral penicillins. Noting that some brands cost three to four times as much as the same dose in generic form,* the item went on to point out that "there is no evidence of clinically important differences in the bioavailability [a measure of quality] of oral generic and brand-name products." The same issue also cautioned against the inappropriate prescribing of ampicillin (a related drug), which in brand-name form can cost six to seven times as much as unbranded penicillin, although for many purposes it "offers no important advantage over oral penicillin" while producing "a higher incidence of skin rashes and diarrhea." [5]

Unless the physician has access to reliable information from noncommercial sources, he tends to be unduly influenced by advertisements and detail men. The problem is particularly acute for physicians who practice alone, whereas rational prescribing is facilitated in an organized group setting where each physician can more easily benefit from the experience of his colleagues and where joint efforts at systematic appraisal of new drugs can be made to determine efficacy, toxicity, and cost.

Drug Retailing

About one-fourth of the drug industry's total output is sold to hospitals, governments, and other bulk buyers, while three-fourths is distributed through retail pharmacies. More than half of all the drugs sold by retailers come to them through drug wholesalers, whose markup is usually small (about 10 percent of the retail price) and covers the cost of such essential functions as storage, credit, and delivery. Unlike drug manufacturing and drug retailing, the wholesaling sector of the drug business has never seemed to pose any special problems for public policy.

The drug retailer's markup is typically about 40 to 50 percent of his selling price, although these are average figures and the actual markup can and does vary greatly. Retailers sharply disagree regarding the basic policy they should follow in charging for their services. Some apply a fixed percentage markup to every drug, while others charge a fixed dispensing fee, such as two dollars per prescription, regardless of the drug's retail price. The latter practice makes more sense from the economic

---

* Many drugs are manufactured in generic form—i.e., without a brand name—as well as under various brand names. Thus many companies produce *penicillin* (the generic term), some of them under brand names like V-cillin (Lilly), Veetids (Squibb), and Iticillin VK (Upjohn).

point of view because the costs to the retailer that are involved in dispensing a drug are not likely to vary much or at all with the price of the drug.

There are about fifty thousand retail drugstores in the United States—or one for every four office-based physicians. About 90 percent are independently owned; the others are owned by chains. The chain stores are, on average, about five times larger than the independents, but most of the difference in size reflects sales of merchandise other than prescription drugs. The bulk of prescriptions are still dispensed by independent owner-operated pharmacies. There is, however, growing price competition from discount chains, and this competition is changing the retail drug market, especially in large cities. No one knows how significant discounting has become, but it appears that careful shopping for drugs can result in substantial savings.

According to a recent editorial in Drug Topics, a leading trade publication for pharmacists, some observers predict that "the quality chain drugstore and the highminded independent [are] on the way to becoming as extinct as the passenger pigeon," being driven out by "aggressive discounters." The editorial goes on to criticize the discounters for skimping on services, and concludes by recommending state administered price controls that "would make it illegal to sell a prescription drug below a certain level." [6]

The controversies concerning drug retailing should be viewed in the context of the changing role of the pharmacist. In earlier decades, the pharmacist manufactured many of the drugs he dispensed. Now the pills and liquids are usually compounded at the factory, and the production part of the pharmacist's job consists of transferring the prescribed quantity from a large jar to a smaller one. Even that task is being made unnecessary by the increasing use of prepackaged prescriptions in quantities most frequently ordered by physicians.

These trends have prompted some observers to contend that the pharmacist is overtrained for the few simple tasks he actually performs. Evidence that this is the case is fairly strong, and many large pharmacies now make extensive use of pharmacist's aides (typically high school graduates with on-the-job training). They work under the supervision of a licensed pharmacist (who ordinarily has had five years of specialized training beyond high school). There is a completely different way of viewing the situation, however. Given the potency of modern drugs to do harm as well as good, there is a need, some argue, for pharmacological experts to keep track of all the drugs their customers take, to know what drugs their customers are allergic to, to keep abreast of new drugs and new findings about old drugs (including possible adverse interactions and side effects), and to be well versed in drug costs and drug quality. It is unlikely that many pharmacists currently fulfill this role, but the need exists and, therefore, it is plausible to suggest that, in another sense, pharmacists are "undertrained."

Another controversy surrounding drug retailing today concerns the advertising of prescription drug prices by pharmacies. The traditional position is that such advertising is "unprofessional," that patients should choose their pharmacist on the basis of convenience, service, and reputation, without regard to cost. At the instigation of pharmacy owners, most states have passed laws prohibiting the advertising of prescription drug prices, although recent court decisions have called into question the constitutionality of such legislation.

Public opinion, moreover, has been aroused by the discovery that the price for the same prescription item in the same city can vary by as much as 200 to 300 percent depending upon the pharmacy selling it. Studies have also revealed that some pharmacies charge different prices for the same prescription depending on the race or social class of the customer. A few large drug chains have begun to display their prices openly, and the city of Boston, for example, *requires* drugstores to post the prices of a specified list of nearly a hundred drugs.

Drugstores do differ in the services provided. Variations in the range of stock maintained, location, store hours, credit policy, and delivery services all affect the cost of doing business. Perhaps most important from a health point of view, pharmacists differ in the extent to which they keep accurate records, note side effects and allergic reactions, and work with physicians as members of the health team.

From the economic point of view, customers should be free to buy where they think they are best served, and with as much information as possible, including price. Price, however, should not be the only consideration. The problem is, of course, greatly complicated by the fact that the patient often lacks any familiarity with the product he is purchasing. In many cases the physician may not have even told him the name of the drug he prescribed.

The prescribing and taking of drugs is a critical part of the health care process. Questions about the organization of drug dispensing are best handled, in my view, by integrating them with the broader questions of the overall organization and delivery of medical care. As previously suggested, the surest way to get physicians to give more thought to their prescribing is to give them a financial stake in keeping down the cost of drugs. Capitation prepayment that includes drugs does this. Moreover, establishing a closer relationship between the pharmacist and the physician would contribute to the improvement of health care by assuring the more efficacious use of drugs and fewer adverse reactions.

New Drugs

The drugs developed in recent decades have been major factors in improving the prevention, cure, and alleviation of disease and pain. These drugs have, for the most part, been developed by drug manufacturers through their own research-and-development programs. Publicly supported medical research has also played a role, but even when basic breakthroughs occur in the laboratory of a university or other nonprofit institution, private industry is responsible for transforming the research discovery into a marketable product.

During the past decade the rate of introduction of new drugs has decreased appreciably. The average number of new chemical entities (i.e., truly new drugs) annually placed on the market since 1962 is roughly one-half the average for the preceding decade. According to Sam Peltzman, professor of economics at the University of Chicago, this decrease is attributable to the 1962 Kefauver-Harris Amendments to the Pure Food and Drug Act.[7] These amendments, which Congress passed in the emotional aftermath of the thalidomide tragedy, impose much more stringent requirements on drug companies for proof of efficacy and safety.

Drug manufacturers claim that, as a result, two to four additional years are now required to obtain the necessary approval for a new drug from the federal Food and Drug Administration (FDA), with a considerable attendant increase in costs. Expenditures by drug manufacturers for research and development are now much greater than they were in the period when the number of new drug products was so much higher. Drug industry spokesmen contend that the delay in FDA approval places an even greater burden on them than the accompanying increase in costs by making it that much more difficult for manufacturers to anticipate the state of the market and technology. Peltzman further argues that the delay in the introduction of new drugs and the reduction in their number as a result of the more stringent FDA regulations is far more costly to the nation's health than the possible cost of some unsafe or inefficacious drug that might be marketed under less stringent legislation.[8]

The process of developing a new drug and bringing it on the market is indeed a long and expensive one. It may begin with (for example) the deliberate modification of a natural product that has a desired therapeutic effect, or with the accidental discovery that some compound acts in a desired way. Initial screening using rodents and other animals usually follows. Specialists in numerous disciplines, including biology, chemistry, and biochemistry, become involved at this stage. Developmental chemists undertake large-scale synthesis of the drug, and if continued testing reveals a significant therapeutic effect, toxicity studies are initiated. Usually dogs or monkeys are given the drug in the same way that it would be used with humans, and careful examinations are conducted to determine toxic effects.

If a compound gives promise of both efficacy and safety, at this point it is administered to humans under controlled conditions by physician investigators. If after extensive clinical trials the FDA approves the new drug application, the product can then be marketed.

Dr. Louis Lasagna, professor of pharmacology at the University of Rochester, has also commented on the inhibiting effects of the Kefauver-Harris Amendments. In addition, he speculates that perhaps "the fantastic output of the pharmaceutical industry (prior to 1962) preempted many additional contributions by tackling successfully the 'easier' development problems, and that post–'Golden Age' research is necessarily less productive because the nuts left to crack are the tougher ones." [9]

Comparing the dates of introduction of new drugs in the United States with dates for the same drugs in France, Germany, and England, Lasagna finds that for the period 1965–1969 the United States lagged an average of one year behind France, 1.6 years behind Germany, and 2.1 years behind England.[10] On the other hand, he notes that in the case of L-dopa, a spectacular new drug for the management of Parkinson's disease, FDA approval was obtained relatively swiftly. The drug was quickly placed on the market with the understanding that experience with it would be carefully assessed so that if unforeseen major problems arose, approval could be rescinded.

A 1971 FDA report contends that the number of new drugs representing "important therapeutic advances" has not been adversely affected by the 1962 amendments.[11] An extremely comprehensive comparison of new drugs in Great Britain and in the United States by Dr. William Wardell, however, reveals that since 1962 there has been "a substantial lag and a deficit . . . in the introduction of new drugs to the American market." [12] Between 1962 and 1971, seventy-seven new drugs were introduced in Great Britain that were not available in the United States, while only twenty-one were available in the United States but not in Great Britain. Of eighty-two new drugs that became available in both countries, forty-three appeared first in Great Britain, with an average lead of 2.8 years, while twenty-five appeared first in the United States, with an average lead of 2.4 years. Fourteen were introduced in the same year in both countries.

Wardell identified several drugs that were available in Great Britain, but not in the United States, which British physicians considered of significant therapeutic value, including the use of salbutamol (albuterol) in asthma, the beta blocker in angina, co-trimoxazole in pyelonephritis, and carbenoxolene in gastric ulcer. A survey of American specialists revealed that very few of them were aware of the existence of these drugs, although those who were aware expressed a desire to have them available in the United States.[13] (The fact that so few American specialists knew of these drugs' existence—despite extensive discussion of them in professional journals—seems to testify to the importance of the detail man and drug industry advertising as sources of information on drugs for American physicians.)

The principal thrust of Wardell's and of Peltzman's work is that the present FDA regulations are heavily biased in the direction of keeping drugs off the market. This is done in the name of saving lives (by preventing unsafe drugs from reaching the market) and saving money (by preventing inefficacious drugs from reaching the market). The net result, however, may be unnecessary suffering or even loss of life because some drugs that would be efficacious for some patients are not available.

Wardell's analysis points to the fact that most adverse drug reactions in both Great Britain and the United States are associated, not with the new or relatively untried drugs, but with drugs that have been long in use. He argues that paying more attention to postmarketing surveillance (which is much poorer in the United States than in many other countries) would do more to reduce drug hazards than the current American practice of relying on extensive animal testing and other premarketing screening procedures. The limitations of animal testing are highlighted by the fact that penicillin and fluroxene, two valuable drugs, are both lethal to some laboratory animals. Thus if these drugs were just being developed today, the clear evidence of their toxicity in animals would probably result in their rejection long before approval was sought to market them. On the other hand, it is not at all clear that present regulations would prevent a thalidomide from being marketed.[14]

Another crucial point underscored by both Lasagna and Wardell is that the availability of an efficacious drug for a particular condition is not sufficient reason to bar a less efficacious alternative from the market. Suppose, for example, that drug A is already on the market and is successful in the treatment of a disease 50 percent of the time, has no effect in 40 percent of cases, and is actually harmful in 10 percent. Further suppose that a new drug—drug B—is proposed for the same disease and that tests indicate it is effective only in 30 percent of cases and is harmful in 20 percent. Should approval to market drug *B* be withheld on the grounds that a more efficacious drug (drug *A*) is already available? Not necessarily. Drug *B* may actually be effective in a substantial number of cases where drug *A* is not; if so, to bar *B* from the market would be to deny a number of patients their only opportunity for effective therapy.

It is interesting to speculate what would happen if the regulatory standards that are applied to drugs in the United States were also applied to surgical procedures. Suppose no operation could be undertaken unless there was significant and conclusive evidence of both the efficacy and the safety of the procedure. Would tonsillectomies pass the test of efficacy? About a million are performed annually in the United States, yet many physicians are skeptical of their value except in special cases. Would surgery for lung cancer meet such a test? In Great Britain such surgery is undertaken much less often than in the United States. The ostensible reason these standards are not applied to surgery is that reliance is placed on the physician (and hospital) not to undertake or permit inappropriate procedures. Also, a patient who undergoes surgery that should not have been performed always has recourse to a malpractice suit (or at least his family does).

Could the traditional approach to surgery be used with respect to prescription drugs? Under law a patient cannot obtain such drugs without a physician's prescription. No physician is under any compulsion to prescribe a drug unless he believes that its possible therapeutic benefits outweigh possible harm. Moreover, patients still have recourse to malpractice suits in cases of the physician's gross negligence.

The present approach of strict market controls on drugs really amounts to a vote of "no confidence" in physicians' ability to prescribe with judgment and care. If such a vote is warranted, it raises serious questions about the state of medical education, the organization of medical practice, and the usefulness of medical licensure.

A critical question for social choice in the drug field at this time is whether the United States should continue to place heavy emphasis on barring potentially unsafe drugs from the market at the cost of possibly delaying the introduction of helpful new drugs. A policy of extreme caution hardly seems warranted a priori since human lives are at stake either way the choice is made. If physicians are in fact ill equipped to function within a more permissive regulatory framework, perhaps the solution lies in the reform of medicine rather than in regulation of drugs.

Drugs and Ill Health

The overuse, abuse, and misuse of drugs constitute a major health problem in the United States. From the medical point of view, overuse occurs whenever a drug's net effect on health is harmful. Drug abuse is simply an extreme version of overuse, and usually refers to drug addiction. From the economic point of view, however, overuse must be defined differently. On the one hand, any drug use which did not yield a benefit equal to its cost would constitute economic overutilization, even if it were not detrimental to health. On the other hand, some use that *is* detrimental to health would not be characterized as overuse in economic terms if it increased satisfaction in other ways. Good health and long life are not the consumer's only goals.

From a health point of view one of the most overused drugs in the United States is alcohol. At least one of every twenty adults, and possibly as many as one in ten, consume alcohol at a level harmful to their health. Other drugs that are commonly overused include nicotine, caffeine, and aspirin. Prescription drugs that are believed to be objects of widespread overuse include tranquilizers, barbituates, and amphetamines. The abuse of heroin, cocaine, LSD, and other illegally obtained drugs is, of course, a major problem, but beyond the scope of this discussion.

What, if anything, should be done about the overuse of drugs? Education is one possible answer. If overuse is the result of ignorance, there is a clear and proper role for both private and public institutions in trying to help people make more intelligent use of their purchasing power. What about the adult who knows that he is harming his health but persists in drug overuse because the drug provides him with other satisfactions? Should he be free to make and carry out his own decisions regarding drug use? The answer to this, in my view, is that it depends on the nature and extent of the consequences of such use for others. For instance, overuse of alcohol, particularly outside one's home, may well imperil the comfort and safety of others, and in such a case government has the clear right to intervene. But the notion—so popular in some quarters—that government has the obligation and capacity to keep people from doing anything that seems foolish (even when there is no harm to others) should be firmly rejected by all who value a free society. In the case of health, the possibilities for intervention are almost without limit: one could first prohibit alcohol and then cigarettes, then try to curb overeating, then compel exercise, and so on.

That which government should refrain from compelling, however, the physician has every right and duty to try to accomplish by persuasion. The physician who is successful in persuading patients to reduce weight or eliminate cigarette smoking may be doing more for health than the one who has mastered the most esoteric diagnostic and therapeutic techniques.

A related problem concerning drugs is their misuse. It has been estimated that 1½ million persons are hospitalized each year as the result of adverse drug reactions. Many millions more experience adverse reactions not requiring hospitalization but producing considerable pain, discomfort, and disability.[15] Some "misuse" is inevitable so long as it is impossible to predict with certainty the way every patient will react to every drug. Other cases of misuse are clearly the fault of patients who fail (or refuse) to follow instructions. Much of the misuse, however, represents a failure of the medical care delivery system. Correction of such failure should be high on the agenda of health care educators and researchers. What is needed is more knowledge and more concern on the part of physicians and a closer articulation of the prescribing and dispensing functions. The current proliferation of specialization in medicine, for example, causes situations where a patient may be simultaneously taking several drugs prescribed by different physicians. The potential for harm, obviously great here, could be reduced if all the drugs were dispensed by a single knowledgeable pharmacist.

Drug Costs

Drug costs do not present as big a problem for social policy as do the effects of drugs on health. Drug expenditures account for about 10 percent of total health expenditures, and this share has tended to decline over time. The drug portion of the consumer price index has been relatively stable for many years, and has actually decreased during some. Even the average price of prescriptions, which was rising rapidly in the 1950s when new, expensive drugs were flooding the market, has been rising at only a moderate rate, and most of this change is due to an increase in the size of the average prescription.[16]

Although the problem of drug costs is not among the most pressing in the health field, several aspects are worthy of consideration. First, it should be noted that only a small part of the cost of drugs goes to pay for the materials and labor used to produce them. Of every dollar received by drug manufacturers, only about 40 cents is used for materials and supplies, production-worker wages, and other payroll. This is a smaller percentage than in almost any other industry, even including cosmetics.

Much of the drug sales dollar is used for marketing, including advertising. The exact percentage is not known, although Senator Gaylord Nelson (D.–Wisc.), a long-time critic of the drug industry, claims that it is as high as 25 percent of total sales—a much higher proportion than is spent by most manufacturing industries. The share of sales spent for research is more than 5 percent and less than 15 percent, but there is no agreement on the exact figure.

The rate of profit in drug manufacturing has been very high throughout the past quarter-century. In most years the drug industry has led all manufacturing in rate of return on stockholders' equity, and the rate has been one-and-one-half times the average of all industries combined. The reported rate is biased upward because the drug industry's heavy investment in research and development is not capitalized (as is investment in physical capital), but this accounting peculiarity would explain only a part of the "excess" profits. Other factors offered by the industry to explain its high rate of return, such as the high risk involved in marketing individual drug products or the need for research-and-development funds, are unconvincing. The major reasons for high profits are, rather, product differentiation and the absence of price competition among existing firms, aided by the role played by patents and exclusive process know-how in inhibiting competition from new firms.

There can be little doubt that drug prices could be reduced substantially if sharp cuts were made in advertising, research expenditures, and profits. Whether this would be desirable or not is another matter. It is naïve to assume that the public interest always lies in the direction of lower prices. If lowering drug prices were to inhibit the development of useful new drugs, for instance, the public interest might be poorly served.

High profits have probably helped fuel the rapid expansion of the drug industry in the past. If there is less need for expansion now, profits could and probably should be lower. The charge that expenditures for drug marketing are excessive seems well supported, but these expenditures are likely to continue as long as they pay off for the manufacturers. Significant changes in drug marketing, therefore, are not likely to occur without significant changes in physicians' behavior.

One such change that has been urged on physicians is to prescribe "generically" whenever possible instead of specifying brand names. By prescribing generically the physician affords the pharmacist the option of filling the prescription with any manufacturer's version of that drug, including (presumably) the cheapest version. When a physician prescribes by *brand* name, the anti-substitution laws in most states forbid the pharmacist from substituting a generic equivalent. Those who defend brand-name prescribing, however—including, of course, brand-name drug manufacturers—maintain that generic prescribing would not result in significant savings for the patient. While acknowledging individual instances of huge price differences between the brand-name and generic versions of the same drug, they argue that there are so many drugs where the difference is small and so many where no generic version exists that total possible savings would be less than 10 percent.

Considerable controversy has arisen over whether generic drugs are in fact therapeutically equivalent to their brand-name counterparts. It has been shown, for example, that two manufacturers' versions of the same drug, although chemically equivalent, may not be therapeutically equivalent because of differences in rate of absorption within the body, among other reasons. Advocates of generic prescribing admit that not all chemically equivalent drugs dissolve at the same rate, but they question whether this is true for most drugs and they also note the lack of agreement among pharmacologists regarding therapeutically adequate rates of absorption and blood levels.

Yet another hot argument is now raging over whether pharmacists should be granted the right to substitute one manufacturer's version of a drug for another when the physician has prescribed a brand name. Those in favor of the right to substitute—including the American Pharmaceutical Association (a pharmacists' organization)—argue that if the pharmacist is aware of a cheaper alternative which he believes to be just as good, or better, than the brand name prescribed, the patient should be allowed this potential saving. Opponents of this right, however—including the Pharmaceutical Manufacturers Association (representing the drug industry)—argue that the physician knows his patient best and is in the best position to decide not only which drug but which brand of drug the patient should have.

A useful compromise position is the one adopted by the Kaiser Medical Group in California. On the bottom of their prescription blanks there is a little box and the notation, "Authorization is given for dispensing by nonproprietary name unless checked here." Thus if the physician wants to insure that the pharmacist dispenses the specific brand he has prescribed, he checks the box; if he does not mind a substitution being made, he leaves the box empty. The system, according to Kaiser officials, works quite well. It allows the physician to exercise strict control of treatment when he considers it necessary while permitting opportunities for savings in the cost of drugs in other cases.

The mere existence of alternatives, however, is no guarantee of savings. Lowering drug costs, it has been emphasized throughout, requires that physicians become more concerned with and knowledgeable about the drugs they prescribe. The prescription drug program of the Group Health Cooperative of Puget Sound in Washington State provides a good example of this. The cost per prescription in this prepaid plan—which covers hospitalization, physician's services, and out-of-hospital prescription drugs—is about one-half the national average. The principal reason for this is that the group's physicians have given a good deal of thought and attention to their prescribing. They will not prescribe a high-price brand-name drug if they know that an equally good lower-price version is available or that some cheaper drug product will do the same job. In addition, the group is able to buy drugs at more favorable rates because of its larger volume. Very little of the saving comes from greater technical efficiency in the running of the pharmacy; nearly all of it is in lower costs of the drugs purchased.

There are a substantial number of important drugs now available from only a single source whose patents will be expiring shortly. After the patents expire it is likely that these drugs will become available from several sources. The potential savings from generic prescribing or, what amounts to almost the same thing, from permitting pharmacists to practice brand substitution, will increase.

While many economists believe that drug prices are higher than they should be according to criteria of efficiency and equity, a few believe that even higher prices might be warranted as an inducement to develop and market drugs to treat relatively rare diseases. Some physicians have also expressed concern about the cost of developing drugs to treat rare diseases. If the potential market is small, and the cost of development high, it is clear that a profit-seeking firm will not undertake the required research. It has been proposed that some kind of subsidy is desirable to encourage such research. This argument runs counter to the economic point of view. Following that logic the state should subsidize guard rails on roads that are very seldom traveled (to prevent the "rare accident") and should spend money in many different ways that might conceivably result in saving a few lives.

Suppose those with the rare disease would be willing to pay a very large sum for an effective drug? At present, drug firms assume that even if their research produces an extremely valuable drug, they will not be able to charge anything close to its value to consumers. Fear of public opinion, government intervention, and the like preclude such a possibility. Because of this assumption potentially useful research and development, especially for rare diseases, may be shelved.

Ethical Problems

Significant ethical problems surround all aspects of medicine and several of the most troublesome ones involve drugs. Consider, for instance, the widespread use of placebos in medical practice. *Placebo* is the term applied to any harmless concoction (e.g., sugar and water) given to a patient under the pretense that it is an active drug. If definition is broadly construed to include things like vitamins (when no vitamin deficiency is apparent), it appears that a significant proportion of all prescriptions are placebos. One British physician who kept a careful record of his prescriptions reported that 30 percent were in the placebo category.

Why do physicians prescribe placebos? To some extent because they constitute the safest therapy for treating hypochondria. By prescribing a placebo and thus pretending to acknowledge the seriousness of the patient's condition, the physician may be preventing him from resorting to harmful self-medication or to treatment from some unqualified or unscrupulous third party. Some physicians defend their practice of prescribing placebos by arguing that it "cements the physician-patient relationship": the patient who expects to be given a prescription may feel that the physician who fails to write one hasn't really done anything for him or doesn't really care to.

Cynics might say that physicians prescribe placebos in order not to lose customers; but the practice is also widespread in charity clinics and other settings where the question of patronage loss is less relevant.

Because of the strong psychological component in many illnesses, placebos often in fact work—i.e., have a favorable effect on health. On the other hand, they can of course be downright dangerous—by being totally useless—if prescribed after inadequate diagnosis or as a substitute for concentrated efforts to deal with serious problems.

The use of placebos undoubtedly adds to the public's expenditures for drugs, but it is not clear whether there is any less expensive way of dealing with the cases for which they are typically prescribed. Some might argue that if no prescription is indicated, the physician should take the time to explain the situation carefully to the patient in order to save the patient's money. But this may not be the most cost-effective way of dealing with the case; the physician's time also costs money—if not to the patient, then to the physician. Under fee-for-service where the patient pays for the drug separately, the physician's impulse is to write a prescription and get on to the next case without unnecessarily wasting time. Under a prepayment plan that covers the cost of prescriptions, the physician is more likely to weigh the cost of his time against the cost of a placebo—ideally with the help of some organization formula.

Another ethical question is whether physicians should themselves dispense drugs for profit. One school of thought regards this as unethical, arguing that physicians would be tempted to overprescribe in order to increase their incomes. Exactly the same point, however, could be made concerning the tests and X rays that physicians recommend (and charge for), the surgery they perform, and the return visits they suggest. Indeed, if all drugs had to be administered by injection, this issue would not even arise. This is not to deny that abuses occur in the other areas just mentioned, but to say that the problem of insuring responsible physician behavior doesn't begin or end with the prescribing and dispensing of drugs. If a physician wants to take advantage of his patient's lack of medical knowledge, he can do so in many ways other than overprescribing.

The phenomenal rise in the importance of drugs during the past few decades, uncertainty concerning some of the basic facts about drug research, sales, and usage, and the limited amount of objective analysis of drug industry performance make it difficult to reach firm conclusions for social policy in this area. Whereas well-meaning critics of the drug industry continue to press for stricter government controls on drug development and marketing, other analysts are arguing that such controls seriously impede the war on disease. With respect to drug prices, my own view is that they are currently higher than they need be as a result of a wasteful distribution system and the lack of price competition within the industry. The crucial questions regarding drugs, however, relate not to cost but to the consequences of drugs on health. One weakness of the present system is the almost total absence of any connection between the retail sale of drugs and the practice of medicine. A related weakness is the limited knowledge many physicians have concerning drugs. Given the central role of the physician in medical care, it seems to me that the best way to achieve more rational prescribing and a more efficient, effective drug industry is by physicians becoming more knowledgeable about drugs. Education can help, but probably the strongest incentive, as in the case of hospital care, would be the inclusion of prescription drugs in prepaid capitation medical insurance plans so that the physician had a clear financial stake in the cost of drugs.

CHAPTER 6

Paying for Medical Care

Some saw health insurance primarily as an educational and public health measure, while others argued that it was an economic device to precipitate a needed reorganization of medical practice. . . . Some saw it as a device to save money for all concerned, while others felt sure that it would increase expenditures significantly.

DANIEL S. HIRSCHFIELD,
The Lost Reform, commenting on the campaign for compulsory health insurance in the United States at the time of World War I

How to pay for medical care? This question, which periodically has been the subject of vigorous debate in the United States for more than half a century, has moved to the forefront of public attention in the wake of rapid increases in the cost of care and heightened concern about inequality of access. More than a dozen different proposals for some type of national health insurance have been submitted in Congress, and major interest groups—private insurance companies, hospitals, organized medicine, and organized labor—have staked out their positions in great detail. Before considering the pros and cons of national health insurance and the implications of alternative proposals, a few general remarks about medical care finance and the present U.S. system are in order.

The most basic point, often obscured in public discussions, is that the public must pay for care under any system of finance. That is, the ultimate cost falls on families and individuals even when the payment mechanism makes it appear that the bills are being sent elsewhere. Except during an economic depression, no magic wand of finance can divert labor, capital, and other resources to medical care without resulting in a reduction in resources available for food, housing, education, recreation, or other goods and services. Nor is there any secret formula that can transfer the cost of health care to "government" or "business" without the burden eventually being borne by the public through more taxes, higher prices, or lower wages. Granted, the choice of financing system can make a significant difference to families at the highest and lowest levels of income, but the average family will have to pay the same share under any system.

Not that the method of financing medical care is irrelevant. On the contrary, the choice of financing system can have significant implications, especially for cost and access. This is particularly true when one considers that the financing system has two sides: how people pay for care and how providers are paid.

The two sides are sometimes linked in a single transaction, as in the traditional system when a patient buys services directly from a physician: the patient pays fee-for-service, and the physician is paid fee-for-service. Under the medical foundation system, however, as pioneered by the San Joaquin County Medical Society in California and now being copied in many other states, the patient (or his employer) pays an annual insurance premium, while the physician continues to be compensated on a fee-for-service basis. On the other hand, in the world-famous Mayo Clinic (and in several other large private group practices patterned after it), patients (or their insurance companies) pay fee-for-service, but the physicians receive a salary from the organization.

Besides fee-for-service, the principal ways in which consumers pay for medical care is either directly, through insurance premiums and taxes, or indirectly, through higher prices or lower wages if the taxes are levied on business firms. The principal ways of compensating physicians, aside from fee-for-service, are capitation (an annual fee for each person covered regardless of actual utilization of services), salary, or profit sharing (in group practices). Hospitals can be paid on the basis of their charges, retrospective costs, negotiated rates, or prospective budgets.

The Present System

The present system for financing medical care in the United States reflects the diversity and pluralism characteristic of American life in general. Unlike the small homogeneous democracies of Western Europe or the large centrally controlled nations such as the USSR and China, the United States has refrained from establishing a national medical care system just as it has refrained from a national system of education, police, and many other basic services. Of the more than $90 billion spent on health care in the United States in 1973, however, government was the source of about 40 percent, two-thirds of it federal monies and one-third from state and local governments. The next largest source was direct payment by patients, which amounted to about one-third of the total. Payments by private insurance companies (including Blue Cross, Blue Shield, and other nonprofit plans) amounted to about one-fifth, and the balance was supplied by philanthropy, company-operated health services, and miscellaneous other sources.

The relative importance of different financing sources varies greatly depending upon the type of expenditure. For instance, dental services, drugs, and eyeglasses, which together account for almost 20 percent of total expenditures, are paid for almost exclusively by patients, although there is a minor trend toward providing insurance coverage for these items.

Private insurance is most important in paying for hospital and physician costs. In general, the distribution between private insurance and direct patient payment tends to be influenced by the size of the expenditure and its variability. The more expensive the item and the more variable it is from family to family, the more likely it is that the insurance mechanism will be brought into play. Insurance is a method of avoiding risk, or, more accurately, of sharing risk. In some societies risk is shared through extended-family and kinship obligations, but organized insurance, either private or public, has become a major factor in the more impersonal, individualistic societies of the modern world.

Apart from the desire to share risk, many people seem to prefer the convenience of having medical care payments periodically deducted from their wages in the form of insurance premiums. The alternative would be voluntary saving in order to be able to pay for services when utilized. Even if the question of risk did not arise, that is, if a family knew for certain that its total medical expenditures would be $520 over the year, they might still prefer to have $10 per week deducted to cover the cost, rather than having to come up with the money at the time of treatment.

The government supplies most of the funds for public health programs (e.g., control of epidemics) and for medical research. This makes a great deal of economic sense inasmuch as these activities indirectly benefit large numbers of people. It would hardly be efficient to let individual consumer demand determine the size of public health or medical research programs. For instance, although basic scientific research on cancer stands to eventually benefit millions, which makes the *collective* demand for this research quite strong, the incentive for *individuals* to pay for cancer research is weak, since any future benefits will be made widely available regardless of who pays for the research now.

Whenever the action taken by an individual, household, or firm confers benefits (or imposes costs) on others and no feasible way exists of arranging direct compensation for these benefits (or costs), economists say there is an "externality." When externalities arise, there is an a priori case for some kind of governmental or collective action. For instance, if I am debating whether to be vaccinated for a contagious disease, my self-interest requires weighing the personal cost (time, money, side effects) against the personal benefit (immunity). Such a calculation ignores the external benefit, that is, the benefit to others, whose chances of getting the disease decrease as the number of immunized people increases. A calculation based on self-interest thus leads to an *undervaluation* of vaccination; hence economic efficiency requires that the decision not be left to a free market choice. Self-interest weighs private cost against private benefit; the optimum for society requires comparing social costs and social benefits. An example of an external cost is the pollution attributable to a factory smokestack. In choosing between a low-price dirty fuel and one that is cleaner but higher in price, the factory owner will probably ignore the pollution costs unless the government intervenes. His private interest leads him to choose the "cheaper" fuel—even though the other fuel might really be cheaper if all costs (including pollution) are considered.

Most medical care does not involve externalities in the sense discussed above. The benefits of surgery, for instance, accrue primarily to the patient and his family. This is equally true of most medical interventions, with the notable exception of treatment of communicable diseases. Nevertheless, the share of government in paying for hospital care and physicians' services has grown rapidly in recent years for reasons that will be discussed below.

Before World War II the roles of both government and private insurance in health care were relatively much smaller than they are today; direct patient payment and philanthropy were relatively more important. Private insurance grew particularly rapidly in the 1940s and 1950s; in recent years its share of total expenditures has been fairly stable. Part of the original impetus for the private expansion of health insurance came from the health care providers, especially the hospitals, who were concerned about achieving certainty of payment and stability of revenue. Additional impetus stemmed from the increasing demand for medical insurance premiums as a fringe benefit in labor contracts. During World War II, for example, increases in fringe benefits were often exempt from federal ceilings on wages. And despite the lifting of wartime controls, the fact that employer contributions for medical insurance are not taxed as employee income continued to make this method of finance attractive to workers throughout the recent decades of high and rising personal taxes.

Another factor that has undoubtedly contributed to the growth of both private and public insurance is the increasing complexity of medical technology. Today it is possible and sometimes desirable to provide care at a level of expense far beyond the means of the average family except through the insurance mechanism.

The decline in the relative importance of voluntary philanthropy has been offset (some say more than offset) by "compulsory philanthropy"—i.e., by redistribution of income through government. This shift may reflect recognition that philanthropy frequently involves "external" benefits analogous to those discussed above. Suppose Mr. X is poor and sick and both Mr. A and Mr. B would like to see him better off. If A voluntarily gives X some money or arranges medical care for him, B will derive some pleasure from seeing the improvement in X without having spent a cent. If B is the one who makes the gift, A derives the same kind of benefit at no cost (to himself). Under a system of voluntary philanthropy, neither A nor B is likely to give X as much as they would if full account were taken of their collective desire to see X better off. A good solution would be for A and B to get together and agree on a tax-supported program—that is, compulsory philanthropy. The undervaluation of philanthropy in the free market is thus similar to the undervaluation of vaccination previously discussed. The solution is also similar—some kind of government intervention to insure that the choices facing individuals reflect social costs and social benefits.

The rapid expansion of the government's share of health expenditures in recent years is probably due in part to an increase in egalitarian attitudes. It is not entirely clear, however, why there is apparently more support for redistributing income through subsidized medical care than for simply redistributing income directly and letting individuals decide how they want to spend their money. Where medical care for the poor involves using such groups for teaching and research purposes, as under much private philanthropy, significant external benefits probably accrue to those who are not poor. Many government-supported programs, however, are trying to eliminate these discriminatory practices.

Other motives may underlie changes in financing arrangements. For instance, some supporters of government health insurance predict that it will increase patients' bargaining strength vis-à-vis hospitals, physicians, and other providers, since a single large buyer (in this case, the government) is in a much better position to negotiate prices and supervise quality. It is also thought that national health insurance would provide the leverage to bring about needed changes in the organization and delivery of care. By changing the incentives facing the providers, the payment mechanism could be used to eliminate unnecessary hospitalization, to control drug prescribing, and to limit costs in general.

Sometimes the motivation for change is to improve the care process through integration of the payment and delivery systems, as in the Group Health Cooperative of Puget Sound (discussed in Chapter 5), which is a true consumers' cooperative. Patients own the hospital, engage the physicians, and serve as volunteers. Interestingly enough, where consumers have almost complete control, as in this system, they do not necessarily opt for maximum coverage: although the co-op has a very comprehensive plan, it has refused to cover abortion services or out-patient tranquilizing drugs.

Although motives are diverse, support for a change in medical care finance is widespread. Republicans and Democrats, liberals and conservatives, the AMA and the AFL-CIO all agree that *some* kind of national health insurance is desirable. Underlying this consensus, however, are sharp disagreements concerning *who* should be covered, *what* kind of coverage should be provided, and *how* the plan should be financed, administered, and implemented.

Who?

The debate over *who* should be covered boils down to determining whether there should be universal coverage or whether federal payment for insurance should be limited to families and individuals with low income.

Those who favor the latter approach argue that the primary objective of a national health insurance program should be to remove the financial barrier to care for the poor. Since the average family has to pay for care one way or another, it is argued, the simplest solution is to let everyone but the poor buy their own insurance, perhaps with the encouragement of tax deductions for premiums paid. Expenditures for medical care, it has been noted, account for a significant proportion of national income. Why, it is asked, should many additional tens of billions of dollars be brought into the federal budget only to be dispersed again in local communities to pay for the care of individuals who could have financed that care through nongovernmental mechanisms? Some observers further contend that a system of universal insurance would put an unnecessary burden on the federal fiscal system and possibly endanger other important government programs.

Arguments made in support of universal coverage take many forms. One is that access to medical care should be a matter of right, just as police and fire protection and other essential services are provided by the government to all citizens regardless of income. A particularly strong case is made for providing children with access to care regardless of whether their parents can afford it or have made provision for it. Access for children is held to be an essential ingredient in the American commitment to equality of opportunity, and a comparison is drawn between medical care and schooling. The analogy is not perfect, however: free public education is often justified partially in terms of significant externalities, which is more difficult to establish with regard to many types of medical care.

Coupled with the philosophical argument that medical care is everyone's "right" is a practical argument that cautions against making too many benefits conditional on low income. If the price one pays for medical care, housing, children's college education, child care, and other goods and services depends on having a low income, there will be less incentive for individuals to try to raise their incomes.

Universal compulsory coverage is also advocated as the only effective way to deal with the problem of the "free rider." There are many people, it is argued, who can afford to buy health insurance but don't. If they or their dependents become seriously ill and incur huge bills, the community feels obliged to provide care. These people are in effect "free riders" on the rest of the community.

One telling argument in favor of universal coverage is that the level of benefits and the quality of administration would have to be high enough to satisfy the majority of Americans, whereas a special plan for the poor might quickly degenerate to a second-class level. True, theoretically the best way to help the poor is to redistribute income, but it might be more feasible politically to achieve some redistribution with a national health insurance plan.

This seems to be the case in Great Britain, where the National Health Service (NHS) makes care available to all segments of the population. There are admittedly regional differences in quantity and quality of facilities, and the ability to use the system effectively tends to vary with social class. On balance, however, the NHS is regarded as having introduced a significant element of equality and justice into British life, and it commands wide public approval on that account.

What?

The debate over *what* should be covered by a U.S. national health insurance plan takes many forms, including quibbles over such details as cosmetic surgery and types of eyeglasses. The most basic cleavage, however, is between those who favor insurance only for "catastrophic" costs (major-risk insurance) and those who favor comprehensive "first-dollar" coverage. One argument for limiting insurance to catastrophic costs proceeds from fairly orthodox principles of public finance. Several leading health economists, including Martin Feldstein of Harvard, have been among the leading proponents of major-risk insurance. The essential point is that insurance lowers the net price to the consumer and therefore encourages him to buy more care than if he had to pay the whole cost out of pocket. Feldstein argues that the more comprehensive the coverage, the greater the "welfare loss" entailed in society collectively "overconsuming" medical care at the expense of other goods and services which, at the margin, they value more highly.[1]

It is the "restaurant check" problem, writ large. When a group goes to a restaurant and decides to split the bill evenly, there is a tendency for individuals to spend more than they would if each paid for his own order. In Feldstein's terms, there is a "welfare loss" from check splitting; nevertheless, the practice is widespread, and not without reason. One advantage is the reduced cost of "administration"—figuring out who ordered what and how much each owes. A second reason is that to the extent that a group meal is a social event, a party where each person is both host and guest, check splitting is conducive to the group feeling. These observations have some relevance to the question of medical insurance as well.

The catastrophic or major-risk approach has a great deal of political appeal because the premiums would be very much lower than for comprehensive plans, but a number of questions and objections may be raised concerning it. First, since initial expenditures would be paid by the patient and only large subsequent expenditures by insurance, there would be less incentive for persons to seek early care or preventive treatment; rather, the emphasis would be on expensive tertiary care. Second, the catastrophic approach would impose a large administrative burden on both patients and the government. Every family would have to maintain comprehensive records on all medical care expenditures in anticipation of eventually exceeding the deductible amount and becoming eligible for insurance coverage, and the government would have to establish means for checking these records. Most proposals call for the deductible to vary with the level of income of the family, so additional checking would be required to determine each family's income level in relation to its medical expenditures. The incentive to try to lump expenditures into the year when the deductible is exceeded, as well as the temptation to indulge in more flagrant forms of chicanery, would be very great.

Major-risk insurance would not deter utilization once the deductible had been satisfied, but it is the marginal expenditure over which the patient frequently has the most discretion. In hospital care, for example, the marginal decision frequently is whether to remain an extra day or so. The first several days' stay is often determined primarily by medical considerations; the last day or two are usually much more likely to be subject to patient preference. Given the size of the deductibles now proposed for major-risk insurance (about 10 percent of income, with an upper limit of about a thousand dollars), the average hospitalized patient would satisfy the deductible in the first several days and thereafter be under little or no financial pressure to cut short his stay.

Moreover, it is not clear how the provision of major-risk insurance by the federal government would prevent families from also acquiring "first-dollar" or "shallow" coverage from private insurance companies if they so desired. It should be noted that although major-risk insurance in various forms is now available from private insurance companies, the demand for it is less that overwhelming. If major-risk insurance is really what people desire in the way of medical care coverage, why don't they buy it now? And why do union leaders and representatives of other groups seek more coverage? I believe one reason is because people want an easy, convenient, systematic way of *paying* for medical care. It is a great mistake to view the purchase of health insurance as simply the result of the desire to avoid risk.

Finally, it should be noted that the major-risk approach concentrates exclusively on the patient and does nothing about organization of care, problems of access, or efficiency of delivery systems. In my view, its appeal is extremely deceptive. It seems like a cheap way of getting out of a crisis, but it offers little hope of solving the major health care problems now facing the American public.

How?

The disagreements over the *how* of national health insurance fall into three main categories: how to raise money; how to administer the plan or plans; and how (or whether) to use the financing system to change the organization and delivery of care.

Governments raise money through taxes. The principal taxes being proposed for national health insurance—indeed, the only ones likely to yield sufficient revenue—are the income tax and the payroll tax. The former is believed to be more progressive (that is, taking a greater proportion of income as income rises) and thus likely to result in more redistribution to the poor. Professor Mark Pauly of Northwestern University points out, however, that while this is certainly true of an ideal income tax, the existing system is "shot through with exclusions, deductions and special categories of income," and that the higher income tax rates required for national health insurance may cause more distortion.[2]

Much time and effort have been spent debating whether an increased payroll tax should be paid by the employer or the employee or both. This is largely a spurious issue because the ultimate burden would be borne by the public in the form of either lower wages or higher prices. As Pauly notes, "The 'employers share' is really a piece of political jim-crackery, designed to get the people, most of whom are employees, to agree to levy a higher tax on themselves than they would if the true tax burden were made clear."[3]

A question related to the choice of tax is whether expenditures and tax receipts should be linked through a medical insurance trust fund or whether the level of expenditures should be set independently and financed from the government's general revenue. Under a payroll tax trust fund arrangement, the size of the program would be affected by fluctuations in business conditions. Some people believe that it would be desirable to have benefits closely related to costs, while others prefer to have the benefit level set independently of the government's revenue position. The two groups apparently agree that closely gearing benefits to tax receipts would make the government more reluctant to raise benefit levels, but they differ over whether this restraint would be desirable.

One of the bloodiest battles over national health insurance concerns the manner in which the plan or plans should be administered. At one extreme is the proposal for a single insurance fund administered by the government. At the other extreme is the argument that universal coverage could be achieved by requiring every individual (or his employer) to obtain coverage from a private insurance company, with the government's role limited to setting minimum standards and paying premiums for the poor. Not surprisingly, the private insurance companies regard any proposals for a single government-managed fund as a threat to their very survival. They have consequently been fighting tenaciously in an effort to reserve an important role for themselves in whatever system is finally adopted, an effort which most knowledgeable political observers believe will succeed.

Advocates of a single government plan are fond of pointing out the efficiency with which the old age and survivors program is administered by the federal government. The analogy, however, is imperfect. Social Security payments are relatively simple to administer; the provision of medical services or reimbursement for same is a much more complex task, as shown by the problems of payment delay and overpayment encountered with Medicare and Medicaid. Some degree of pluralism and competition in the administration of national health insurance is in my view desirable, if only because it would allow for more flexibility and innovation than is likely to be forthcoming from a single government agency.

One beneficial consequence of a single plan, however, is that it would facilitate control of total health expenditures. This has been demonstrated in England, which has a single national plan and devotes a much smaller proportion of its gross national product to health care than does the United States. Indeed, close control of expenditures and the greater equality mentioned previously seem to be the principal benefits of Britain's National Health Service. The expectation that it would emphasize preventive and early care, or that it would encourage great efficiencies in the production of medical care, do not, in the main, seem to have been realized.

The final point of major disagreement is over whether any new financing system should be used to change the organization and delivery of care. Present-day organized medicine is, on the whole, opposed to any changes in the traditional system; most physicians would like to see any national financing system limited to the payment of bills. The opposing view is that unless national insurance is used to modify current practices, costs will skyrocket and possibly destroy the system—a compelling argument, especially in view of the experience of Medicare and Medicaid. Thus if national health insurance is to be successful in improving access to services for the poor without resulting in a diminution in needed services for everyone else, then the financing system will have to put pressure on the delivery system to eliminate waste and inefficiency or else face ruinous inflation.

HMOs

National health insurance proposals that seek to use the financing mechanism to change the organization of medical care rely heavily on the creation and encouragement of health maintenance organizations (HMOs). Dr. Paul Elwood, one of the most active proponents of this concept, describes an HMO as "an organization which provides comprehensive medical care, including preventive, diagnostic, outpatient, and hospital services, to a voluntarily enrolled consumer population in return for a fixed, prepaid amount of money." [4] The key elements are comprehensive coverage, prepayment, and an organization that takes responsibility for availability and quality of services.

Two principal types of HMOs are already in operation. One is the prepaid group-practice plan as developed by Kaiser, the Group Health Cooperative of Puget Sound, and a few other organizations; the other is the medical care foundation as developed by the San Joaquin County Medical Society. In the former type, there is only one insuring agency, the physicians are either salaried or share the income of the group partnership, and the hospitals are usually owned and managed by the plan. The foundation approach is more varied, typically involving many insurance companies, physicians compensated by fee-for-service, and independent hospitals. The foundation is considered an HMO, however, for it undertakes to monitor the utilization and charges of the individual physicians and guarantees to third-party payers that annual per capita costs will not exceed a specified amount. The foundation approach is less organized in the sense that patients can seek care from any physician who is part of the plan. Also, physicians may practice either alone or in groups, and are free to work as much or as little as they wish.

Many advantages are claimed for HMOs. First, membership in an HMO implies more than simply having health insurance (which has been likened to having a "shopping license"), because the organization undertakes the responsibility of providing care—i.e., it guarantees *access*. According to the late Ray Brown, a health care expert, "The greatest worry and frustration of the American public with the health care system does not have to do with cost, but rather has to do with the public's feeling that it is medically disengaged. . . . By having a single and known organization responsible for a particular set of individuals, those individuals are by this means wired or plugged into the health care system; that is, they know where they are supposed to go, and they know who is responsible to do something about it when they get there." [5]

Because the HMO provides *comprehensive* coverage, it alters incentives for the patient. In particular, patients are less likely to seek hospitalization for diagnostic work and other care that could be provided on an ambulatory basis than under health insurance plans where coverage is limited to care provided in the hospital. The HMO also alters incentives for physicians whose income is determined by annual capitation payments and who are consequently less likely to provide or order unnecessary care as a way of increasing their incomes. True, the temptation still exists in the foundation HMO, where physicians are paid fee-for-service, but the foundation acts as a counterweight through education, persuasion, and threats to withhold payment.

One advantage to providers in prepaid group practices is that they know approximately what their income will be and what services they will be called upon to provide, making it much easier to plan budgets and manpower requirements. Some HMO enthusiasts even maintain that health levels will be raised because providers will be more strongly motivated to keep patients healthy (in order to minimize the use of services).

Opponents of the HMO concept are both skeptical of its supposed advantages and critical of what they consider its drawbacks. Some health economists, for example, doubt whether there are significant economies of scale to be realized in large groups of physicians. Other health experts question whether physicians can do much to maintain the health of their patients even given the incentives to do so. A few critics have even questioned whether HMOs really lower hospitalization rates.

One specific disadvantage of HMOs, it is argued, is that providers will

skimp on patient care because their income is unaffected by the amount
of care delivered. Indeed, in some HMOs the physician's income is
increased if there is less hospitalization or few prescriptions. Furthermore, the concern has been expressed that HMOs will try to enroll only
the best risks. It is alleged that even if they do a wonderful job for their
members, they will not serve the total community, and they will tend to
throw the greatest burdens on other providers.

What does experience with existing HMOs suggest about these claims
and counterclaims? With respect to hospital utilization the evidence is
reasonably clear-cut: hospitalization (measured in patient-days) is lower
for those covered by HMOs than for comparable populations covered by
conventional insurance. The savings involved are at least 15 percent and
may be as high as 30 percent. Moreover, these savings do not seem to be
offset by higher out-of-hospital utilization. The savings are more depen-
dable for prepaid group-practice plans than for foundations, although the
San Joaquin Foundation, the oldest and best-established one, has an excellent record.

There is still considerable controversy, however, concerning *how*
HMOs reduce hospitalization. Is it because physicians stand to benefit
from lower hospitalization? Is it because patients have equally good coverage for ambulatory care? Health economist Herbert Klarman has suggested that control of bed supply may be the critical variable. If beds are
not available, they can't be used. Just restricting the bed supply may not
be enough to lower hospital utilization over the long run, however. If
physicians and patients regard the supply as unduly restrictive, they will
press for expansion or drop out of the plan. What is needed, apparently,
is fewer beds plus an "approach" to medical practice that makes the
smaller supply tolerable. This "approach" encompasses the incentives
and constraints facing the physician, his training and professional
"socialization," and a feeling on the part of the patient that his needs are
being met.

The skepticism about HMOs improving the health of their members
seems to be justified. Apart from some old studies of infant mortality in
HIP (Health Insurance Plan of Greater New York), no major health effects of HMOs have been reported. Indeed, it is significant that none of
the best-known HMOs make any important claims with respect to health.
This is consistent with my view that health differences are determined
largely by genetic factors, environment, and life-style. It is unlikely that
variations in the quantity, quality, or organization of medical care can

make a significant difference for the health of populations as a whole, although obviously the impact in individual cases can be very great.

If there is little evidence that HMOs improve health, there is even less evidence that HMO physicians tend to neglect the legitimate health needs of their patients. Indeed, so long as enrollment in a HMO is voluntary and alternative modes of care are available, the HMO must satisfy its customers or lose them.

On balance, then, existing HMOs have demonstrated that it is possible to control cost without jeopardizing patient health. When a group of physicians sets out to eliminate unnecessary utilization and curb wasteful practices, great savings are possible, particularly regarding hospitalization and drugs. Many physicians are resisting changes in the way they are paid, but unless the financing system is used to modify the behavior of physicians and hospitals, a national health insurance plan might do more harm than good. Forward-looking physicians might well consider August Heckscher's observation: "The prevailing structure of medical care—the doctor in solo practice dealing on a fee-for-service basis with the individual patient—is not part of the eternal order of things. It is a social convention, and like all social conventions, it is subject to reexamination, to development, to change." [6]

Concluding Comments

More than fifty years ago, at the time of World War I, there was a strong movement for compulsory health insurance in the United States. Its advocates, however, were divided (as are present advocates of national health insurance) over its ultimate purpose. Some wanted to control costs, others to improve health, and still others to make access more equal. In contrast to the present situation, significant opposition to compulsory health insurance came from many important labor leaders (including Samuel Gompers, then head of the American Federation of Labor), who opposed social insurance as "paternalistic." The medical profession, originally in favor of the proposal, gradually became a significant source of opposition, partly in response to the influence of the commercial insurance companies.

According to Daniel S. Hirschfield, the fundamental reason for the original failure of compulsory health insurance was that its major proponents were reformers who argued that traditional personal liberty and individual responsibility had to give way to new social and economic conditions—a position that the great majority, the public, did not share.[7]

At present, according to journalist Jonathan Spivak, "rising costs are the forcing factor for political action." I think he is correct, but I am not so sure of the corollary he adds—namely, that "cost considerations will also dominate the changes in the delivery system." [8] A serious attempt to deal with the cost problem—say, by moving to a capitation system of payment (including hospitalization, tests, and drugs)—is likely to run into opposition from physicians, drug companies, and possibly the insurance companies. Because the groups that think they have a great deal to lose will fight tenaciously, the most likely result will be a compromise that protects their interests. If the past is a good guide to the future, the emphasis is likely to shift to getting legislation that *appears* to serve great and noble purposes. Then, if the system in fact fails to live up to the expectations, the failure can be blamed on the administrators or on subsequent Congresses for failing to pass sufficient funds, or on the health professionals for sabotaging the programs.

Significant compromises are likely in order to overcome the objections of specific interest groups. Such compromises will probably tend to increase spending, while leaving organization and delivery unchanged. The only hopeful possibility is that representatives of other organized groups, such as business and union leaders—who in a sense represent workers, consumers, and taxpayers—will insist on changes that really make a difference. The time is past for either superficial measures or just pouring more money into the present system.

I am not so naïve as to think we can or should develop a system of paying for medical care incongruent with the approach to other major problems in our society. The degree of equality, the nature of incentives and constraints, and the character and extent of government intervention must bear some relationship to arrangements in other sectors. The significance and economic importance of health care, however, are now so great that decisions taken with respect to this sector can substantially influence other areas. A responsible and effective policy for health and medical care therefore, could become a cutting edge to help reshape our approach to other social problems.

CONCLUSION

Health and Social Choice

The organization of medicine is not a thing apart which can be subjected to study in isolation. It is an aspect of culture whose arrangements are inseparable from the general organization of society.

WALTON H. HAMILTON
Medical Care for the
American People

In the preceding chapters, I have discussed the major problems of health and medical care now facing the American people and have delineated the different social choices that must be made. These problems—high cost, inadequate access, and unsatisfactory health levels—have been examined from the economic point of view, which stresses the need to allocate scarce resources efficiently in order to best satisfy diverse human wants. For most Americans, better health is not the only, or even the most important, goal. For most Americans, more medical care is not the only, or even the most promising, route to better health.

The approach of this book has been to explore the relationship between health and such socioeconomic factors as income, education, and lifestyle and to examine in detail the principal elements of medical care: the physician, the hospital, and drugs. Economic analyses of these elements reveal significant opportunities for reorganizing care in order to moderate costs and improve access. In particular, Chapter 6 (on paying for medical care) indicated the central role of the financing system in this process.

Review

In this chapter I shall summarize my policy recommendations, but before doing so it will be useful to restate here some of the principal conclusions about health and medical care that form the basis for the recommendations. One such conclusion is that health status (as measured by mortality, morbidity, or other indexes), depends on many things besides medical care. For most of man's history, his health has depended on his economic well-being (his real income). Adequate food supply, clean water, protection from the elements—these are historically critical factors affecting life expectancy and the avoidance of disability. In modern developed countries, income no longer seems to be a significant determinant of health except for the very poor, and particularly with regard to infant mortality (although even here differences in income have less effect than formerly).

Current variations in health among individuals and groups are determined largely by genetic factors, environment, and life-style (including diet, smoking, stability of family life, and similar variables). To be sure, changes in the health of the population over time are influenced by medical care—but mainly through scientific advances, not through changes in the quantity of care. The most rapid of these gains occurred between 1930 and 1955, largely due to the development of relatively inexpensive, highly effective drugs for the prevention or treatment of influenza and pneumonia, tuberculosis, and other infectious diseases. The current major health problems—heart disease, cancer, accidents, emotional illness, and viral infections—are more difficult to solve with the available medical technology.

In developed countries the marginal contribution of medical care to life expectancy is very small. That is, variations in mortality across and within countries do not seem to be related to differences in the availability of physicians or other medical care inputs. Medical care, however, performs other functions besides reducing mortality and morbidity. Particularly important are the caring function (sympathy, reassurance, relief of anxiety) and the validation function (provision of professional information about health status). Moreover, some of the high cost of medical care, especially in hospitals, is for amenities consistent with the general level of affluence in our society. People who live comfortably when they are well expect to do the same when they are sick.

Another aspect of medical care that preceding chapters have underlined is the overwhelming importance of the physician as principal decision maker. Even though only 20 percent of health care expenditures are for physicians' services and less than 10 percent of all health care workers are physicians, it is the physician who determines most of what happens in the health care process, His role is particularly important with respect to the *cost* of care, for his are usually the pivotal decisions concerning hospitalization, surgery, tests, and drugs. Given the uncertainties about the effect of medical care on health, there is frequently a wide range of choice open to the physician on these matters. It follows that a concern with cost requires concentrating on the physician—particularly the criteria for admission to medical school, the nature of the physician's education and training, and, most important, the incentives and constraints that he faces once he has set up practice.

The physician is also important with regard to the problem of access, although the common notion that simply increasing the number of physicians will provide a quick and easy solution is a mistaken one. The general problem of access to medical care is mainly a question of access to primary care and to emergency care. It is furthermore a question of finding a physician or an organization to take complete, continuing responsibility for all of a family's health needs. The problem arises principally from the growth of specialty and subspecialty medicine, not from an overall shortage of physicians. The general solution does not lie in increasing the number of such specialists, but in reorganizing the delivery system to make greater use of nurse clinicians and other physician extenders working under the supervision of physicians.

While the physician's behavior is of critical importance, the hospital is where the most money is spent and where costs have been rising most rapidly. Thus the hospital is where the greatest potential exists for stemming the increase in medical care costs. Moderating hospital costs can be accomplished primarily by moderating utilization—that is, by eliminating unnecessary admissions and reducing unduly long stays. Additional savings could be achieved by closing inefficient hospitals—thus bringing about higher occupancy rates—and by establishing better coordination among the remaining institutions. It is particularly important right now to stop subsidizing the creation of new hospital capacity, which at present is creating excess capacity and consequently inappropriate utilization.

Whereas cost considerations are central to the hospital problem, drugs are important primarily because of their tremendous potential to affect health for good or for harm. Most of the major advances in health over the past forty years are traceable to the introduction of new drugs. Inappropriate use of drugs (to say nothing of drug abuse), on the other hand, is now a significant source of ill health. For most people, drugs are only secondarily an economic or cost problem; drug expenditures and prices have not been rising at an unduly rapid rate in recent years. The sharp decrease in the number of new drugs coming onto the American market since the Kefauver-Harris Amendments of 1962, however, may indicate that this country is putting too much emphasis on premarketing controls and not enough on postmarketing surveillance.

Although the cost of drugs is not a crucial problem, significant opportunities for savings nevertheless exist. In the main, it is up to the physician to take advantage of these opportunities, which he is most likely to do if he is given a financial stake in the cost of drugs. With respect to both drugs and hospitals, it has been shown that physicians can reduce costs without harming their patients' health, although they have little incentive to do so under the conventional fee-for-service payment system. When payment is made on an annual capitation basis that includes hospitalization, tests, and drugs, physicians are motivated to examine more closely the way they practice. Inasmuch as the financing of medical care, its organization, and its delivery are closely interrelated areas, it is naïve to think that solutions can be found in one without considering the others.

The Limits of Economics

One of the principal objectives of this book has been to show how the economic point of view can help us understand health problems. It is not my intention, however, to suggest that economics provides easy and ready solutions to the basic social problems that underlie questions of health and medical care. On the contrary, there are important limitations to economics.

One kind of limit is set by what economics can contribute *now;* that is, there are deficiencies in our theoretical framework and in our empirical knowledge that currently prevent us from answering particular questions about the health field. For instance, available economic theory is weak in explaining the behavior of nonprofit institutions and professional organizations, both of which are so important in medical care. Application of the traditional "theory of the firm," which assumes that organizations producing goods and services try to maximize profits, can yield many useful predictions regarding business decisions about prices, wages, composition and rates of output, and so on. In a voluntary nonprofit hospital, however, such decisions are usually the result of a "tug-of-war" among hospital administrators, the medical board, trustees, and the house staff. Furthermore, the motives of each of these groups differ, and their relative strengths vary, from hospital to hospital. Thus additional "theories of the firm" are needed to reflect the complexities.

Another troublesome aspect of economic theory is the assumption of perfect information. The elementary competitive model assumes that patients, physicians, and other decision makers possess all the necessary relevant information—about prices, production possibilities, usefulness of various therapies, and so on. In the real world, of course, such information may be difficult or even impossible to obtain. High information costs are characteristic of many health care markets; frequently the only way a person can know whether he needs to see a physician is to see a physician. At present most economic research on information costs and search is purely theoretical, but some day it may yield fruitful empirical insights into the behavior of patients and physicians.

Still another area of behavior that has important implications for health involves what goes on within the family. Whereas economists frequently treat the family (or household) as a basic unit of analysis and then seek to explain its behavior vis-à-vis the rest of the world, there has been relatively little effort so far to explain behavior *within* the household. The importance of the concept of investment in human capital is now recognized, however, and we know that much of this investment takes place within the family in the form of preschool learning and health care.

The consequences of intrafamily behavior for matters of health and general welfare can thus be significant. To take an intractable health problem of increasing concern as an example: Why do some parents go to extraordinary lengths to maintain and improve their children's health, while others are neglectful and still others even abuse and maim their children? These are difficult subjects to study empirically, however, because they involve no formal markets, no exchange of money, nor even the kind of input data available for studies of schooling or medical care.

In addition to theoretical weaknesses, there are serious limits to economists' current ability to estimate quantitative relationships between variables, even where theory predicts the direction of effects. For instance, economics can be used to predict that a decrease in the price of medical care will result in *some* increase in the amount of care demanded, but an effective policy decision would require an accurate estimate of the *degree* of response (termed "elasticity"). A consensus regarding the probable range of demand and supply elasticities in medical care markets is emerging only slowly. Similarly, we need better estimates of how cost is related to scale of production in medical care before making definitive judgments about the advantages or disadvantages of encouraging group practice or other changes in organization. Furthermore, every so often these relationships must be reestimated because, unlike relationships studied by natural scientists, economic relationships can and do change over time. Thus one of the limits of economics is that we must periodically discover anew the quantitative answers to old questions.

To keep these limitations in proper perspective, it should be noted that health economics is a relatively new field. The first national conference on the subject was held in 1962, the first international conference in 1973. There are perhaps only a hundred economists in the United States who devote all or most of their time to problems of health and medical care; by contrast, there are five times as many agricultural economists even though health care accounts for a much larger share of the gross national product than does agriculture. Nevertheless, the field has made considerable progress in the past decade, and the deficiencies mentioned above are, in principle at least, remediable. New theoretical insights, better data, and more sophisticated analyses will no doubt cause present limits to recede.

There are, however, other limits of an even more fundamental nature. At the root of most of our major health problems are *value choices:* What kind of people are we? What kind of life do we want to lead? What kind of a society do we want to build for our children and grandchildren? How much weight do we want to give to individual freedom? how much to equality? how much to material progress? how much to the realm of spirit? How important is our own health to us? How important is our neighbors' health to us? The answers we give to these questions, as well as the guidance we get from economics, will and should shape health care policy.

My own view is that we must quickly come to grips with the tremendous inequality in our nation. Imagine how critical we would be of a family which permitted some of its members to live in great luxury while other members lacked a minimum of basic goods and services? At the community level this is precisely the condition we tolerate. It is only a short walk from the opulence of upper Park Avenue to the rat-bitten, lead-poisoned children of East Harlem, but for our institutions that distance represents a chasm they seem powerless to bridge. Not that New York City is the only or the worst offender. The gap between the oil barons of Texas and the state's Chicano migrant farm workers is as large as any that can be found in New York. Paradoxically, the survival of our treasured personal freedom and independence may depend on our explicitly acknowledging a decent amount of interdependence and responsibility for one another.

The problem of inequality should be faced head on—in ways that do least damage to the efficient performance of the economy. Too often a concern for the poor has been used to justify minimum wages, price regulations, rent controls, and other devices that interfere with the competitive price system. This system (as Soviet planners have discovered), provides the most efficient mechanism for allocating scarce resources, even though it may result in a distribution of income which is socially and morally unacceptable.

While elementary justice seems to require greater equality in the distribution of medical care, the question is complicated by the fact that the poor suffer deprivation in many directions. Economic theory suggests it might be better to redistribute income and allow the poor to decide which additional goods and services they want to buy. As a practical matter, however, it may be easier to achieve greater equality through a redistribution of services (such as medical care) than through a redistribution of money income.

Recommendations

The recommendations that follow are based not only on my understanding of the economics of health and medical care, but also on my value judgments regarding what constitutes responsible policy in this field. As economist John Maurice Clark once wrote, "There are two worlds, the world of impersonal investigation of cause and effect, and the world of desires, ideals and value judgments. The natural sciences deal with the first, ethics with the second. . . . The peculiarity of economics is that it is called upon to bridge this gap." [1]

These are my principal policy recommendations:

1. *Universal comprehensive insurance.* Universal health insurance that meets nationally established minimum standards of benefits, with periodic upward readjustment of the minimum as technology changes and per

capita income rises, should be established by Congress. The program should be universal because the best way of meeting the nation's responsibility to the poor is by integrating them into the same system covering the great mass of society. Another reason is that when care is provided only to those receiving less than a specified income, benefits are very difficult to administer and the system generates antisocial incentives. Participation should be compulsory to overcome the "free rider" problem and to improve the equality of opportunity for children.

A national health insurance plan to which all (or nearly all) Americans belonged could have considerable symbolic value as one step in an effort to forge a link between classes, regions, races, and age groups. It will be more likely to serve that function well if not too much is expected of it—if it is not oversold—particularly with respect to its probable impact on health. If too much is promised, then instead of being of positive symbolic value it may serve as another source of divisiveness. For each group may become convinced that they alone are being cheated, that the promised benefits are being realized by others but not by them.

2. *Decentralized delivery systems*. Most health services should be produced and delivered locally. While there are very few advantages in centralized control of delivery, there are many disadvantages, including a greater likelihood of high costs, bureaucratic rigidity, low morale among providers, and an inability to meet the diversity of local needs. A few, less frequently used, tertiary services should not be provided locally but at regional medical centers.

3. *Capitation payments for enrolled populations*. Capitation payment that covers hospitalization, medical care, and drugs has proven in practice to be convenient for the patient and easy to administer; most important of all, it leads to significant reductions in cost without jeopardizing health. Moreover, within a capitation system individual providers can be compensated in a variety of ways.

4. *Competition* (wherever possible) *among alternative health plans*. Although coverage should be compulsory, choice of plan should be voluntary. The economies of scale in medical care are not so great as to justify the creation of huge, monopolistic organizations. Except in areas of low population density, it would be more efficient to have most services (primary and secondary care) provided by several organizations in order to benefit from competitive pressures and to increase the range of choices available to consumers and providers.

5. *Elimination of many of the restrictions on use of health manpower; experimentation with institutional licensure; and greater use of "physi-*

cian extenders.'' Improved access requires round-the-clock availability, an organization that takes continuing responsibility for its patients, and a good fit between the needs of the patient and the skills and training of the provider. There is a continuum of health needs, and there should be a continuum of health care personnel to meet those needs. Such personnel would function best in an organized setting with proper supervision, training, and assistance.

6. *Rational physician supply.* The number of residencies in specialties in oversupply, such as general surgery, should be sharply reduced. The number of physicians in other specialties and subspecialties where over-supply may be developing (e.g., in the various branches of internal medicine) should be closely monitored. And although we need more physicians to supervise primary care, appeals for heroic increases in the overall supply of physicians should be considered with caution.

7. *Rational hospital utilization.* The danger of overcapacity in community hospitals is more obvious than with respect to physicians. A five-year moratorium on new bed capacity would be salutary, and would provide an opportunity to reassess our medical priorities. Restrictions on bed supply should be accompanied by expansion of home and ambulatory care programs and extended care facilities.

Implementation of these recommendations should have a significant impact on the problems of *cost* and *access*. They should not be expected, however, to produce a dramatic improvement in the overall *health* of the population. Such improvement will more likely come as a result of advances in medical knowledge or of changes in human behavior. By changing institutions and creating new programs we can make medical care more accessible and deliver it more efficiently, but the greatest potential for improving health lies in what we do and don't do for and to ourselves. The choice is ours.

Health,
Economics,
and
Social Choice

What Every Philosopher Should Know About Health Economics*

The Great Health Care Debate of 1994 was like the uses of this world to Hamlet—"weary, stale, flat, and unprofitable." Why did so much effort by so many produce so little understanding and no reform? The finger of blame has pointed in many directions: "the Clinton Plan was unworkable"; "the plan was poorly explained to the public"; "the political strategy was misconceived"; "special interests triumphed over the general interest." Each of these explanations has some merit, but I believe the fundamental reason has been the unwillingness of policy makers and the public to make the difficult choices that are inevitable if the U.S. is to improve its approach to health care. What are the difficulties?

If You Don't Know Where You're Going, Any Road Will Get You There

Part of the problem is that we have not decided what it is we want our health care system to do. There are several possible goals or criteria

* Originally published in *Proceedings of the American Philosophical Society*, Vol. 140, No. 2, June 1996.

for assessing the performance of a health care system. Health economics suggests three dimensions of "output": technological, public health, and access to service. In addition, each of these must be considered from the perspectives of distributional equity and efficiency in the use of scarce resources.

Until now the U.S. system has emphasized pushing the technological frontier; we have the most advanced medical technologies in the greatest abundance. The U.S. is where the world's ambitious young physicians go for advanced training, and where the super-rich from Third World countries go when they want high-tech medical care. In this sense the U.S. has the best health care system in the world. But another way of judging the merits of a system is by the health of the population. This could be based on simple measures such as life expectancy or on more complex ones that take into account quality of life, as indicated by the absence of morbidity or disability.

From this perspective the U.S. ranks below average among economically developed countries, according to most measures. Physicians may argue that poor health levels in the United States are the result of social and cultural factors, and there is much truth in this argument. But if improvement in health is an important goal, and if physicians concede that they are not effective in modifying diet, exercise, drinking, and smoking, and that they are incapable of changing the physical and psychosocial environments that affect health, some reallocation of resources to research and services that have more impact on health may be in order.

Health *care* has always meant more than improving health outcomes. Particularly important are the caring function (sympathy and reassurance) and the validation function (provision of professional certification of health status). Until this century, the service, caring, and validation offered by health professionals were undoubtedly more valuable than their therapeutic interventions. Even today many health problems are either self-limiting or incurable, but people who are sick or in pain want access to physicians, nurses, and other health professionals. Thus, an important criterion for evaluating a health care system is the availability of services. Is it easy to get to see a physician? Or to reach one by telephone? How long does a bedridden hospital patient lie in urine before someone responds to a call? Do health aides regularly visit the homebound elderly? Are dying patients treated with compassion?

Each of the three dimensions of technology, public health, and service can be looked at from the perspective of distributional equity. All else held constant, many people believe that a more equal system is a better and more just system. Indeed, they might even be willing to sacrifice a little from one of the other goals in order to achieve more equality. Consider, for instance, a country that has an average life expectancy of seventy-six years, but that also has great inequality. Some of its citizens die in childhood or as young adults while others live past ninety years of age. Given any reasonable assumption about risk aversion, most people would prefer to be born into a country in which everyone lives to age seventy-five. Similar arguments can be made about the distribution of technology or of service.

Efficiency in the use of scarce resources is another criterion that can be applied to technology, public health, and the provision of services. At any given time, resources used for health care are not available for education, housing, automobiles, and the thousands of other goods and services that people want. Much of the criticism of the U.S. health care system arises because Americans spend 40 percent more than Canadians for health care, and the excess over European countries is even greater. In England, high-tech medicine is severely rationed, but the level of public health is about the same as in the U.S., and per capita spending for health care is less than half the American average. Without some consensus regarding the goals of our health care system it is unrealistic to expect any agreement about the means of achieving them.

Two Necessary and Sufficient Conditions
for Universal Coverage

Why are thirty-five million to forty million Americans without health insurance? There are only two logical explanations. First, most of them are too poor or too sick to afford the premiums. A family with an annual income of $15,000 or $20,000 per year is too affluent to qualify for Medicaid but can hardly afford to pay directly $5,000 for health insurance or to forego that amount in wages by seeking employment-based insurance. Even a middle income family with serious health problems cannot afford the very high premiums that would be actuarially appropriate, given their expected utilization of care.

Second, there are those who can afford to pay but are unwilling to do so. To achieve universal coverage there must be subsidization for the first group and compulsion for the second. No nation achieves universal coverage without subsidization and compulsion. Both elements are essential. Subsidies without compulsion will not work; indeed, they could make matters worse since the healthy flee from the subsidized common pool, only to return when they expect to use a great deal of care. Compulsion without subsidies would be a cruel hoax for the millions of poor and sick who cannot afford health insurance.

There are two principal ways to achieve universal coverage: an explicit tax earmarked for health care with implicit subsidies for the poor and sick, or mandates (an implicit tax) with explicit subsidies based on individual or family income. The U.S. could have universal coverage next year if the public (and the policy makers) were prepared to bite the bullet of subsidization and compulsion. Last year's policy debacle reflected, in part, the unwillingness of the administration and Congress to mount a meaningful, informative debate on this issue.

Cost-Containment: "No Pain, No Gain"

There is widespread belief in the U.S. that expenditures for health care are too high and growing too rapidly. The basic facts are clear. In 1994 Americans spent about $3,600 per person for health care, for a total bill of close to one trillion dollars. By comparison, spending for education from kindergarten through graduate school was less than half as large, and defense expenditures were even smaller, about $280 billion. Over the last forty years health care expenditures have grown 3 percent per annum faster than expenditures for all other goods and services. If health spending continues to outpace the rest of the economy at that rate by 2030, the health sector will consume almost one-third of the Gross Domestic Product.

Why should the health sector's share of the GDP be a cause for concern? Every country must spend 100 percent of its GDP on something. If the U.S. spends a larger share on health care, Japan may spend a larger share on food, Canada on housing, and so on. There are, however, three good reasons for concern about costs. First, there is a presumption (well supported by economic theory and empirical research) that many of the health services currently utilized do not provide benefits to patients that are commensurate with their cost to society. Second, there is a growing body of evidence that suggests that the U.S. health care system uses more resources than necessary to produce the services it currently provides. The waste of resources occurs principally in two areas. First, compared with health care in other countries, the American system requires much more administration (including marketing, billing, and collection).[1] Second, there is considerable excess capacity of facilities, equipment, and specialized personnel.[2] In many American cities there are excess supplies of hospital beds, high-tech equipment, and certain procedure-oriented specialists; charges and fees remain high, however, and the excess capacity has persisted for decades. For example, in 1990 there were 113 California hospitals that offered open-heart surgery, but more than half of these units performed fewer than two hundred procedures per year, a level that experts believe is the minimum necessary for efficient, high-quality care. Another example: the lithotripter (a machine used to dissolve kidney stones) in the Wellesley Hospital in Toronto serves about fifty patients per week. The proliferation of lithotripters in California hospitals is so great that many have fewer than five cases per week.

The least important but still valid reason for cost containment is to eliminate abnormally high returns to some producers of health care goods and services. The drug industry, for instance, consistently earns a rate of return that is far above the average for other manufacturing industries. Also, American physicians enjoy higher earnings (relative to the average employed person) than do physicians in most other industrialized countries.

What can be done to contain health care spending? Expenditures are identically equal to the product of three terms: the quantity of services, the ratio of the quantity of resources to the quantity of services (the inverse of productivity), and the prices of the resources; i.e.,

$$\text{EXP} \equiv Q_{\text{services}} \quad \bullet \quad \frac{Q_{\text{resources}}}{Q_{\text{services}}} \quad \bullet \quad P_{\text{resources}} \cdot$$

Thus, there are only three possible routes to lower costs: reduce services, produce the services with fewer resources, or cut the prices paid to the resources. Each route involves pain for someone.

Consider, for instance, a cutback in services. If the costs of the services to be eliminated are greater than their benefits, there is a gain to society as a whole. But services are not provided to society as a whole; they are received by particular individuals and groups. More than a third of all health care is provided to Americans aged sixty-five or over; any attempt to reduce this care would be vigorously resisted by the American Association of Retired Persons. The Children's Defense Fund would protest cutbacks in services to children; the veterans' organizations want more, not fewer, services for veterans, and so on. Advocacy groups concerned with specific diseases such as cancer or diabetes would surely oppose any reduction in services to the patients that they represent. Reductions in services are also usually opposed by those who provide them. Radiologists are not likely to recommend fewer radiological services, and transplant surgeons typically do not welcome measures to reduce the number of transplantations.

Improvements in efficiency, like reductions in services, also impose burdens on particular individuals and groups. Every dollar spent on administration is a dollar of income to someone; it should, therefore, come as no surprise that where one stands on ''administrative waste'' depends on where one sits. Elimination of excess capacity would undoubtedly inconvenience some patients, either because they would have to wait for procedures or they would have to travel a greater distance to obtain them. The pain experienced by physicians and drug companies when their income and profits are reduced is so obvious as to require no elaboration. Such reductions may also have negative effects on some patients through changes in the behavior of physicians, or in the research activities of the drug companies. In brief, the iron law of cost containment is ''no pain, no gain.''

The Fundamental Problem of Health Economics

The fundamental problem of health economics arises from a conflict between *risk aversion* and *moral hazard*. The utilization of medical care is highly concentrated and often difficult to predict for individuals. In any one year, 5 percent of the population accounts for more than 50 percent of all expenditures.[3] To avoid the risk of large medical bills, most people prefer payment of a known insurance premium. But when they are insured, people tend to use more medical care than when they are not. This is termed ''moral hazard.'' The nature of the problem can be seen in Figure 1. The quantity of medical care

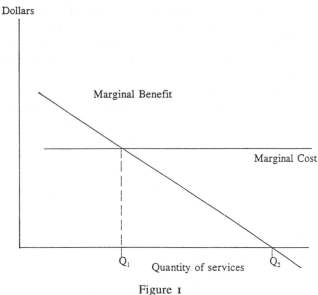

Figure 1
The Fundamental Problem of Health Economics

(i.e., number of physician visits, hospital days, operations, prescriptions, and so on) is measured along the horizontal axis. The vertical axis is calibrated in terms of dollars. The marginal (incremental) benefit of additional units of care declines as the quantity of care increases. (The linear function is a simplifying assumption which does not change the nature of the argument.) Also, for simplicity, the marginal cost of each additional unit of care is assumed to remain constant.

What is the optimal amount of care? For a patient without insurance, the optimal amount is the level at which the marginal cost and the marginal benefit are equal, i.e., Q_1. If a patient were uncertain about the marginal benefit, a conscientious physician acting as a perfect agent of the patient would also recommend Q_1. From a social point of view Q_1 is also the optimal amount of care because of the equality between marginal cost and marginal benefit. Any smaller quantity of care would result in a marginal benefit greater than the marginal cost, and any amount greater than Q_1 would have the reverse effect.

Because people are typically risk-averse, they seek health insurance. But with full insurance, the marginal cost of care to a patient is zero, i.e., the horizontal axis. In that case the patient would want care up to the point where the marginal benefit is zero, i.e., Q_2. A conscientious physician, acting as a perfect agent of an insured patient, would also recommend Q_2, which is the technological optimum. The social optimum, however, is still at Q_1 where the marginal cost to society is equal to the marginal benefit.

Any care to the right of Q_2 has a negative marginal benefit, i.e., it does more harm than good; it is "unnecessary." Care between Q_1 and Q_2 is not "unnecessary," although the fact that the cost exceeds the benefit makes it socially undesirable. This is the fundamental problem; insured patients want Q_2, and their physicians would like to provide Q_2, but the extra cost is excessive, relative to the benefit. Every health plan, private or national, faces this problem, and no perfect solution for it has yet been found.

The Second Fundamental Problem of Health Economics

The conflict between risk aversion and moral hazard would pose a major problem even if everyone with the same medical condition had

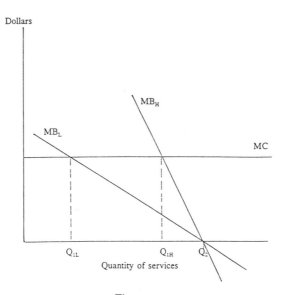

Figure 2
The Second Fundamental Problem of Health Economics

the same marginal benefit for any given amount of care, as depicted in Figure 1. But the problem is exacerbated when the marginal benefit differs among individuals, as shown in Figure 2. Differences in marginal benefit for a given medical condition arise for several reasons, the most important of which is differences in income. Individuals with higher income will usually place a higher value on care (i.e., have higher marginal benefits) than those with lower income. This is true for every level of care up to the point where the marginal benefit for all becomes zero. This amount (Q_2) is defined by the technology and is the same for all individuals. With this scenario we can see there is an additional conflict between pressure for equality of care across individuals as opposed to allowing freedom of choice and achieving closer correspondence between marginal cost and marginal benefit for each individual.

We Must Learn to Cope with an Aging Society

At the beginning of this century there were ten children (under age eighteen) in the United States for every person age sixty-five or older. By 1960 the ratio had fallen to four to one; by 1990 it was two to one; and the ratio continues to fall. This demographic revolution has major implications for politics, economics, and social dynamics. The implications for health care are particularly striking because the elderly now consume almost 40 percent of all health care in the United States, and the proportion grows every year. In principle, the amount of health care that the elderly can consume is limited only by the imagination and ingenuity of scientists, physicians, drug companies, and other producers of health care goods and services. Beyond some age, which varies from person to person, almost every part of the body can benefit from repair or replacement. Rehabilitation therapy and assistance with daily living for the frail or disabled elderly create two other potentially huge sources of demand. What kind of health policy will keep insured elderly from demanding and receiving all of the care that might do them some good without regard to cost?

Currently there is considerable discussion and debate over the right to death with dignity. The goal is to give terminally ill patients or their families the right to refuse certain kinds of treatment that will prolong their dying. Some states are moving farther; they propose to give terminally ill patients the right to request physician assistance in ending their lives. As financial and ethical pressures mount, we probably will see the right to death with dignity transformed into an expectation and eventually into an obligation. This development will create enormous stresses for patients and their families, health professionals, and government.

The nation must confront the question of not only how much health care to provide the elderly, but also what kind of care. Americans who turn sixty-five in 1995 can expect to receive, on average, about $200,000 worth of health care before they die. This estimate assumes no further inflation in health care prices and no further advances in technology; the actual figure will probably be larger. Much of this money will go for high-tech, high-cost interventions. Between one-fourth and one-third of the total will be spent in the last year of life. At the same time many of the sick elderly will suffer from a lack of low-tech, "high-touch" services such as visiting nurses and nurses' aides and will experience hardships with respect to housing, transportation, shopping, and social services. If the elderly, at age sixty-five, could choose the pattern of spending that they prefer, many might opt for a mix very different from the one they will actually receive. They might prefer more focus on the quality of life, even at the expense of a small decrease in average life expectancy.

In conclusion, neither the policy makers in Washington nor the public have been willing to make the difficult choices that are inevitable if the U.S. is to improve its approach to health care. These include establishing priorities for the health care system, accepting the necessity of subsidization and compulsion if we wish to achieve universal coverage, recognizing that containment of expenditures must impose burdens on patients and providers, coping with an aging society, and balancing the competing demands of efficiency, justice, freedom, and security.

Poverty and Health: Asking the Right Questions[*],[1]

Gertrude Stein, noted author and confidante of the leading writers, artists, and intellectuals of her time, lay dying. Her closest friend and lifetime companion, Alice B. Toklas, leaned forward and said, "Gertrude, what's the answer?" Gertrude looked up and with her last breath said, "Alice, what's the question?"

Regarding the issue of medical care and the health of the poor, we must indeed ask "what is the question?" Or, more appropriately, "what are the questions?" Unfortunately, too often the only questions addressed by writers on health policy are those for which they have predetermined answers. I propose to inject a different perspective by raising several theoretical questions about poverty and health so as to elicit answers that might improve public policy.

Who Are the Poor?

A logical place to begin is by asking what we mean by poverty—that is,

* Originally published in *Medical Care and the Health of the Poor*, edited by David E. Rogers and Eli Ginzberg (Westview Press, 1993), pp. 9–20.

who are the poor? This question has a long history within economics and even from the perspective of that single discipline gives rise to considerable controversy over definition and measurement. The question becomes even more important, however, when poverty is discussed in relation to health. As an economic concept, there is general agreement that poverty refers to some measure of income (or wealth) that indicates "inadequate" command over material resources. In the health care field, however, the concept often gets transformed into an amorphous set of "socioeconomic conditions" or an ill-defined "culture of poverty."

Let us try to avoid such confusion. This is not to deny that people can be "poor" in ways other than economic. They can be "spiritually impoverished," "morally bankrupt," "unhealthy," and so on. But to the extent possible, let us strive for clarity. If we mean low income, let us say low income. If we mean education, let us say education. And if we mean alcoholism, cigarette smoking, crime, drug abuse, fragmented families, hazardous occupations, sexual promiscuity, slum housing, social alienation, or unhealthy diets, let us say so explicitly. If we constantly redefine poverty to include anything and everything that contributes to poor health, we will make little progress either in theory or practice.

Even when poverty is defined in terms of income, there are numerous questions still to be answered, such as adjustment for size and composition of household, but we can leave them to the specialists.[2] There is one conceptual issue, however, that is so important as to require explicit discussion. Should poverty be defined according to some fixed standard (absolute income) or according to position in the income distribution (relative income)? In my judgment, we need to combine both approaches. If we cling only to a fixed standard, economic growth gradually raises almost everyone out of poverty so defined, but the problems we usually associate with poverty persist. So-called subsistence budgets are adjusted to new social norms. Alternatively, to define poverty in terms of the bottom 10 or 20 percent of the income distribution does not help us get to the heart of the problem either. In a society with little inequality of income, being at the lower end need not have the same negative implications as when the distribution is very unequal.

People usually think of themselves as poor (and are regarded as poor) when their command over material resources is much less than others. Poverty as an economic concept is largely a matter of economic distance. Thus, in 1965, I proposed a poverty threshold of one-half of median income.[3] The choice of one-half was somewhat arbitrary, but the basic idea would not change if a level of four-tenths or six-tenths were chosen instead.

There is considerable resistance to such a definition because a reduction in poverty so defined requires a change in the distribution of income—always a difficult task for political economy. But I believe it is the only realistic way to think about poverty. In this respect, as in so many others, Adam Smith had a clear view of the matter more than 200 years ago when he wrote, "By necessaries I understand not only the commodities which are indispensably necessary for the support of life but whatever the custom of the country renders it indecent for creditable people even of the lowest order to be without." [4]

What Is the Relation Between Poverty and Health?

Once we have identified the poor, the next question concerns their health relative to the rest of the population. We know in general the answer to this question—on average those with low income have worse health. There are, however, several aspects of the question that deserve further exploration. How does the relation vary with different measures of health, such as morbidity, disability, or mortality? Is the relation different for different diseases? Is it different at different stages of the life cycle? Is the relation stronger in some countries than in others? If any of these questions are answered in the affirmative (and they surely will be), the next step is to determine the reasons for the variation. Such inquiries can provide valuable inputs into the next stage of analysis when we seek to make inferences about causality.

Is Low Income the Cause of Poor Health?

Many writers simply assert, without rigorous testing, that poverty is the cause of poor health. In England, social class is often used as a proxy for poverty, but this is problematic, as illustrated by the following figures. There is a large differential in mortality between the lowest and the highest class and a large differential in income as well, but more detailed inspection reveals a complex pattern. Class II has only 5 percent greater mortality than class I, even though income is 23 percent lower. In contrast, the differential in mortality between classes IV and V is 21 percent, but

Indexes of Mortality and Income in England and Wales by Social Class,
1971 (class I = 100)

SOCIAL CLASS	AGE-ADJUSTED MORTALITY, MEN 15–64	GROSS WEEKLY INCOME
I. Professional	100	100
II. Managerial	105	77
III. Skilled	136	58
IV. Semiskilled	148	51
V. Unskilled	179	50

Source: Adapted from R. G. Wilkinson, "Socioeconomic Differences in Mortality: Interpreting the Data on Their Size and Trends," in R. G. Wilkinson, ed., *Class and Health: Research and Longitudinal Data* (London: Tavistock, 1986), pp. 2, 11.

the income difference is only 2 percent. It may be tempting to explain these data by asserting that the relationship between income and mortality is nonlinear. Thus, at low levels of income (classes IV and V) even a small increase in income has a strong effect on mortality, whereas at high levels (classes I and II) the effect is very weak. This explanation will not wash, however, once we note that the mortality differentials between classes I and V were no smaller in 1971 than in 1951. During those two decades, real earnings rose by more than 50 percent for all classes; thus, if non-linearity is the explanation for the pattern shown above, there should have been an appreciable narrowing in the class mortality differentials between 1951 and 1971. No such decrease occurred. Furthermore, there was no decrease between 1971 and 1981 despite additional increases in real income.

England is not alone in experiencing persistence of class (occupation) differentials in mortality in the face of rising real income and universal coverage for medical care. In Scandinavia, the age-standardized mortality ratio for male hotel, restaurant, and food service workers is double that of teachers and technical workers.[5] A Swedish study of age-standardized death rates among employed men aged forty-five to sixty-four found substantial differences across occupations in 1966–1970 and slightly greater differentials in 1976–1980. In Sweden, there is growing recognition that these differentials cannot be explained by differential access to health care. Johan Calltorp writes, "There is no systematic evidence that the health care system is inequitable in the sense that those in greater need get less care or that there are barriers towards the lower socio-economic groups."[6]

What Explains the Correlation Between Poverty and Health?

That variables A and B are correlated does not, of course, prove that A is the cause of B. Two other possibilities must be considered. First the causality may run in the opposite direction: B may be the cause of A. The possibility that health affects social class has been explored extensively by British writers.[7] Almost all agree that there is some "selective mobility," but no consensus has emerged regarding its importance. R. G. Wilkinson concludes that "its contribution to observed class differences in health is probably always small." [8] But Roy Carr-Hill writes, "There is an effect which should not be ignored: the size of the effect could be substantial, but it cannot be estimated properly without a lifelong longitudinal study." [9]

Second, one or more "third variables" may be the cause both of low income and poor health. These variables could include genetic endowment as well as numerous socioeconomic factors. Among the latter, most U.S. studies have focused on schooling. There is a vast literature that explores the relation between health and education.[10] To be sure, income and education are correlated, but the correlation is not so high as to preclude sorting out their separate relationships with health. In the United States, the coefficient of correlation between education and income within age–sex–race groups never reaches as much as .50 and is typically around .40.

When health is regressed on both income and schooling, the latter variable always dominates the former. Indeed, in some studies income is negatively related to health once years of schooling are controlled for.[11]

Why Is the Correlation Between Schooling and Health So Strong?

One possible answer, of course, is that schooling is the cause of good health. That is, at any given level of income, those with more education know how to use medical care more effectively, choose better diets and other health behaviors, and so on. This line of reasoning has been developed most fully by Michael Grossman.[12] But again, as a matter of logic, we must consider two other possibilities. Good health may lead to more schooling, or there may be third variables that affect both schooling and health. Among the third variables, my favorite candidates are time preference and self-efficacy.[13]

Time preference is an economic concept that refers to the rate at which people discount the future relative to the present. Individuals with high rates of time preference will tend to invest less in the future: on average they will have less education, lower income, and worse health. A perfect capital market would enable those with low rates of time discount to provide funds to those with high rates until their rates were equal at the margin, but the real world bears little resemblance to this theoretical model. For one thing, low-income individuals who want to borrow a great deal cannot provide effective collateral. Also, many choices about health do not involve money; thus, there is no effective market in which individuals with different rates of time preference can make trades.

Self-efficacy is a psychological term that describes people's beliefs in their capability to exercise control over their own behavior and their environment. Differences among individuals in self-efficacy are probably correlated across several domains, such as health and education, thus helping explain the close relationship between these variables.

How Does Low Income Affect Health?

Let us return to the line of inquiry that has poverty as a cause of poor health. Within that framework the central question concerns the mechanism through which low income translates into bad health. To what extent does the health of the poor suffer because they have inadequate access to medical care? To what extent is their poor health the result of deficiencies in other health-producing goods and services such as good food, good housing, and a safe environment? If poor health is attributable to inadequate medical care, are the barriers faced by the poor simply a matter of purchasing power, or are there other impediments?

What Are the Most Important Health Problems Facing the Poor?

In addressing this question, I want to distinguish between relative risk and absolute risk, a distinction that is often obscured in the media and even in policy discussions. For example, infant mortality may be twice as high among the poor as the nonpoor (a relative risk of 2 to 1), whereas the differential in mortality from heart disease may be only 50 percent (a relative risk of 1.5 to 1). The absolute level of risk of infant mortality, however, may be very low relative to heart disease mortality; thus, the poor might benefit more from efforts devoted to heart disease rather than to infant mortality.

To illustrate this point, let us consider the tremendous attention given by the media (and many health policy experts) to black-white differences in infant mortality and the relative neglect of other black-white health differentials. It is true that the black infant death rate is double the white rate, while the difference in overall life expectancy is only 9 percent (75.9 years versus 69.7 years in the United States in 1989). But if the black infant mortality rate were reduced to the white level (and all other age-specific rates remained unchanged), black life expectancy would rise only by six-tenths of a year. More than 90 percent of the black–white difference in life expectancy would remain. Is there not a danger that undue emphasis on attention-grabbing headlines results in a misallocation of health care resources from the perspective of those whose health problems are being addressed?

Which Health Problems of the Poor Are Most Amenable to Solution?

To make rational allocations of resources to alleviate the health problems of the poor, it is necessary but not sufficient to know the relative importance of the problems. It is also necessary to know how readily the problems can be solved or alleviated. Unfortunately, the bulk of health policy research dwells on documenting the problems of the poor, while it neglects the more difficult task of assessing the efficacy of alternative interventions. Policymakers and the public need to know both the costs and benefits of such alternatives. For example, treatment for infectious diseases may be very efficacious, whereas treatment for cancer may not be. Some prevention programs, such as immunizations, may provide a great deal of benefit for little cost, but others, such as mass screening of cholesterol levels, may use a vast amount of resources for limited benefits.

Are There Reasons for Providing Medical Care to the Poor Other Than Improving Health Outcomes?

Suppose the contribution of medical care to health at the margin is quite small. Is that sufficient reason to ignore the provision of care to the poor? Not necessarily. In his critique of the Oregon plan for rationing medical care to the poor, Bruce Vladeck writes, "We expect the health system to take care of sick people whether or not they are going to get better."[14]

Medical care may be valued by the poor (as it is by the nonpoor) for the caring and validation services that it provides. If this is the case, serious questions arise concerning the kind of care provided to the poor. In particular, is "high-tech" care overemphasized at the expense of simpler, more valuable services? That medical care has value apart from improving health outcomes provides no grounds for rejecting a cost-benefit approach to resource allocation. But it does highlight the need to incorporate the value of all services in such analyses.

What Policy Instruments Are Available to Help the Poor?

A sociologist tried to explain poverty to a colleague in economics. "You know, the poor are different from you and me." "Yes," replied the economist, "They have less money." This apocryphal exchange highlights a continuing controversy over the best way to help the poor with respect to health or anything else. If more resources are to be allocated to the poor, is it better to provide cash and allow the poor to decide how to spend it, or should the transfers be tied to particular goods and services? The arguments for tied transfers usually derive from a paternalistic assumption that the poor, left to their own devices, will not spend the money "wisely"—that is, they will buy cake when those making the transfers think they should buy bread. A more sophisticated version of this argument invokes "externalities." It may be the case that forcing the poor to spend their additional resources on immunizations rather than on alcohol helps the nonpoor because the former creates positive externalities, whereas the latter creates negative ones.[15] But the same is true of expenditures by the nonpoor.

Paternalism aside, there is the practical question of whether tied transfers can alter consumption patterns. If a family that previously spent $250 per month on food receives $100 worth of food stamps, there is no reason to expect spending on food to rise to $350. Indeed, food expenditures are not likely to increase by any more than if the family received $100 in cash. The relative price of food at the margin is no different after the transfer than before. The only way to assure a disproportionate increase in food consumption would be to provide food stamps greater in amount than what the family would voluntarily spend on food, given its income plus the cash value of the food stamps.

In devising programs for the poor, physicians usually advocate more medical care; educators, more schooling; the construction industry, more housing; and so on. But what area(s) would the poor give highest priority? This question is beyond the scope of this chapter, but it cries out for attention from policy analysts in some setting.

In choosing between in-kind and cash programs, policymakers should also consider the pecuniary effects of alternative transfers to the poor.[16] One result of Medicare and Medicaid, for example, was higher incomes for physicians—surely not a goal of the Great Society. These programs also led to an increase in the price of medical care for the general public, including many low-income persons who did not qualify for Medicaid. If instead of Medicare and Medicaid, the government had transferred to the elderly and the poor an equivalent amount of cash, some of it would have been used for medical care, but much of it would have been used for other goods and services, including food, clothing, consumer durables, and the like. The income and price effects would probably have been very different from those of Medicare and Medicaid and possibly more egalitarian.

Why Are Americans Less Willing Than Others to Subsidize Medical Care for the Poor?

The health policy literature abounds with articles that describe and decry the difficulty faced by poor Americans in obtaining health care. But these articles are typically silent as to why the United States is the only major industrialized country that does not have national health insurance. In 1976, I proposed several answers to this question: distrust of government, the heterogeneity of the population, the weakness of *noblesse oblige*, and a robust voluntary sector. In the following chapter, I reappraise these explanations in the light of subsequent political, social, and economic developments. I have a healthy respect for my opinion, but it would be useful to hear other views on this question.

What Is the Most Efficient Way to Provide Medical Care for the Poor?

The debate on this issue is clear-cut. On the one hand are those who want to provide the poor with health insurance and leave it to them to obtain the care they need. On the other hand are those who advocate special programs directly aimed at providing care for the poor. Inasmuch as both approaches have been tried in the United States and abroad, it should be possible to make some judgments about their relative costs and benefits.

Is it acceptable to provide highly cost-effective care for the poor although the care is different from that available to the nonpoor? A good example is prenatal care and delivery of babies. The Maternity Center Association can provide high-quality midwifery service in its childbearing center for less than half of what Medicaid pays for in-hospital normal childbirth.[17] At present, some poor women get the high-cost care, and some get little or no care.

The question of efficient provision of care to the poor is complicated by the fact that there may be gross inefficiencies in care provided to the nonpoor—overtesting, inappropriate surgery, and so on. Should programs for the poor aim at reproducing these misallocations of resources?

What Is "Two-Tier" Medical Care?

Discussions of medical care for the poor frequently invoke the phrase *two-tier medicine*. For strict egalitarians this is a deplorable concept. But others have argued that an explicit two-tier system would serve the U.S. poor better than does the present jumble of services that range from no care (e.g., prenatal) to the most sophisticated (e.g., neonatal intensive). In thinking about this issue, we can note that two-tier systems can vary greatly, as shown in Figure 3. In both systems, the people in the first tier receive more and better service than those in the second. But in version A most of the population is in the first tier, and only the poor are in tier two. In version B the proportions are reversed; most of the population

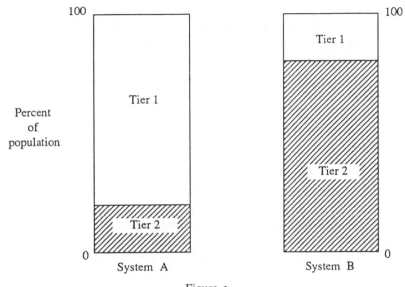

Figure 3
Two Versions of Two-Tier Medical Care

is in the second tier, and only the affluent and/or well connected are in tier one.

Version A provides a "safety net"; version B provides an "escape valve." Most Americans tend to associate two-tier medicine with version A; most other countries have opted for version B. Several interesting questions may be posed about these alternative approaches. Do the two versions have different consequences for cost, access, and quality?

For example, consider cost. Suppose per capita expenditures in tier one are identical in the two systems and the same is true for tier two except that in each country they are 50 percent less than tier one. Suppose that in system A 80 percent of the population are in tier one and 20 percent in tier two, and that the proportions are reversed in system B. In that case, the average expenditure per person in system A will be 50 percent greater than in system B.

What political, social, and economic factors lead a country to adopt one version or the other? It seems that individuals who are certain they would be in tier two under either system would prefer B. Similarly, individuals who are certain they would be in tier one under either system may also prefer B. Supporters of A are likely to be individuals who think they would be in tier one under A but in tier two under B. Many Americans probably fit that category.

What Is Basic Medical Care?

A frequent conclusion of health policy discussions in the United States is that everyone should have access to "basic" medical care. Many observers believe that the nonpoor would be more willing to subsidize a "basic" package than they would complete equality of care. Problems arise, however, in trying to define the contents of that package. Moreover, no matter how they are defined at any point in time, no one should imagine that the contents can remain fixed over time. In a world of changing technology and rising real income, a fixed approach to basic care will prove no more satisfactory than will a fixed poverty standard based on some notion of subsistence. The basic care package will constantly have to change to include "whatever the custom of the country renders it indecent for creditable people, even of the lowest order, to be without."

Summary

In summary, there are numerous questions about poverty and health that need to be addressed. Many of them concern the relation between poverty and health: its extent, pattern, and explanations. Other questions revolve around possible confounding variables such as education, which is correlated with income and health. Still other questions focus on medical care: its efficacy in improving health, its value to the poor, the best way to provide it. In pursuing these questions, we need to find a middle road between a mindless optimism that ignores reality and a constricting pessimism that denies the possibility of creating a more efficient and more just society.

From Bismarck to Woodcock: The "Irrational" Pursuit of National Health Insurance*

> Uniformity of practice seldom continues long without good reason.
> —SAMUEL JOHNSON, 1775

> If an economic policy has been adopted by many communities, or if it is persistently pursued by a society over a long span of time, it is fruitful to assume that the real effects were known and desired.
> —GEORGE STIGLER, 1975

Almost a century ago Prince Otto Eduard Leopold von Bismarck, the principal creator and first chancellor of the new German nation-state, introduced compulsory national health insurance to the Western world. Since then, nation after nation has followed his lead until today almost every developed country has a full-blown national health insurance plan. Some significant benchmarks along the way are the Russian system (introduced by Lenin after the Bolshevik Revolution), the British National Health Service (Beveridge and Bevan, 1945), and the Canadian federal-

* Originally published in *The Journal of Law and Economics*, Vol. XIX (2), August 1976, pp. 347–359.

provincial plans (hospital care in the late 1950s, physicians' services in the late 1960s). In nearly all cases these plans built on previous systems of medical organization and finance that reflected particular national traditions, values, and circumstances.[1]

In some health plans, such as those in the communist countries, the government has direct responsibility for providing services. In others, the production of medical care is still at least partially in the private sector, but the payment for care is through taxes or compulsory insurance premiums which are really ear-marked taxes. Even in the United States, the last major holdout against the worldwide trend, government funds pay directly for almost half of all health care expenditures and pay indirectly for an appreciable additional share through tax exemptions and allowances.[2] Moreover, most observers believe it is only a question of *when* Congress will enact national health insurance, not *if* it will.

Almost as obvious (to many economists) as the rise of public subsidy of health insurance is the "irrational" aspect of such programs. Health insurance, in effect, reduces the price the consumer faces at the time of purchase of medical care and therefore induces excessive demand. Because the direct cost to the consumer is less than the true cost to society of providing that care, he tends to over-consume medical care relative to other goods and services. This misallocation of resources results in a significant "welfare loss," which Martin Feldstein has estimated at a minimum of $5 billion per annum in the United States.[3]

Not only does society seem to be irrationally bent on encouraging people to overuse medical care, but in the free market for health insurance people also tend to buy the "wrong" kind. Most economists agree that to the extent that health insurance serves a useful purpose it is to protect consumers against large, unexpected bills for medical care. All insurance policies are actuarily "unfair," that is, they carry a load factor for administrative costs, but, if consumers are risk averse, it is worthwhile for them to pay these costs in order to protect themselves against unpredictable (for the individual) large losses. It follows, therefore, that consumers should prefer major medical (catastrophe) insurance, that is, plans with substantial deductibles or copayment provisions for moderate expenses but ample coverage for very large expenses. Instead, we observe a strong preference for "first dollar" or shallow coverage. Of the privately held hospital insurance policies in the United States, the number covering the first day of hospitalization are several times greater than the number covering long-term stays.

Another apparent irrationality with respect to health insurance was alleged by Milton Friedman in a *Newsweek* column in April, 1975. He noted that Leonard Woodcock, President of the United Automobile Workers (UAW), is leading the drive for universal comprehensive national health insurance despite the fact that such a measure is

... against the interest of ... members of his own union, and even of the officials of that union.... The UAW is a strong union and its members are among the highest paid industrial workers. If they wish to receive part of their pay in the form of medical care, they can afford, and hence can get, a larger amount than the average citizen. But in a governmental program, they are simply average citizens. In addition, a union or company plan would be far more responsive to their demands and needs than a universal national plan, so that they would get more per dollar spent.[4]

Friedman says that Woodcock is an "intelligent man," and therefore finds his behavior a "major puzzle."

From Bismarck to Woodcock, it seems that economists are drowning in a sea of irrationality. But other economists warn us against jumping to the "irrationality" conclusion. In particular, George Stigler has taught us to look beyond the surface appearance of political actions in search of their actual consequences and of the interests that they serve. He writes,

It seems unfruitful ... to conclude from the studies of the effects of various policies that those policies which did not achieve their announced goals, or had perverse effects ... are simply mistakes of the society.[5]

In short, when confronted with some consistent and widespread behavior which we cannot explain, we should not blithely assume that it is attributable to lack of information or bad judgment. We should be wary of what might be called the "fallacy of misplaced ignorance." It may be that the behavior we observe is more consistent with the self-interest of particular individuals or groups than it first appears.

It is to George Stigler that we are also indebted for the "survivor principle," one of his many contributions to the study of industrial organization.[6] The basic notion is simple: if we want to learn something about the relative efficiency of differently sized firms in an industry, Stigler tells us to look at that industry over time and notice which size classes seem to flourish and which do not. Can the "survivor principle" be applied to institutions as well? If so, national health insurance seems to pass with flying colors. No country that has tried it has abandoned it, and those that have tried it partially usually expand it. It may not be unreasonable to infer, therefore, that national health insurance does serve some *general* interests. That is, there may be some *welfare gains* lying below the surface that more than offset the losses so apparent to many economists. An exploration of some of the special or general benefits that might explain the widespread pursuit of national health insurance follows.

The U.S. Already Has Implicit National Health Insurance

Some of the observed behavior would seem less irrational if we assume that the U.S. already has *implicit* national health insurance, especially for catastrophic illness. If it is true that most uninsured people who need care can get it one way or another—through government hospitals, philanthropy, or bad debts—then it may be rational for people to buy only shallow coverage, or indeed, not to buy any insurance at all. To suggest that there is implicit insurance in the United States covering nearly everyone is not at all to suggest that there is equal access to equal quality care. We know that so-called free care may often have some stigma attached to it, may be less pleasant and less prompt, and may fail in other ways as well. But it cannot be denied that a good deal of medical care is delivered every year in the United States to persons who do not have explicit insurance or the money to pay for it.

Those persons without explicit insurance are essentially free riders. Those who do carry extensive insurance, such as the automobile workers, in effect pay twice—once through the premiums for their own insurance and again through taxes or inflated costs to cover care for those without explicit insurance. If this is a significant factor, it could be perfectly rational for the automobile workers to support *universal compulsory* insurance. Why society provides implicit or (in most countries) explicit coverage for all remains to be explained.

An Attempt to Control Providers

Another reason why the UAW leaders and others may favor a single national health plan is the hope of gaining some control over the providers of medical care—the hospitals and the physicians. In recent years one of the major frustrations faced by the auto workers and other groups with extensive insurance coverage is the rapid escalation in the price of medical care. They may believe that only a single source national health insurance plan will be in a position to control provider behavior and stop the escalation in costs. Moreover, there is strong evidence that they are not alone in this view. One of the puzzles for economists has been to explain the traditional opposition of the medical profession to legislation which, at least in the short run, increases the demand for their services. This opposition probably stems in part from the belief that national health insurance would ultimately result in an increase in government control over providers.

Tax Advantages

Why do people buy shallow coverage—where the administrative load is high and the risk element relatively small? One reason is that when the premium is paid by the employer the implicit income is free of tax. Even health insurance premiums paid by the individual are partially deductible from taxable income. If the tax laws allowed employers to provide tax-free ''food insurance,'' we would undoubtedly see a sharp increase in that type of fringe benefit. But again the explanation is not very satisfactory. Why do the tax laws encourage the purchase of medical care but not food, clothing, or other necessities? In an attempt to answer this question, we should consider some of the characteristics of medical care and health insurance that are different from conventional commodities.

Externalities

One explanation for the popularity of national health insurance that has great appeal for economists at the theoretical level is that there are substantial external benefits associated with the consumption of medical care. If this were true, then governmental subsidy of care need not be irrational; indeed it might be irrational not to provide that subsidy. The best example of potential externalities is the prevention or treatment of communicable diseases such as tuberculosis. In earlier times these diseases constituted a very significant portion of overall health problems, but are much less important today. Furthermore, if a concern with externalities were the chief motivation, it would be logical and feasible to subsidize those services (for example, venereal disease clinics) which are clearly addressed to the communicable diseases. However, even economists who are strong advocates of national health insurance, such as Lester Thurow, do not rely on the externality argument. Thurow writes, "Once a society gets beyond public health measures and communicable diseases, medical care does not generate externalities." [7]

Mark Pauly has called attention to one special kind of externality which probably is operative. It involves the satisfaction people get from knowing that someone else who is sick is getting medical attention.[8] This satisfaction could be purchased by voluntary philanthropy, but the total amount so purchased is likely to be less than socially optimal since each individual's giving tends to be based on his or her private satisfaction, ignoring the effects on others. The solution may be compulsory philanthropy, that is, tax-supported programs.

A Matter of "Life or Death"

Another explanation for national health insurance that has great appeal at the theoretical level but carries less conviction empirically is that "the market should not determine life or death." This theme is advanced by Arthur Okun in his new book, *Equality and Efficiency, the Big Tradeoff*, and is a basic tenet of those who argue that "health care is a right." [9] There is considerable logic in the argument that society may be unwilling to accept the consequences of an unequal distribution of income for certain kinds of allocation decisions, such as who serves in the army during wartime, who gets police protection, and who faces other life-threatening situations. It may be easier and more efficient to control such allocations directly than to try to redistribute money income (possibly only temporarily) to achieve the desired allocation.

Although this explanation has a certain theoretical appeal, one problem with it is that the vast majority of health services do not remotely approach a "life or death" situation. Moreover, the ability of medical care to make any significant contribution to life expectancy came long after Bismarck and Lenin advocated national health insurance. Even today, when some medical care is very effective, it is possible that housing, nutrition, and occupation have more influence on life expectancy than does medical care, yet we allow inequality in the distribution of income to determine allocation decisions in those areas. According to Peter Townsend, there is no evidence that the British National Health Service has reduced class differences in infant mortality, maternal mortality, or overall life expectancy.[10] If equalizing life expectancy were society's goal, it is not at all clear that heavy emphasis on national health insurance is an optimal strategy.

The emphasis on medical care rather than other programs that might affect life expectancy is sometimes defended by the statement that it is more feasible. Although diet or exercise or occupation may have more effect on life expectancy than does medical care, it may be technically simpler to alter people's consumption of medical care rather than to alter their diet, etc. It has also been argued that it is politically more feasible to push medical care rather than alternative strategies. The distinction between technical and political feasibility is not, of course, clear-cut because the former depends in part on what we are willing to do in the way of permitting government to intrude on personal decisions—a political question. However, to the extent that the popularity of national health insurance is said to be attributable to its political feasibility, we have really not explained much. Its political popularity is precisely the question we started with.

The Growth of Egalitarianism

Life expectancy aside, one way of interpreting the growth of national health insurance is an expression of the desire for greater equality in society. British economists John and Sylvia Jewkes have written,

The driving force behind the creation of the National Health Service was not the search for efficiency or for profitable social investment. It was something quite different: it was a surging national desire to share something equally.[11]

An American economist, C. M. Lindsay, has developed a theoretical model which analyzes alternative methods for satisfying the demand for equality of access to medical care. Among other things, he shows that if this demand for equality is widespread, there are externalities similar to those discussed by Pauly in connection with philanthropy. Thus a free market approach will result in less equality than people really demand.

He also shows that the British National Health Service can perhaps best be understood as an attempt to satisfy this demand for equality. He concludes, ". . . the politician's sensitive ear may read the preferences of his constituents better than the econometrician with his computer."[12]

Why the demand for equality has grown over time and why it should find expression in medical care more than in other goods and services are not easy questions to answer. Is there really more altruism in society now than before? Were Bismarck and Lenin the most altruistic political leaders of their time? Is it simply the case that equality is a normal "good," that is, we buy more of it when our income rises? If this is the explanation, what are the implications for equality in a no-growth economy?

Perhaps there has been no real increase in altruism at all. Perhaps what we observe is a response to an increase in the ability of the less well-off to make life miserable for the well-off through strikes, violence, and other social disruptions. In this view health insurance is part of an effort to buy domestic stability. It may be that industrialization and urbanization make us all more interdependent, thus increasing the power of the "have-nots" to force redistributions of one kind or another. Or perhaps there has been a decline in the willingness of the "haves" to use force to preserve the status quo.

Such speculations, if they contain some validity, would explain a general increase in egalitarian legislation, but they would not help much in explaining why this legislation has focused heavily on medical care. Indeed, is it not curious that society should choose to emphasize equality in access to a service that makes little difference at the margin, in life expectancy or to economic or political position and power? A cynic might argue that it is not curious at all since it is precisely because medical care does not make much difference that those with power are willing to share it more equally with those with less. Indeed, one might argue that the more a society has significant, enduring class distinctions, the more it needs the symbolic equality of national health insurance to blunt pressures for changes that alter fundamental class or power relationships.

One egalitarian goal that has always had considerable acceptance in the United States is equality of opportunity. Thus, a popular argument in favor of national health insurance is that it would help to equalize access to medical care for children. Some recent theoretical work on the economics of the family, however, calls into question the effectiveness of such programs. Gary Becker has argued that the thrust of programs aimed at increasing investment in disadvantaged children can be blunted by parents who can decrease their own allocation of time and money to their children as investment by the state increases.[13] The increase in the welfare of the children, therefore, may be no greater than if a cash subsidy equal to the cost of the program were given directly to the parents. The ability of the "head" to reallocate family resources may not, however, be as unconstrained as Becker's model assumes. There may be legal or social constraints, or there may be a desire on the part of the head to maintain the child's obedience, respect, or affection. Thus the importance of the reallocation effect is an empirical question, about which at present we know virtually nothing.

Paternalism[14]

An argument advanced by Thurow in favor of transfers in kind—such as national health insurance—is that some individuals are not competent to make their own decisions. He writes,

Increasingly we are coming to recognize that the world is not neatly divided into the competent and the incompetent. There is a continuum of individuals ranging from those who are competent to make any and all decisions to those who are incompetent to make any and all decisions.[15]

Thurow argues that if society desires to raise each family up to some minimum level of *real* welfare, it may be more efficient to do it through in-kind transfers than through cash grants. Even if we agree with this general argument, it does not follow as a matter of logic that subsidizing medical care brings us closer to a social optimum. It may be the case, for instance, that the "less able" managers tend to *overvalue* medical care relative to other goods and services, in which case Thurow ought to want to constrain their utilization rather than encourage it.

More generally, there is the question whether government will, on average, make "better" decisions than individuals. As Arrow has stated in a slightly different context, "If many individuals, given proper information, refuse to fasten their seat belts or insist on smoking themselves into lung cancer or drinking themselves into incompetence, there is no reason to suppose they will be any more sensible in their capacity as democratic voters."[16] Two arguments have been suggested to blunt Arrow's critique. The first is that the "less able" are less likely to vote; therefore the electoral process produces decisions that reflect the judgment of the more able members of society. Second, it has been suggested that there is considerable scope for discretionary behavior by elected representatives; they do not simply follow the dictates of their constituents.[17] It may be that their judgment is generally better than that of the average citizen.

An Offset to an "Unjust Tax"[18]

Suppose the U.S. were defeated by an enemy in war and had to pay an annual tribute to the enemy of $100 billion. Suppose further that the enemy collected this tribute by a tax of a variable amount on American citizens chosen at random. The U.S. government might decide that this tribute tax was unjust and that it would be more equitable for the federal government to pay the tribute from revenues raised by normal methods of taxation. If the enemy insisted on collecting the tribute from individual citizens on a random basis, the government could choose to reimburse those paying the tribute.

Some observers believe there is a close parallel between the tribute example and expenditures for medical care. They see ill health and the consumption of medical care as largely beyond the control of the individual citizen—the cost is like an unjust tax—and the purpose of national health insurance is to prevent medical expenditures from unjustly changing the distribution of income. There is, of course, the question whether, or how much, individuals can influence and control the amount of their medical expenditures. Putting that to one side, however, and assuming that the analogy is a good one, there are still some questions that arise.

One might ask why the government has to intervene to protect people against the tribute tax. Why couldn't citizens in their private lives buy insurance against being taxed for tribute? The total cost and the probabilities are known; therefore private insurance companies could easily set appropriate premiums. One answer might be that this is also inequitable to the extent that some people can afford the insurance more easily than others. The government could easily remedy this, however, by some modest changes in the distribution of income.

Another problem, of course, is that some people might not buy the insurance. They would be "free riders" because if they were hit with a big tribute tax they would be unable to pay and others would have to pay in their place. Furthermore, they would be wiped out financially, so that society would have to support their families.

To be sure, the government could both redistribute income to take care of the premium and make insurance compulsory, but that becomes almost indistinguishable from a national insurance plan. The only difference then would be whether there is a single organization, the government, underwriting the insurance, or whether there are several private insurance companies.

In the tribute tax example we have assumed that the probability of loss would be identical across the population, but this is clearly not true for health insurance. One argument advanced in support of national health insurance is that it does not require higher-risk individuals to pay higher premiums. A counter argument is that individuals do have some discretion concerning behavior that affects health and concerning the utilization of medical care for given health conditions. National health insurance, it is alleged, distorts that behavior. A related argument is that medical care will always have to be rationed in some way and that national health insurance requires the introduction of rationing devices other than price and income. These devices carry their own potential for inequity and inefficiency.

The Decline of the Family

Illness is as old as mankind, and, while frequently in the past and not infrequently today, there is little that can be done to change the course of disease, there is much that can be done to provide care, sympathy, and support. Traditionally most of these functions were provided within the family. The family was both the mechanism for *insuring* against the consequences of disease and disability and the locus of the *production* of care. The only rival to the family in this respect until modern times was the church, a subject to be considered below.

With industrialization and urbanization, the provision of insurance and of care tended to move out of the family and into the market. Thus, much of the observed increase in medical care's share of total economic activity is an accounting illusion. It is the result of a shift in the production of care from the home, where it is not considered part of national output, to hospitals, nursing homes and the like, where it is counted as part of the GNP. Unlike the production of bread, however, which also moved from the family to the market (and stayed there), medical care, or at least medical insurance, increasingly became a function of the state.

One possible explanation is that the state is more efficient because there are significant *economies of scale*. With respect to the production of medical care, the economies of scale argument can fairly safely be rejected. Except for some exotic tertiary procedures, the economies of scale in the production of physicians' services and hospital services are exhausted at the local or small region level. For the insurance function itself, there may be significant economies of scale. Definitive studies are not available, but the proposition that a single national health insurance plan would be cheaper to administer than multiple plans cannot be rejected out of hand.[19] To be sure, a single plan would presumably reduce consumer satisfaction to the extent that the coverage of the plan would represent a compromise among the variety of plans different individuals and groups might prefer.

The relationship between the declining importance of the family and the growing importance of the state is complex. Not only can the latter be viewed as a consequence of the former, but the causality can also run the other way. Every time the state assumes an additional function such as health insurance, child care, or benefits for the aged, the need for close family ties becomes weaker. Geographic mobility probably plays a significant role in this two-way relationship. One of the reasons why people rely more on the state and less on their family is that frequently the family is geographically dispersed. The other side of the coin is that once the state assumes responsibilities that formerly resided with the family, individuals feel freer to move away from the family, both literally and figuratively.

It has often been alleged that these intra-family dependency relationships are inhibiting and destructive to individual fulfillment. Whether a dependency relationship with the state will prove less burdensome remains to be seen. There is also the question whether the efficient provision of *impersonal* ''caring'' is feasible.

The Decline of Religion

In traditional societies when the family was unable to meet the needs of the sick, organized religion frequently took over. Indeed, practically all of the early hospitals in Europe were built and staffed by the church and served primarily the poor. The development of strong religious ties, with tithes or contributions frequently indistinguishable from modern taxes, can be viewed as an alternative mechanism for dealing with the philanthropic externalities discussed previously. Moreover, at a time when technical medical care was so ineffective, religion offered a particular kind of symbolic equality—in the next world if not in this one. Thus, the decline of organized religion, along with the weakening of the family, may have created a vacuum which the state is called upon to fill.

The "Political" Role

When refugees from the Soviet Union were interviewed in Western Europe after World War II, they invariably praised the West and disparaged life in Russia—with one notable exception. They said they sorely missed the comprehensive health insurance provided by the Soviet state.[20] It may be that one of the most effective ways of increasing allegiance to the state is through national health insurance. This was undoubtedly a prime motive for Bismarck as he tried to weld the diverse German principalities into a nation. It is also alleged that he saw national health insurance as an instrument to reduce or blur the tension and conflicts between social classes.

We live at a time when many of the traditional symbols and institutions that held a nation together have been weakened and have fallen into disrepute. A more sophisticated public requires more sophisticated symbols, and national health insurance may fit the role particularly well.

Why Is the U.S. Last?

One rough test of the various explanations that have been proposed is to see if they help us understand why the U.S. is the last major developed country without national health insurance. Several reasons for the lag can be suggested. First, there is a long tradition in the U.S. of distrust of government. This country was largely settled by immigrants who had had unfavorable experiences with governments in Europe and who had learned to fear government rather than look to it for support and protection. Second, it is important to note the heterogeneity of our population compared to some of the more homogeneous populations of Europe. We are certainly not a single "people" the way, say, the Japanese are. Brian Abel-Smith has noted, for instance, that the U.S. poor were often Negroes or new immigrants with whose needs the older white settlers did not readily identify.[21]

The distrust of government and the heterogeneity of the population probably account for the much better developed non-governmental voluntary institutions in the U.S. Close observers of the American scene ever since de Toqueville have commented on the profusion of private non-profit organizations to deal with problems which in other countries might be considered the province of government. These organizations can be viewed as devices for internalizing the philanthropic externalities discussed earlier in this paper, but the organizations are frequently limited to individuals of similar ethnic background, religion, region, occupation, or other shared characteristic.

Another possible reason for the difference in attitudes between the U.S. and Europe is the greater equality of opportunity in this country In the beginning this was based mostly on free or cheap land, and later on widespread public education. Moreover, the historic class barriers have been weaker here than in countries with a strong feudal heritage. To cite one obvious example, consider the family backgrounds of university faculties in Sweden and the U.S. Sweden is often hailed as the outstanding example of a democratic welfare state, but the faculty members at the leading universities generally come from upper-class backgrounds. By contrast, the faculties at Harvard, Chicago, Stanford, and other leading American universities include many men and women who were born in modest circumstances. With greater equality of opportunity goes a stronger conviction that the distribution of income is related to effort and ability. Those who succeed in the system have much less sense of *noblesse oblige* than do the upper classes in Europe, many of whom owe their position to the accident of birth. In the U.S., even those who have not succeeded or only partially succeeded seem more willing to acquiesce in the results.

Summing Up

The primary purpose of this inquiry has been to attempt to explain the popularity of national health insurance around the world. My answer at this point is that probably no single explanation will suffice. National health insurance means different things to different people. It always has. Daniel Hirshfield, commenting on the campaign for national health insurance in the United States at the time of World War I, wrote:

Some saw health insurance primarily as an educational and public health measure, while others argued that it was an economic device to precipitate a needed reorganization of medical practice. ... Some saw it as a device to save money for all concerned, while others felt sure that it would increase expenditures significantly.[22]

Externalities, egalitarianism, the decline of the family and traditional religion, the need for national symbols—these all may play a part. In democratic countries with homogeneous populations, people seem to want to take care of one another through programs such as national health insurance, as members of the same family do, although not to the same degree. In autocratic countries with heterogeneous populations, national health insurance is often imposed from above, partly as a device for strengthening national unity. The relative importance of different factors undoubtedly varies from country to country and time to time, but the fact that national health insurance can be viewed as serving so many diverse interests and needs is probably the best answer to why Bismarck and Woodcock are not such strange bedfellows after all.

National Health Insurance Revisited[*][1]

Proposals for national health insurance are once again making the headlines, as they have periodically in the United States since World War I.[2] Advocates of national health insurance have, as always, diverse goals: to expand access to health care for millions of uninsured Americans; to stem the rapid escalation in the cost of health care; and to improve the overall health status of the population and reduce socioeconomic differentials in life expectancy. Vigorous opposition to national health insurance is not a new phenomenon. Insurance companies, physicians, and others directly involved in the health field see national health insurance as a threat to their roles and interests; in addition, many Americans with no direct involvement in health issues oppose expansion of government on general principle. The huge federal budget deficit contributes to the difficulty of enacting a major new domestic program, in health or any other area. Thus, the debate among those for and against national health insurance does not appear to be headed for resolution any time soon.

* Originally published in *Health Affairs*, Winter 1991, 10(4), pp. 7–17.

In the preceding chapter, I discussed the popularity of national
health insurance around the world and offered four reasons why the
United States was the last major holdout: distrust of government;
heterogeneity of the population; a robust voluntary sector; and less sense
of *noblesse oblige*. In this essay, I consider whether these explanations
are as relevant today as they were in the past. First, however, I discuss
several issues that put the universal insurance controversy in clearer
perspective. Why are so many Americans uninsured? How do conflicting
views of health insurance shape attitudes toward national health insurance?
What is the connection between national health insurance and the cost
of care? Would national health insurance reduce socioeconomic differentials in health?

The Uninsured

With some exceptions, such as Medicare, health insurance in the United
States is a private, voluntary matter. The demand for insurance, like the
demand for any product or service, depends on consumers' ability and
willingness to pay for it. Some of the uninsured cannot afford health
insurance; others are unwilling to acquire it. In all, the uninsured can
be grouped into six categories.

THE POOR

The largest group of uninsured consists of individuals and families
whose low income makes it infeasible for them to acquire insurance,
either on their own or as a condition of employment. About 20 percent
have no connection with the work force, but nearly 80 percent either
are employed or are the dependents of employed persons.[3] The Health
Insurance Association of America (HIAA) estimates that 31 percent of
the working uninsured earned less than $10,000 in 1989; another estimate
puts the figure at 63 percent.[4] In any case, it is clear that the great majority
of uninsured workers cannot afford to give up a substantial fraction of
their wages to obtain health insurance.

Most uninsured workers are employed in small firms, but the frequently
heard explanation, "Small employers can't afford health insurance," is
as misleading as the phrase "employer-provided health insurance."
Employers do not bear the cost of health insurance; workers do, in the
form of lower wages or forgone nonhealth benefits. A more accurate

description of the problem would be, "Many workers in small firms can't afford health insurance." Note that lawyers, accountants, computer consultants, and other highly paid professionals organized in small firms usually have health insurance, although they often face extra costs, as discussed below.

THE SICK AND DISABLED

Many men and women who are not poor are still unable to afford health insurance because they have special health problems and therefore face very high premiums or are excluded from coverage entirely.[5]

THE "DIFFICULT"

Some individuals are neither poor nor sick but have difficulty obtaining insurance at average premiums. They may be self-employed, work in small firms, or be out of the labor force entirely. To insure such individuals, insurance companies incur abnormally high sales and administrative costs. They also encounter the problem of adverse selection: if an insurance company offers a policy to individuals or small groups at an average premium, those who expect to use a great deal of medical care are likely to buy, and those who do not will refrain from buying.

THE LOW USERS

Some people do not expect to use much medical care. They may be in particularly good health; they may dislike going to physicians; or, like Christian Scientists, they may not believe in the efficacy of medical care. For them, health insurance is a "bad buy" unless they can acquire it at a below-average premium.

THE GAMBLERS

Most people buy health insurance in part because they are risk averse. They would rather pay a fixed, known premium (even above the actuarial level) than risk a huge expense in the event of serious illness. But not everyone is risk averse about health expenditures, or risk averse to the same degree. People in this category prefer to take their chances with continued good health and save the premium payment.

THE FREE RIDERS

The final category consists of individuals who remain uninsured because they believe that in the event of serious illness they will get care anyway, and others will pick up the bill. They save the cost of insurance and "ride free" on the coattails of those who pay into the health care system. There may be elements of free riding in the behavior of the low users and the gamblers as well; it is often difficult to distinguish among the three categories of individuals who are able to pay for insurance but are unwilling to do so.

From an analytical perspective, it is not difficult to achieve a national health insurance system; all it requires is subsidizing those who are unable to afford insurance and requiring purchase by those who are unwilling to acquire it voluntarily. No nation achieves universal coverage without subsidization and compulsion. Thus far, Americans have resisted both.[6]

Two Models of Health Insurance

Part of the current debate over national health insurance is rooted in two conflicting visions of how the cost of health care should be shared. We can designate one as the casualty insurance model and the other as the social insurance model. Casualty insurance, which usually refers to automobile collision, residential fire, and similar risks, is premised on the idea that premiums should (to the extent feasible) be set according to expected loss. Other things being equal, policyholders with better driving records or with smoke detectors in their homes pay lower premiums; poorer risks pay higher premiums. Social insurance, which is the basis for national health insurance, provides for extensive cross-subsidization among different risk groups; it ignores expected loss in allocating costs.

Advocates of the casualty approach argue that, as applied to health insurance, it is more efficient and more equitable than the social insurance model. They assert that use of care depends, to some extent, on personal behavior and choice. If premiums vary with expected use, individuals have an incentive to choose healthier behavior and to make more cost-conscious decisions about their use of care for any given health condition.[7] A clear example is charging cigarette smokers higher premiums than nonsmokers are charged. This may decrease the number of smokers, and even if it does not, advocates of the casualty model argue that it is fair for smokers to bear the extra cost of their unhealthy habit.

Even when there is no possibility of altering behavior, and even if use of care is unrelated to insurance coverage, the casualty model still offers an efficiency advantage in any system of voluntary health insurance. The alternative—a uniform premium for all individuals, including those with major health problems—will discourage purchase of insurance by those without such problems because the premium would be unreasonably high.

Advocates of the social insurance model rely heavily on arguments that appeal to one's sense of justice or collective responsibility. In earlier times, these feelings of mutual responsibility were often evident within families and within religious communities. In modern times, many countries have extended the concept to encompass the entire nation. The philosophical foundation for such arguments can be discerned in John Rawls's discussion of making choices behind a veil of ignorance.[8] For example, suppose, before you were born, you did not know if you were going to be rich or poor, sick or healthy; you might (assuming some risk aversion) prefer to be born into a society that would provide health care on the same basis for, say, persons born with a genetic disease as for those born without such a problem. Advocates of the social insurance model also point to efficiency arguments. Because everyone must participate, there can be savings in sales and administrative costs that offset other efficiencies achieved through the casualty approach.

Whether one model or the other is more conducive to an efficient health care system is primarily an empirical question (interwoven with value judgments) that cannot be answered a priori. Which approach is more just is primarily a value question (individual versus collective responsibility), but empirical information concerning the reasons for variation in use of care is relevant. In my experience, the same audiences that overwhelmingly approve charging smokers a higher premium because they use more care strongly oppose a premium surcharge for individuals whose high use is attributable to genetic factors. If cigarette smoking should turn out to have a significant genetic component, opinions concerning the smoker surcharge would presumably change. One consequence of the genetics revolution may be to shift public sentiment toward the social insurance model.

National Health Insurance and Health Care Costs

Opponents of national health insurance frequently assert that it would result in a substantial increase in total health care costs. Both theoretical and empirical research support the view that the lower the price of care to the patient, the more care he or she will want. The logic of this argument suggests that those countries with universal coverage spend more on medical care than does the United States. In fact, the reverse is true. Adjusting for differences in real income, the United States spends much more per person on medical care than does any other country. For instance, the average American spends about 40 percent more than the average Canadian, even though the difference in real income per capita is less than 10 percent. And Canada spends more per capita than does any European country. How can this be? Countries with universal coverage find other methods to contain health care spending, methods that apparently are more effective than financial constraints on patients.

The most obvious source of savings under a national health insurance system is in reduced administrative costs. Approximately 6 percent of U.S. health expenditures are in "program administration and net cost of private health insurance." Several additional percentage points must be added to account for costs incurred by providers for billing and other administrative activities directly attributable to the U.S. system of financing care. By contrast, the Canadian system of provincial health insurance imposes minimal administrative and billing costs on providers and payers; the insurance plans themselves are inexpensive to run because everyone must join, and premiums are collected through the tax system.

But savings in administrative costs are only part of the answer. Nearly all countries with national health insurance rely heavily on what I call "upstream resource allocation." The key to this is control over capital investment in facilities and equipment, specialty mix of physicians, and the development and diffusion of high-cost new technologies. Such control usually results in less excess capacity, in both physical and human capital. In Canada, for example, relatively scarce high-tech equipment, such as magnetic resonance imaging (MRI) or computerized axial tomography (CT) scanners, is used intensively, while the proliferation of such equipment in the United States results in considerable idle time. There are more physicians per capita in Canada than in the United States, but fewer physicians there specialize in complex surgical and diagnostic procedures. As a result, the average Canadian specialist has a full workload, while his or her American counterpart does not.[9]

The price that Canadians and Europeans pay for such controls is delay or inconvenience in receiving high-tech services, or sometimes not receiving such services at all. Whether such delays or denials have a significant effect on the health of the population is not known with certainty; the limited evidence now available suggests that they do not.

Countries with national health insurance also contain costs by using their centralized buying power to squeeze down the prices of resources, especially drugs and physician services. Drug prices in the United States usually contain significant monopoly rents as evidenced by the willingness of the drug manufacturers to sell the identical products overseas at much lower prices.

Canadian and European physicians do not enjoy net incomes that are as high as those of American physicians, even after adjustment for international differences in the general level of wages. But this does not mean that American physicians are more satisfied with their lot or that American medical schools find it easier to attract high-quality, well-motivated applicants. Compared with physicians in most countries with national health insurance, American physicians experience more bureaucratic supervision from public and private insurance plans and greater interference with day-to-day practice of medicine.

It is important not to overestimate the amount that can be saved by reducing physicians' incomes. U.S. physicians' net incomes account for about 10 percent of all health care spending. If these incomes were reduced by 20 percent (the approximate differential between the United States and Canada after adjusting for specialty mix, the exchange rate, and the general level of wages), the saving would be only 2 percent of health care spending.[10] Also, this is not a saving of real resources, but only a money transfer from physicians to patients and taxpayers.

Cost containment under a national health insurance system often relies on single-source funding set prospectively (for example, the global budget given to each Canadian hospital at the beginning of each year). Samuel Johnson once said, "When a man knows he is to be hanged in a fortnight, it concentrates his mind wonderfully."[11] Much the same seems to be true of health care. When physicians and hospital administrators know that there is a certain pool of resources at their disposal and that no more will be forthcoming, they seem to figure out ways to do the job with what they have. To be sure, this inevitably involves limitation of some services, but most health professionals prefer having some control over the allocation of the scarce resources available to them.

National Health Insurance and Health

Does national health insurance improve the health of the population by increasing access to care, or does it worsen health by constraining the introduction of new technology and destroying incentives for physicians and hospitals? There is no conclusive answer to this question; in my judgment, such a system has little effect on health one way or the other.[12]

The evidence regarding life expectancy differentials, however, is more compelling. Universal coverage does not eliminate or even substantially reduce differentials across socioeconomic groups. In England, for instance, infant mortality in the lowest socioeconomic class is double the rate of the highest class, just as it was prior to the introduction of national health insurance.[13] The relatively homogeneous populations of Scandinavia not only enjoy universal coverage for health care but also have many other egalitarian social programs. Nevertheless, life expectancy varies considerably across occupations; the age-standardized mortality ratio for male hotel, restaurant, and food service workers is double that for teachers and technical workers.[14] A study of age-standardized death rates in Sweden among employed men ages forty-five to sixty-four found substantial differentials across occupations in 1966–1970 and slightly greater differentials in 1976–1980.[15]

The failure of national health insurance to eliminate or reduce mortality differentials is not necessarily a decisive argument against its adoption. Bruce Vladeck argues that curing disease and improving functional outcomes are not the only benefits of medical care. He writes, "We expect the health system to take care of sick people whether or not they are going to get better, as much for our benefit as theirs."[16] The caring services provided by health professionals have value even when they do not change health outcomes.

Prospects for National Health Insurance in the United States

What changes have occurred since 1976 that might modify Americans' resistance to national health insurance? Here I evaluate the four factors that I advanced in 1976 to explain the absence of national health insurance in the United States in light of recent sociopolitical trends.

DISTRUST OF GOVERNMENT

The typical American's distrust of government is probably stronger now than it was in the mid-1970s. Jimmy Carter was elected as an "outsider," and he did little to enhance the image of the presidency or of government in general during his four-year term; Ronald Reagan maintained an antigovernment posture throughout his two terms; and George Bush, while he may be more pragmatic and less ideological, still commands wide support with the message, "Government is the problem, not the solution."

The recent debacle with the savings and loan industry also provides ample cause for concern. It did not come upon us suddenly; it was a well-diagnosed, localized cancer that government allowed to metastasize to its present level. What is particularly disturbing is that the blame cannot be laid on one political party or branch of government. Moreover, not just the federal government was derelict; state regulatory agencies and legislatures also failed to meet their responsibilities to the public.

Our government is built on checks and balances. If these checks and balances failed so badly with savings and loan institutions, many observers wonder how well they would do with health care, which is so much larger, more complex, and more vulnerable to mismanagement and dishonesty.

HETEROGENEITY OF THE POPULATION

In 1976, I argued that the heterogeneity of the U.S. population helped explain a reluctance to embrace national health insurance. Unlike the Swedes, Germans, Japanese, and many other peoples, most Americans do not share centuries of common language, culture, and traditions; thus, there is less sense of national identification and empathy. In 1991, this explanation probably has even more force. The celebration of "multiculturalism" in the United States in the past fifteen years appears to have led to a heightened sense of separateness among the country's many ethnic, religious, and racial groups. Glorification of the "pluribus" at the expense of the "unum" does not enhance the prospects for national health insurance.

Heterogeneity of values also fuels resistance to national health insurance. No nation should expect or desire uniformity of opinion, but the name calling and physical violence that often accompany debates in the United States over values undermine the ability of the nation to undertake collective efforts for collective well-being. Americans might consider the words of British historian R. H. Tawney: "The condition of effective action in a complex civilization is cooperation. And the condition of cooperation is agreement, both as to the ends to which efforts should be applied and the criteria by which its success is to be judged."[17]

A ROBUST VOLUNTARY SECTOR

The United States has always been distinguished by its highly developed private, nonprofit institutions devoted to health, education, and social services. These institutions, often founded and supported by religious groups, perform many of the functions that government undertakes in other countries. During the past fifteen years, however, the ability of nonprofit hospitals and the Blue Cross/Blue Shield organizations to provide a form of social insurance through free care, cost shifting, and community rating of insurance premiums has been seriously compromised. The "competition revolution" has imposed the casualty approach to health insurance as a condition for survival.[18] The growth of managed care entities and tough bargaining by all third-party payers have sharply diminished the capacity of nonprofit institutions to act as redistributive agents. The declining importance of philanthropy relative to private and public health insurance also decreases the ability of nonprofit institutions to act as quasi-governmental agencies. In health care, the "thousand points of light" are fainter now than in the past. I conclude that the "voluntary sector" explanation for the absence of national health insurance in the United States has less force now than it had in the 1970s.

LESS *NOBLESSE OBLIGE*

The two central ideological forces of American society have been a commitment to individual freedom and, at least in the abstract, to equality. Tension has always existed between these forces, with the emphasis on individual opportunity and achievement prevailing most of the time, but the egalitarian emphasis much in evidence in the 1930s and 1960s. Even the egalitarian ideology, however, has focused more on equality of social status, equality under the law, and equality of opportunity than on equality of outcomes. Because so many Americans of humble origins could and did gain wealth and high social position, the sense of *noblesse oblige* that motivates many of the well-born in other nations to vote for social programs to aid the less fortunate has never been as evident in the United States. While I find it difficult to judge accurately, I suspect that the absence of *noblesse oblige* may be slightly more relevant today than in 1976. In the 1980s, the rhetoric of most of the American right wing was "laissez faire," not "Tory conservative." Moreover, the left wing's infatuation with the vocabulary of "rights" (divorced from obligations) often diminishes a feeling of mutual responsibility.

In summary, the distrust of government, the population heterogeneity, and the lack of *noblesse oblige* explanations are probably more relevant today than in 1976. Only one explanation—the robustness of the voluntary sector—is definitely weaker now. It is ironic that the "competition revolution," which erodes the ability of not-for-profit health care institutions to provide a modicum of social insurance, may prove to be a significant factor leading the country toward national health insurance.

Nevertheless, in my view, the prospects for national health insurance in the short run are poor. The forces actively opposed to it are strong, are well organized, and have a clear sense of what they do not want. The forces actively in favor are relatively weak, disorganized, and frequently at odds regarding the reasons for wanting national health insurance or the best way to obtain it. The great majority of Americans are not actively involved in the debate one way or the other but tend to be opposed for the reasons I have indicated. Some public opinion polls seem to indicate a readiness for national health insurance, but they are not credible indicators of political behavior.

In the long run, national health insurance is far from dead; the need to curb cost while extending coverage will continue to push the country in that direction. The process will accelerate as nonprofit health care institutions lose their ability to provide some social insurance as an alternative to national health insurance. Moreover, the current trend of basing insurance premiums on expected utilization will strike more people as unjust because most disease will be found to have a significant genetic component. Also, as employers' hiring decisions and employees' job choices become increasingly constrained by health insurance considerations, there will be more appreciation of the efficiency advantages of making health insurance independent of the labor market.

The timing of adoption of national health insurance will depend largely on factors external to health care. Major changes in health policy, like major policy changes in any area, are political acts, undertaken for political purposes. That was true when Bismarck introduced national health insurance to the new German state over a hundred years ago. It was true when England adopted national health insurance after World War II, and it will be true in the United States as well. National health insurance will probably come to the United States in the wake of a major change in the political climate, the kind of change that often accompanies a war, a depression, or large-scale civil unrest. Short of that, we should expect modest attempts to increase coverage and contain costs, accompanied by an immodest amount of "sound and fury."

The Clinton Plan: A Researcher Examines Reform*

A scholar, wrote George Stigler, winner of the Nobel Prize in economics, "ought to be tolerably open-minded, unemotional and rational. A reformer must promise paradise if his reform is adopted. Reform and research seldom march arm in arm."[1] As a longtime researcher and teacher about America's health care system, I congratulate President Bill Clinton, Hillary Rodham Clinton, and their aides for the phenomenal job they have done in getting the nation to focus on health care. The current problems are so big and complex partly because of the unwillingness or inability of previous administrations to address them. The Clintons deserve praise for their courage and their skill in bringing health policy to the top of the domestic agenda. I also applaud them for giving priority to universal coverage and for their recognition that universal coverage requires subsidies for the poor and the sick, and compulsion for those who can obtain insurance but choose to "free ride" instead. Commendation also is in order for the Clintons' insistence that the gap between the rate of growth of health spending and the rate of growth of the rest of the economy must narrow. Finally, I believe

---

* Originally published in *Health Affairs*, Spring 1994, 13(1), pp. 102–114.

that they are on the right track in encouraging the formation of integrated health care plans that will have responsibility for defined populations.

In this paper I summarize the basic elements of the Clinton plan and then I comment on several false assumptions that underlie not only the Clinton plan but most alternative proposals for health care reform. Next, I critique the plan, limiting myself to what I believe are its major shortcomings, and I suggest a few changes. The next section focuses on one particular aspect of health policy: the relation (or lack thereof) between medical care and the health of the population. Finally, I discuss three issues that I believe are crucial for progress in health policy over the long term.

How does one describe a plan, the short version of which runs to about 250 pages and the longer version more than five times that length? The problem is somewhat analogous to describing a house that one is thinking of buying. You can come back and tell your spouse that the kitchen is painted yellow, the dishwasher has two extra cycles, the bedroom has blue wallpaper, and there are lovely flowers growing in the garden. Some discussions of the Clinton plan are of this character. Who gets which prescription drugs? Are women entitled to a mammogram every year or every two years? And so on. I shall ignore the details, however, and focus on what I believe are the plan's basic elements.

Coverage. The plan calls for universal coverage for a nationally defined benefit package. Some groups (the Medicare population and patients served by the Department of Veterans Affairs, the Department of Defense, or the Bureau of Indian Affairs) are excluded. Approximately 60 percent of U.S. health care is financed through the plan.

Financing. The primary source of financing is a payroll tax of approximately 10 percent earmarked for health care.[2] The temper of the times requires that this levy be called a "mandated premium," and I do not mind using that terminology as long as everyone understands that the distinction is of little analytical significance. (Americans currently pay a tax on each gallon of gasoline they buy, but it could also be described as a mandated premium earmarked for road construction and maintenance.) The Clinton plan also is financed partially through higher cigarette taxes and from general revenues.

Subsidies. Subsidies are provided for low-wage workers, the unemployed, and retirees ages fifty-five to sixty-four.

Community rating. The mandated premiums are community rated in four categories, depending on family status.

Health alliances. Everyone covered by the plan becomes a member of a regional (or corporate) health alliance; the alliances make contracts with health care plans, and members choose from among the plans that have contracts with their alliance.

Risk adjustment. Health plans receive capitation payments that are risk-adjusted for demographic characteristics, health and poverty status, linguistic and cultural barriers, and location. The alliances also contract with fee-for-service plans.

Cost containment. The principal mechanism for cost containment is price controls on increases in the charges that health plans can make to the alliances.

National Health Board. A seven-member National Health Board, appointed by and responsible to the president, refines congressionally determined scope and depth of benefits, develops the risk adjusters, implements a system to control increases in premiums, and assumes many other tasks.

False Assumptions?

Americans desperately need comprehensive change in health care, both to contain costs and to assure universal coverage with equitable financing. These goals will remain elusive, however, as long as both the supporters and the opponents of the Clinton plan base their arguments on the following false assumptions.

"Employers pay for health care." It is a commonplace in the current health care reform debate to assume that health insurance is now paid for by employers. Nothing could be further from the truth. Let me illustrate with an example close to home—my home. I am employed by Stanford University, and the university nominally "provides" my health insurance. But who really pays for it? The chairman of my department? The president of the university? The members of the Board of Trustees? Surely none of the above. Most of the premium undoubtedly comes from money that otherwise would be part of my salary. Some of the cost may be passed on to students in the form of higher tuition. Some may be borne by the agencies that fund research grants and contracts. One thing is certain: Stanford does not pay for my health insurance in any meaningful sense. Much the same story can be told for all employment-based insurance, whether the employer is a nonprofit organization like Stanford, a branch of government, or a for-profit corporation.

Over time, the rising cost of health insurance inevitably reduces the potential earnings of workers or results in higher prices to consumers. Some observers claim that the costs of health insurance come at the expense of corporate profits, but there is no empirical support for that view. Net profits of manufacturing corporations as a percentage of stockholders' equity were just as high in the 1980s as they were in the 1950s, despite huge increases in health insurance premiums over that thirty-year span.[3] The negative effect of rising health insurance premiums and other fringe benefits on wages is readily evident. Between 1970 and 1990 total compensation (wages plus fringe benefits) per hour of work rose 12 percent after adjustment for inflation. During that same period inflation-adjusted hourly earnings fell by 6 percent.[4] Why have fringe benefits such as health insurance become such a large part of the total compensation package? The answer is clear. The fringe benefit portion of total compensation is exempt from federal and state income taxes, Social Security contributions, and other payroll taxes. Workers understandably prefer tax-free compensation when possible. But the illusion that the cost of care is actually borne by employers distorts the search for an efficient and equitable source of financing.

Most policy analysts know that employers do not really bear the cost of health insurance. But some of them regard it as a useful myth for selling universal coverage to an unwilling and unsuspecting public. One Princeton professor, for instance, has been quoted as saying, "If the only way to get everyone insured is to continue the pretense that employers pay, I'm for it." [5] The nation's experiences with similar deceptions in the past provide some cause for alarm. Consider President Lyndon Johnson's success in selling an escalation of the Vietnam War with the message of "guns *and* butter." The public was led to believe that a step-up in our commitments in Vietnam could be achieved without higher taxes or cuts in social programs. This was an effective short-run political tactic, but the long-run results were disastrous in both economic and political terms. The nation would have been better served by an honest debate about the escalation of the war, regardless of the outcome of the debate. The Reagan administration provides another example. President Ronald Reagan achieved short-run success with the promise that he could cut taxes and increase defense spending while not increasing the budget deficit. The nation is still struggling with the consequences of that deception.

"Small employers cannot afford health insurance." This emphasis on the size of the firm is misplaced. It is true that most uninsured workers are employed in small firms, but that is because the majority of those workers earn low wages. Many of the employed uninsured earn less than $10,000 per year, and most earn less than $20,000. They cannot afford to give up a substantial fraction of their wages to obtain health insurance. In contrast, small firms of highly paid professionals such as lawyers and accountants almost always have health insurance.

If there were merit to the argument that the mandated premium rate for health insurance should vary with the size of the firm, why shouldn't firm size also be relevant in setting Social Security payroll tax rates, workers' compensation premiums, and so on? Indeed, steel companies, machine tool manufacturers, public utilities, and other suppliers to business firms should be required to lower their prices for small companies. But that would be absurd. Subsidies based on the income of individuals and families can he justified; subsidies based on size of firm cannot.

"Health care expenditures make U.S. companies less competitive in the global economy." That's nonsense. Health expenditures have no more relationship to competitiveness than do expenditures for hotels or haircuts. Employer contributions to health insurance are part of a total compensation package that includes basic wage rates, overtime premiums, and a wide variety of fringe benefits. If total compensation is high relative to productivity, the firm will not be competitive; that should be obvious. But the form of compensation, such as wages, health insurance, or whatever, is irrelevant. A rise in the price of health care lowers a worker's standard of living, just as a rise in the price of food or any other commodity would. But as long as total compensation is consistent with productivity, the firm's competitiveness is unaffected.

Food is much more expensive in Japan than in the United States, but no one claims that the high price of food has made Japan uncompetitive in the global economy. One reason for confusion and controversy is that many employers were fond of telling their employees that they were "giving" them health insurance. In fact, the insurance was no more of a gift than wages were. But now, when employers need to cut back on insurance benefits or require employee contributions to premiums, they meet fierce resistance because it seems as if they are taking away something that they formerly "gave" to the workers.

"Improved insurance coverage will lead to lower expenditures."
The available evidence on the relationship between insurance coverage
and use of care is overwhelmingly in the other direction. The RAND Health
Insurance Experiment showed conclusively that better insurance coverage led to more physician visits, more admissions to the hospital, and
higher overall expenditures.[6] Nor did more physician visits keep people
out of hospitals—the rate of hospital admissions for groups randomly
assigned to different insurance plans rose almost in proportion to the increase
in visits. And this was not just a short-term effect: The experiment ran
for five years.

What about preventive care? Some preventive interventions clearly
contribute to longer and healthier lives, but they rarely reduce costs. Indeed,
Louise Russell, an economist who has done extensive research on this
question, has concluded that "preventive care usually increases medical
expenditures."[7]

**"Reform of medical care will lead to significant improvements in
the health of the population."** The available evidence, from both this
country and abroad, does not support this assumption. Later in this paper
I attempt to explain why.

Criticisms

Probably the biggest shortcoming of the Clinton plan is its complexity.
The plan has great potential for waste, fraud, and abuse because it has
so many "moving parts." Moreover, it is likely to unleash a huge volume
of litigation and lobbying involving the health alliances, the health plans,
and the National Health Board. The plan may not solve the health care
crisis, but it should substantially increase the demand for lawyers and
lobbyists. Consider the following likely trouble spots.

Benefit package. The plan calls for Congress to define the benefit package in minute detail; thus, the opportunity for special interest groups to
apply political and economic pressure is maximized. Long experience
with congressional micromanagement of defense procurement should serve
as a warning against this approach. (Question: Why does Congress require
the Department of Defense to purchase only colossal-size olives or larger?)

Most other countries do not spell out the details of care in their national
health insurance legislation. One reason is that the appropriate package
constantly changes with changes in medical technology. Also, every clinician

knows that the determination of appropriate care is often patient-specific: It depends on previous medical history, occupation, family status, and other circumstances that are impossible to anticipate in legislation.

If it is deemed essential to have the details of care specified in legislation, I suggest that Congress profit from its experience with the closing of defense bases. An independent commission should be authorized to develop a benefit package; then Congress could vote the total package up or down.

National Health Board. The placement of the National Health Board directly under the president (any president) is an invitation to political control of health care in the worst sense of the term. Consider, for instance, the task of setting the risk adjusters; this is both technically difficult and charged with political dynamite. The same can be said for the board's control over health insurance premiums. There can be little doubt that the board will have power over all Americans rivaled only by that exercised by the Federal Reserve Board. Thus, a comparable degree of independence would be appropriate.

Health alliances. The regional health alliances are assigned a multitude of complex responsibilities. In many states the alliance's budget will exceed that of the state government. Based on past and current performance of most state governments and agencies, there is little reason to think that the alliances will be able to discharge these responsibilities efficiently and honestly. The alliances are supposed to collect the premium for millions of employed persons as well as for other individuals such as those who are self-employed, unemployed, or prematurely retired. The premium is supposed to change every time an individual moves to a new family category through marriage, divorce, childbirth, and so on. The alliances will be responsible for allocating subsidies, monitoring the qualifications of those receiving the subsidies, and collecting retrospectively from those who have been oversubsidized. There is little chance that this will be done well; in any case, the administrative cost is likely to be enormous.

In my judgment, the plan's supporters overestimate the efficiency gains that will be achieved by pooling buyers into health alliances with community-rated premiums. Community rating may be desirable on equity grounds, but it simply redistributes the burden; it does not increase efficiency in the use of medical resources. Although payments by employers and employees will be community rated, payments to health plans will be risk-adjusted to take account of numerous characteristics that affect utilization. Thus, there will be large costs in real resources to calculate and administer these adjustments. Furthermore, there will be a constant battle between the government actuaries who are trying to calculate these risk adjusters and the actuaries in the health care plans who will be trying to outwit the alliances to enroll and keep those patients who are most lucrative. To calibrate and recalibrate the risk adjusters, the government actuaries will need utilization data on individuals and families by each of these various characteristics. While the plan is likely to result in some savings in billing costs, other overhead costs may actually increase. For example, subsidies will be calibrated according to income and other considerations. Resources will be needed to monitor income and the other criteria. Resources also will be needed to recover excess subsidies that have been provided through error or fraud or simply because of unexpected increases in income.

The Relation between Medical Care and Health

What is the relation between medical care and health? In particular, do differences in the financing and organization of care have any substantial effect on the health of populations? I have been intrigued by this question ever since I looked at interstate differentials in mortality some thirty years ago. My conclusion then and now is that if there is any connection, it is dwarfed by the other determinants of health.

First, there is the role of genetic endowment. As genetics research unfolds, it is becoming clear that genetic factors are at work in virtually every disease. Second, there is the importance of the physical environment, including the purity of air and water, the safety of the streets and workplaces, and so on. The psychosocial circumstances of work, family, and community are also critical to health, as is personal behavior such as smoking, diet, and exercise. The proposed tax increase on cigarettes may do more for the health of the population than will the rest of the Clinton plan or any other of the reform proposals.

Those who oppose the Clinton plan or any national insurance program on the grounds that it will hurt the health of Americans by discouraging innovation and bureaucratizing medicine will have great difficulty finding empirical support for their case. On the other hand, there is little evidence either in this country or abroad to suggest that providing universal coverage or changing the delivery system will have significant favorable effects on health, either in the aggregate or for particular socioeconomic groups.[8]

Why is it so difficult for differences in medical care finance and organization to have significant effects in the aggregate? Some insight can be obtained by recognizing that the medical care delivered to a population at any given time falls into three main categories. First, there is care for patients with essentially self-limiting conditions. Examples include viral upper respiratory disorders, gastrointestinal upsets, headaches, sprains, cuts, bruises, and the like. Medical care may provide significant psychological benefits to these patients, but their long-term health condition is not likely to be affected by whether they see a physician or not. Second, there is care for patients with essentially incurable conditions. These may include disease for which there is no effective treatment to prevent early death. An example would be pancreatic cancer. Alternatively, patients may live for a very long time with chronic conditions such as Alzheimer's disease, but effective medical treatment does not exist. The third category consists of medical care that does make a difference in health outcomes as measured by mortality or morbidity. No one knows what fraction of care falls into this category, but it is entirely possible that it accounts for substantially less than half of the total. But that is not the end of the story. The third category can itself be divided into three parts.

First, there are those interventions that are demonstrably effective but are well understood and not particularly expensive. They are provided by most health care systems—for example, antibiotics for bacterial infections or surgery to remove an inflamed appendix. Patients are helped and lives saved, but the results tend to be similar regardless of the health care system.

Second, for many conditions some care is better than no care, but there is no consensus as to which approach is best. Thus, an American who suffers a heart attack usually will be treated very differently from a Canadian with the same condition. The American probably will be treated with TPA rather than the much less expensive streptokinase and is more likely than the Canadian to undergo invasive procedures such as angiogram, angioplasty, and bypass surgery. Some follow-up studies conclude that American patients report less pain and lead more active lives. With respect to mortality or recurrence, however, virtually all of the studies find no discernible difference between the American and Canadian patients.

Finally, there are cases where care is effective, where the care varies from one health care system to another, and where this variation does substantially affect outcomes. It appears, however, that such cases comprise only a small proportion of total medical care—a proportion too small to make a discernible impact on the statistics for national or state populations.

One exception to this generalization concerns the very old. The United States spends more on medical care than other nations at all ages, but the differential is probably greatest after age eighty. For such patients major surgical interventions that are routine in the United States are rare elsewhere. Steven Schroeder, president of The Robert Wood Johnson Foundation, has noted that American intensive care units (ICUs) are full of elderly patients; in European hospitals ICUs care for a younger population. This differential input of medical care seems to make a difference. Life expectancy at age eighty in the United States is the second-highest in the world.[9] The U.S. figure exceeds that of the median Organization for Economic Cooperation and Development (OECD) country by about half a year.

Three Major Issues of Health Policy

The Clinton plan has been attacked as being too radical, but in my judgment it is not radical enough. Indeed, three major issues must be addressed if costs are to be contained while universal coverage is provided and equitably financed.

Separate insurance from employment. First, we must disengage health insurance from employment. This tie never had a rational basis; it is the result of historical accident and misguided tax laws. During World War II wages were frozen, but employer contributions to health insurance were exempt from such control. Thus, employers used insurance as a legal way to bid for scarce workers. The tie was nourished in the post-World War II era by the tax-exempt status of employer contributions to health insurance, an exemption that became more valuable to workers as wages and taxes rose. Sooner or later, the inequities and inefficiencies associated with employment-based health insurance will become so apparent as to dictate disengagement.

The Clinton plan moves in the direction of *de facto* disengagement, but in its efforts to maintain the appearance of an employment-based system it becomes enormously complex while not entirely escaping some of the inefficiencies and inequities of the present system. It is certainly true that if government imposes enough mandates, enough subsidies, enough surcharges, and enough controls and regulations, the tie to employment can be severed. But such a complex system invites evasion, gaming, and litigation. Why pursue such a tortured path when there are more effective mechanisms available?

For example, a national value-added tax, earmarked for health insurance, would be much more efficient and more equitable. It is more efficient than a payroll tax (or mandated premium) because it does not discourage hiring by discriminating against labor. It is also simpler to administer. It is preferable to an income tax because it encourages rather than discourages saving. It is fair because no family can escape its impact through tax loopholes, and the burden rises roughly in proportion to family spending.[10] Financing via a national value-added tax could (and should) be combined with decentralized organization and delivery of care. Diversity among states in geography, population size and density, and cultural norms suggests that it would be foolish to impose a uniform national system of health care delivery.

Technologic change. The second major issue concerns technologic change in medicine, which must be tamed but not destroyed. Technologic change is the most important force behind the escalation of health care expenditures. If health care technology is allowed to develop in the same unconstrained manner as in the past, it will create enormous economic, political, and ethical dilemmas. On the other hand, we must not inhibit technologic change to the point of preventing advancements in medicine that can increase the length and the quality of life at reasonable cost.

From a social point of view, technologic change in medicine suffers from two serious problems. First, there is too much of it, and second, some of it is misdirected. Third-party payment for health care induces too much technologic change because it assures a market for any change that meets standards of efficacy and safety, regardless of costs relative to benefits. In most industries technologic change must exceed a satisfactory benefit/cost threshold; otherwise, it will not be undertaken.

The misdirection of innovation in medicine arises because of the differential valuation of an "identified" as opposed to a "statistical" life. When a patient is facing certain death, the individual, his or her family, and society as a whole are willing to pay heavily for any innovation that offers even a small promise of postponing death. By contrast, the healthy population is not as willing to pay for preventive innovations that would save many

more lives for each dollar of expenditure.[11] The executives who make
decisions about medical research and development know that this bias
exists and therefore understandably fund new projects that offer the
greatest profit potential. Also, legislators and administrators who help
to determine the direction of research and development are influenced
by the greater political pressure generated by the possibility of saving
an identified life.

The new technology assessment must not only assess efficacy and safety,
but must also encompass considerations of quality of life, patient preferences, and especially the evaluation of costs and benefits.[12] Individual
physicians, however, usually lack the incentive or ability to assess new
forms of medical technology; any such assessment is at least in part a
"public good." Even the largest insurance companies each account for
only a small percentage of the health care market. They are, therefore,
understandably reluctant to pay for large-scale assessments that will benefit
all. One possible model for the health care industry is provided by the
electric power industry, which devotes a small portion of each public utility
bill to fund the Electric Power Research Institute. This institute devotes
itself to the development and the assessment of new forms of technology
for electric power. If only a tiny fraction of health care expenditures were
devoted to funding a health care technology assessment institute, the results
could lead to both improved health care for the population and lower
health care expenditures.

Aging society. Finally, we must learn to cope with an aging society.
At the beginning of this century there were ten children (under age eighteen)
in the United States for every person age sixty-five or older. By 1960
the ratio had fallen to four to one; by 1990 it was two to one; and the
ratio continues to fall. This demographic revolution has major implications
for politics, economics, and social dynamics. The implications for health
care are particularly striking because the elderly now consume almost
40 percent of all health care in the United States, and the proportion grows
every year. In principle, the amount of health care that the elderly can
consume is limited only by the imagination and ingenuity of scientists,
physicians, drug companies, and other producers of health care goods
and services. Beyond some age, which varies from person to person, almost
every part of the body can benefit from repair or replacement. Rehabilitation
therapy and assistance with daily living for the frail or disabled elderly
create two other potentially huge sources of demand. What kind of health

policy will keep insured elderly from demanding and receiving all of the care that might do them some good without regard to cost?

Currently there is considerable discussion and debate over the right to death with dignity. The goal is to give terminally ill patients or their families the right to refuse certain kinds of treatment that will prolong their dying. Some states are moving further; they propose to give terminally ill patients the right to request physician assistance in ending their lives. As financial and ethical pressures mount, we probably will see the right to death with dignity transformed into an expectation and eventually into an obligation. This development will create enormous stresses for patients and their families, health professionals, and government.

The nation must confront the question of not only how much health care to provide the elderly, but also what kind of care. Americans who turn sixty-five in 1994 can expect to receive, on average, about $200,000 worth of health care before they die. This estimate assumes no further inflation in health care prices and no further advances in technology; the actual figure may be much larger. Much of this money will go for high-tech, high-cost interventions. Between one-fourth and one-third of the total will be spent in the last year of life. At the same time many of the sick elderly will suffer from a lack of low-tech, "high-touch" services such as visiting nurses and nurses' aides and will experience hardships with respect to housing, transportation, shopping, and social services. If the elderly, at age sixty-five, could choose the pattern of spending that they prefer, many might opt for a mix very different from the one they will actually receive. They might prefer more focus on the quality of life, even at the expense of a small decrease in average life expectancy.

Success in dealing with these three major changes will require significant improvement in our governmental institutions. The market is a powerful and flexible instrument for allocating most goods and services, but it cannot create an equitable, universal system of insurance, cannot harness technologic change in medicine, and cannot cope with the potentially unlimited demand for health care by the elderly. On the other hand, the savings and loan debacle, the cost overruns in defense procurement, and other scandals do not inspire confidence that our government can currently handle the complex issues of health care efficiently and honestly. Thus, major political reform in general, and in health in particular, is a necessary precondition for significant improvements in the health care system.

Is such reform possible? Machiavelli, one of the shrewdest political analysts of all time, observed, ''There is nothing more difficult to manage, more dubious to accomplish, nor more doubtful of success . . . than to initiate a new order of things. The reformer has enemies in all those who profit from the old order and only lukewarm defenders in all those who would profit from the new order.'' With these words Machiavelli provided a prescient commentary on current obstacles to meaningful change in health policy. The problems are formidable, but progress in dealing with them could provide tremendous economic and social benefits to the nation. Moreover, to the extent that we can build a more efficient and equitable health care system, we will strengthen our institutional capacity and resolve to deal with education, child care, and other major domestic problems.

Economics, Values, and Health Care Reform*

Interest in health economics has soared over the past three decades, stimulated by intellectual innovations, greater availability of data, and, most importantly, a surge in health care spending from 6 to 14 percent of GDP.[1] An eleven-fold increase[2] in the number of Ph.D.s has enabled many professional schools, government agencies,[3] and research institutes to add health economists to their staffs. Nevertheless, the health care debate of 1993–1994 benefited much less than it could have from the results of their research.

In this lecture I identify the primary sources of modern health economics and describe interactions between the discipline and the field of health, drawing heavily on my personal experience. I then turn to the question of why economists did not have more impact on health care reform. I report and analyze the answers of health economists, economic theorists, and practicing physicians to a survey I conducted in 1995. My principal conclusion is that value differences among economists, as well as among all Americans, are a major barrier to effective policy-making. I discuss

* Presidential Address delivered at the one-hundred eighth meeting of the American Economic Association, January 6, 1996, San Francisco, CA. Originally published in the *American Economic Review*, March 1996, 86(1), pp. 1–24.

the implications of the importance of values for economics and conclude the lecture with my recommendations for health care reform— recommendations based on my values as well as my understanding of health economics.

The Past

In 1963 a seminal paper by Kenneth Arrow discussed risk aversion, moral hazard, asymmetrical information, philanthropic externalities, and numerous other topics that have since played major roles in health economics research.[4] He saw that *uncertainty* about health status and about the consequences of care was the key to understanding the health sector from both positive and normative perspectives. As Arrow wrote, "Recovery from disease is as unpredictable as its incidence" (1963 p. 951).

At the same time that Arrow was depicting the theoretical landscape, Martin Feldstein was pioneering in the application of quantitative methods such as 2-stage least squares, principal component analysis, and linear programming to the estimation of production functions and other important economic aspects of medical care. His numerous papers analyzing the British National Health Service formed the basis for his Ph.D. thesis at Oxford University (Feldstein, 1967).

A third line of work that has had a significant influence on health economics also began in the early 1960's with the National Bureau of Economic Research Conference on Investment in Human Beings (1962) and Gary S. Becker's treatise on human capital (1964). The NBER conference volume included Selma Mushkin's (1962) paper, "Health As an Investment," and a few years later the application of the human capital model to health was given its fullest development by Michael Grossman (1972).

Predating and postdating the theoretical and econometric innovations of the 1960's is a stream of research that focuses on health care institutions, technology, and policy. As early as 1932, Michael M. Davis and C. Rufus Rorem (1932) were writing about the crisis in hospital finance. Significant contributions to this genre have been made by Henry Aaron, Alain Enthoven, Rashi Fein, Eli Ginzberg, Herbert Klarman, Dorothy Rice, Anne Scitovsky, Anne and Herman Somers, Burton Weisbrod, and many others. Although they are all economists, much of their work does not appear in economics journals, but rather in books and in publications such as the *New England Journal of Medicine*, *Journal of the American Medical Association*, *Milbank Memorial Fund Quarterly*, and *Health Affairs*.

In recent decades several leading health economists have addressed theoretical, empirical, and policy questions in various aspects of their research (e.g., Joseph Newhouse, Mark Pauly). Health economics has also been enlivened and enriched by contributions from economists who are primarily specialists in other fields such as industrial organization, labor, finance, and public economics (e.g., Sherwin Rosen, Richard Zeckhauser). There has also been a welcome infusion from another direction, namely physicians who have earned Ph.D.s in economics and who now contribute to the economics literature (e.g., Alan Garber, Mark McClellan).

Parenthetically, all this name-dropping has a point. I want to underscore the varied intellectual, methodological, and ideological sources that have contributed to the health economics enterprise. Research has often been described as lonely work, and in one sense it is. But in another sense it is the most collective of all human activities. The philosopher Susan Haack (1995) sees scientific research as analogous to an attempt by many participants to fill out a huge crossword puzzle. We have clues; we try out possible answers; we check to see whether they fit together. Occasionally, an Arrow or a Becker comes up with one of the really big answers that runs across the puzzle and makes it easier to discover the smaller words that intersect it. If several of the small answers don't fit, however, we may have to modify or even reject the larger one. It is good to remember that all answers are provisional until the puzzle is completed—and it never will be.[5]

Although I have mentioned only American economists, note should be taken of many fine health economists in England, Canada, and other high-income countries. There is, however, less of a global intellectual community in this field than in some other branches of economics[6]— or in other fields of health[7]—because most health economics research is applied and is (or is perceived to be) country specific. More than 60 years ago Walton Hamilton (1932) noted that "The organization of medicine is not a thing apart which can be subjected to study in isolation. It is an aspect of culture whose arrangements are inseparable from the general organization of society" (p. 190). On the whole I agree with Hamilton; there are, however, important economic questions concerning technology assessment and disease prevention that are common to all high-income countries. This type of research does not receive support commensurate with its importance because funding sources, both public and private, tend to focus on national problems.

My involvement in health economics grew out of my research on the service industries (Fuchs, 1968, 1969). It was motivated in part by a desire to gain a better understanding of the postindustrial society that was emerging in the United States and other developed countries (Fuchs, 1966, 1978a). The growth of the service economy and improved methods of contraception were bringing women into paid employment and dramatically changing gender roles and relationships. Lower fertility and longer life expectancy were transforming the age distribution of the population, and this transformation, along with the fragmentation of the family and the declining influence of traditional religion, were creating new social and economic conditions. The health sector, with its nonprofit institutions, professional dominance, sharply skewed distribution of demand, and the critical importance of the consumer in the production process, seemed like a fruitful area for investigation. I was particularly interested in trying to understand the determinants of health and the determinants of health care expenditures.

With regard to health, my research has led me to emphasize the importance of nonmedical factors such as genetic endowment, the physical and psychosocial environment, and personal behaviors such as cigarette smoking, diet, and exercise. Over time, advances in medical science contribute significantly to reductions in morbidity and mortality; at any given point in time, however, differences in health levels within or between developed countries are not primarily related to differences in the quantity or quality of medical care.[8]

With respect to expenditures on medical care, my research has led me to emphasize the importance of supply factors, especially technology and the number and specialty mix of physicians.[9] To be sure, conventional demand factors such as price, income, and insurance play significant roles, but in my judgment concentration on them to the exclusion of (partly exogenous) supply factors misses a big part of the expenditures story. Despite many attempts to discredit it,[10] the hypothesis that fee-for-service physicians can and do induce demand for their services is alive and well.[11]

My views about health and health care expenditures have been formed not only through research but also through close interaction with medical scientists, practicing physicians, and other health professionals. Since 1968 I have maintained a regular medical school faculty appointment in addition to my appointment in economics, and have participated every year in a wide variety of health-related activities. This dual life would have gained approval from John Stuart Mill who, in *The Principles of Political Economy*

(1848, reprinted 1987), wrote, "It is hardly possible to overrate the value ... of placing human beings in contact with persons dissimilar to themselves, and with modes of thought and action unlike those with which they are familiar ... Such communication has always been ... one of the primary sources of progress" (p. 581).

The proposition that the discipline of economics has a great deal to contribute to health and medical care is not one likely to require elaborate defense before this audience. (I have had audiences that were less receptive to this notion.) It might, however, be useful to report briefly just what it was in economics that I found to be most relevant in the invasion of alien turf. (To avoid undue suspense, let me say at once that it was *not* game theory.)

In my experience, the most important contribution we make is the economic point of view, which may be summed up in three words: scarcity, substitutability, and heterogeneity. This economic point of view stands in stark contrast to the romantic and monotechnic points of view that I found prevalent among health professionals and health policymakers. The romantic point of view refuses to accept the notion that resources are inherently scarce; any apparent scarcity is attributed to some manmade problem, such as capitalism or socialism, market failure or excessive government interference. In the 1960's and 1970's, many physicians said that there was no need to limit expenditures for medical care if only we would cut defense spending. In 1996, when health care expenditures are almost four times as large as the defense budget, this argument is not heard as often. Because it denies the inevitability of choice, the romantic point of view is increasingly seen as impotent to deal with the problems of health care.[12]

To be sure, it is not clear whether economic research or the force of circumstances is bringing about the change in point of view. I suspect that there is a synergistic relationship in which the former provides the language to give expression to the latter. Or, as Max Weber (1915; reprinted 1946) wrote, material and ideal interests are the tracks on which society rides, but ideas throw the switches (p. 280).

The monotechnic point of view, found frequently among physicians, engineers, and others trained in the application of a particular technology, fails to recognize the diversity of human wants, or acknowledge the difference between what is technically best and what is socially desirable.[13] "Optimal" care is defined as the point where the marginal benefit is zero, ignoring the fact that resources used for health care have alternative uses that might yield greater benefit. The "production" of health is viewed narrowly as a function of inputs of medical care, and the appropriate input mix is assumed to be determined by technology without regard to relative prices, explicit or implicit. For example, Feldstein found that average lengths of stay in British hospitals were uniform across regions despite large regional differences in the pressures for admission.[14]

The monotechnic view often fails to consider the heterogeneity of preferences, even though for many health problems there are alternative interventions: one drug versus another, drugs versus surgery, or even "watchful waiting" versus any intervention. Under the influence of economists and other behavioral scientists, physicians are now making such choices with more attention to patient differences in time preference, attitudes toward risk, tolerance of pain, functional needs, and other characteristics.

Among our specific tools, one of the most useful is the idea of the margin. The key to gaining acceptance for this principle is to have people realize that most decisions involve a little more or a little less, and that they will make better decisions if they look at the costs and benefits associated with having a little more or a little less. This formulation is more effective than postulating "maximization," which economists find useful for classroom or research purposes, but sounds unreal to most noneconomists.

David M. Eddy's research on the frequency with which women should get Pap smears provides a fine example of the use of marginal (or incremental) analysis to assist in medical decision-making. This screening test for cervical cancer is of proven safety and effectiveness, and before Eddy's work appeared most experts recommended that women obtain this test annually. Using mathematical models and clinical studies of the natural history of the disease, Eddy (a physician with extensive training in operations research and economics) calculated the incremental cost of one additional year of life expectancy with screening regimes ranging from once every 6 months to once every 5 years. The results were striking. *Some* screening has a high yield at low incremental cost, but as the frequency of screening is increased from once every 2 years to once a year the incremental cost rises to close to one million dollars per additional year of life expectancy (Eddy, 1980, 1987, 1990).[15]

The impact of Eddy's research on health policy is worth noting. The American Cancer Society accepted his conclusions and the Society's recommendation to screen once every 3 years made the front page of

The New York Times. The U.S. Surgeon General, the U.S. Preventive Services Task Force, and the American College of Physicians supported this position, and many individual physicians changed their practice accordingly. Intense opposition came from the American College of Obstetricians and Gynecologists and the American Society of Cytology. The contending groups finally negotiated a compromise along the following lines: "Pap smears should be done annually; after two or more negative examinations the frequency can be decreased."[16]

. The economist's distinction between movement along a function and a shift in the function is a very useful one. It is particularly applicable in discussing the relationship between medical care and health. At any given time in developed countries the effects of additional medical care on health are usually small, but over time advances in medical science have had significant effects on health.[17] Or consider the relationship between infant mortality and per capita income. At any given time income is a good predictor of infant mortality, especially post-neonatal mortality (28 days to one year). In log–log regressions across the 48 states in 1937 and 1965, the income elasticity of post-neonatal mortality was −0.53 (0.11) and −0.49 (0.12) respectively.[18] The decline in post-neonatal mortality between 1937 and 1965, however, was consistent with an elasticity of −2.00. There was undoubtedly a shift in the function associated with the introduction of antibiotics and other advances in medical science (Fuchs, 1974b). In 1991 the elasticity was −0.73 (0.12) but the change from 1965 to 1991 was consistent with an elasticity of −1.08, suggesting a further shift in the function, but not nearly so large as the shift between 1937 and 1965.

Economists have much to contribute to the health field. What can they expect in exchange? The most immediate benefit to me was the pressure to make my lectures and research results accessible, relevant, and credible to intelligent but untutored and often unsympathetic audiences. I was obliged to write clearly and simply and to reconsider assumptions and conclusions in economics that I might otherwise have accepted too readily. My experience was in accord with that of Thomas Henry Huxley (1863) who wrote, "Some experience with popular lecturing has convinced me that the necessity of making things plain to uninstructed people was one of the very best means of clearing up the obscure corners in one's own mind."

For example, one of the questions that troubled me for a long time is why there is such a strong correlation between health and years of schooling. I originally believed that this was another manifestation of the productivity-enhancing effect of education. Schooling could increase an individual's knowledge about the health effects of personal behavior and medical care options or could enable a person to better process and act upon information about health (Grossman, 1975). Or schooling could increase an individual's ability to develop strategies of self control (Richard A. Thaler and H. M. Shefrin, 1981). I began to doubt the schooling-causes-health hypothesis, however, when it was observed that the favorable effect of an additional year of schooling on health does not diminish with increased years of schooling. It is just as strong for those with more than a high school education as for those with less and continues right through graduate school on up to the doctoral level (Grossman, 1975).[19] I began to suspect that perhaps the correlation was the result of some underlying difference among individuals that affects both schooling and health.

To explore this question I examined survey data on smoking behavior collected by colleagues in the Stanford Heart Disease Prevention Program as part of a health education experiment designed to alter smoking and other risks for heart disease (Nathan Maccoby and Douglas S. Solomon, 1981). Identical regressions of smoking on schooling were estimated at age 17 and at age 24, with schooling measured in both cases as the number of years the individual would eventually complete. The most striking result was the absence of any increase in the size of the schooling coefficient between the ages of 17 and 24. The additional schooling could not be the cause of the differential smoking behavior (and by extension the differential health associated with smoking) at age 24 because the differences in smoking were already evident at age 17, before the differences in schooling had emerged (Phillip Farrell and Fuchs, 1982).[20]

In my judgment, the most likely explanation for the high correlation between health and schooling is that both reflect differences in time preference (Fuchs, 1982). Both health and schooling are aspects of investment in human capital; differences among individuals in time preference that are established at an early age could result in different amounts of investment in health and education.[21]

Although I believe there have been many fruitful interactions between economics and health, the political debate over health care reform in 1993–1994 benefited much less than it could have from the insights of economists. Possible explanations for the failure of health economics research to have more impact on policy are explored in the next section.

The Present

George Stigler's Presidential Address to the American Economic Association in December 1964 was distinctive in its emphasis on prophecy over preaching. To be specific, Stigler predicted that economics was "at the threshold of its golden age" (Stigler, 1965 p. 17) because "the age of quantification is now full upon us" (p. 16). The growth of empirical estimation was, for Stigler, "a scientific revolution of the very first magnitude" (p. 17). He believed that empirical research would have an impact on policy far beyond anything possible from theory alone because "a theory can usually be made to support diverse policy positions. Theories present general relationships, and which part of a theory is decisive in a particular context is a matter of empirical evidence" (p. 13).

With regard to health care, Stigler's prediction of a vast expansion in empirical research has been amply fulfilled. During the past 30 years economists have published thousands of empirical articles on various aspects of health and medical care. But the shallow and inconclusive debate over health policy in 1993–1994 contradicts his expectation that this research would narrow the range of partisan disputes and make a significant contribution to the reconciliation of policy differences.[22] What went wrong?

One possibility is that the research was inconclusive. If health economists cannot agree among themselves, why should their research have a salutary effect on public policy? Second, even if the research were conclusive, it would not be of much help to policy if the results were not adequately disseminated to a wider audience. A third possible explanation is that the policy debate foundered on differences in values, differences which could not be reconciled by empirical research, however conclusive and however well disseminated.

To gain some insight into these matters, I prepared a 20-question survey concerning health economics and health policy and sent it to health economists, economic theorists, and practicing physicians. The health economists were those whom I considered to be the leading people in the field, plus some of the more promising recent Ph.D.s. There were 46 respondents (response rate 88 percent). The theorists were also leaders in the field; I was assisted in selecting them by two eminent theorists.[23] There were 44 respondents (response rate 63 percent). The practicing physicians were reached through my personal contacts, and include colleagues and friends of those contacts. Nearly all are in private practice, not teaching, research, or administration. They are located on both the east and west coasts in small towns and large cities. The practice settings vary from solo to a group of over 100 physicians, and in organizational form from traditional fee-for-service to capitation. They include generalists, surgical specialists, and nonsurgical specialists. There were 42 physician respondents (response rate 89 percent).

The participants were asked to indicate whether they agree or disagree with each of 20 relatively short statements; they were also given the option of answering "no opinion." Ten percent of the health economists' replies were "no opinion"; the theorists used that option 19 percent of the time, and the physicians 11 percent.' Participants were also invited to qualify any of their replies by jotting comments on the back of the survey. The percentage of replies that were qualified was 8, 5, and 3 for the health economists, theorists, and physicians, respectively. Participants were told to assume that the statements refer to the United States in 1995, other things held constant. For statements with more than one part, "agree" would indicate that the respondent agreed with all parts of the statement. The order of the questions was determined randomly, and respondents were guaranteed anonymity.

Three experts[24] from three different universities who were not participants in the survey were asked to identify which of the 20 questions were relatively value-free ("positive" questions) and which had substantial value aspects ("policy-value" questions). Their independent replies were almost unanimous in identifying seven of the questions as "positive" and thirteen as "policy-value." Table 1 shows the percent agreeing for each question, with the two types of questions grouped separately. Question numbers refer to the ordering of the questions in the survey. The policy-value questions are presented in three groups: four that pertain directly to national health insurance, three that pertain directly to health insurance company underwriting, and all others. Questions for which the percentage agreeing differs significantly from a 50–50 split (by a chi-square test) are identified with asterisks.

We see in Table 1 that the degree of consensus on positive questions among health economists is extremely high.[25] In six of the seven cases the hypothesis that the observed split differs from a 50–50 split simply by chance is rejected with $p < 0.01$ and the seventh with $p < 0.05$. There is also a high degree of consensus among economic theorists, but for two of the questions (12 and 13) the majority of theorists gave replies opposite to the majority of health economists. Consensus among the physicians on the positive questions was more rare. In no case did the split differ

Table 1—Percentage Agreeing with Positive and Policy-Value Questions[a]

SURVEY QUESTION NUMBER[b]	QUESTION	HEALTH ECONOMISTS ($n \leq 46$)	ECONOMIC THEORISTS ($n \leq 44$)	PRACTICING PHYSICIANS ($n \leq 42$)
A. Positive Questions:				
4	The high cost of health care in the United States makes U.S. firms substantially less competitive in the global economy.	9**	17**	64
9	Third-party payment results in patients using services whose costs exceed their benefits and this excess of costs over benefits amounts to at least 5 percent of total health care expenditures.	84**	93**	73*
10	Physicians have the power to influence their patients' utilization of services (i.e., shift the demand curve), and their propensity to induce utilization varies inversely with the level of demand.	68*	77**	67
12	Widespread use of currently available screening and other diagnostic techniques would result in a significant (more than 3%) reduction in health care expenditures (from what they would otherwise be) 5 years from now.	11**	83**	37
13	The primary reason for the increase in the health sector's share of GDP over the past 30 years is technological change in medicine.	81**	37	68*
18	Differential access to medical care across socioeconomic groups is the primary reason for differential health status among these groups	0**	17**	34*
19	In the long run employers bear the primary burden of their contribution to employees' health insurance.	13**	8**	43
B. Policy-Value Questions:				
National health insurance questions:				
3	The U.S. should now enact some plan that covers the entire population.	62	65*	68*
7	The U.S. should seek universal coverage through a broad-based tax with explicit subsidies for the poor and the sick.	54	56	56
14	The U.S. should seek universal coverage through mandates, with explicit subsidies for the poor and the sick.	38	29*	46
15	Given a choice between the Clinton health care plan or no federal health care legislation for at least 5 years, the Clinton plan should be approved.	36	33*	28**

Table 1—(Continued)

SURVEY QUESTION NUMBER[b]	QUESTION	HEALTH ECONOMISTS ($n \leq 46$)	ECONOMIC THEORISTS ($n \leq 44$)	PRACTICING PHYSICIANS ($n \leq 42$)
Insurance company underwriting questions:				
8	Insurance companies should be required to cover all applicants regardless of health condition and not allowed to charge sicker individuals higher premiums.	51	29**	69*
17	Health insurance premiums should be higher for smokers than for nonsmokers.	71**	90**	85**
20	Health insurance premiums charged to individuals born with genetic defects (that result in above average use of medical care) should be higher than those charged to individuals without such defects.	14**	20**	13**
All other policy-value questions:				
1	It is inequitable for the government to vary subsidies for health insurance by size of firm.	62	36	86**
2	"Any willing provider" legislation (that requires health plans to include any physician who wants to be included) is desirable for society as a whole.	12**	12**	39
5	National standardized health insurance benefit packages should be established.	42	51	63
6	It is inefficient for the government to vary subsidies for health insurance by size of firm.	66*	42	73*
11	Expenditures on medical R&D are greater than is socially optimal.	27*	29*	16**
16	All health insurance plans should be required to offer "point of service" options (that allow patients to obtain care outside the basic plan at additional cost).	30**	55	83**

[a] Of those who agree or disagree.
[b] Question numbers refer to order of questions in original survey.
* Significantly different from 50 percent at $p < 0.05$.
** Significantly different from 50 percent at $p < 0.01$.

from 50–50 with $p < 0.01$, and in only three cases was the split significant at $p < 0.05$. For one question (4) the majority of physicians gave replies opposite to the majority of health economists.[26]

When we turn to the policy-value questions, agreement among the health economists drops sharply. For example, in replies to the four questions dealing with support for national health insurance, the health economists never depart significantly from a 50–50 split. On question 8, which would require insurance companies to cover all applicants regardless of health condition with no premium surcharge for the sick, the health economists are evenly divided: 51 percent agree and 49 percent disagree. Among economic theorists there is slightly more agreement on policy, but not as much as among practicing physicians who, contrary to both groups of economists, show more agreement on policy-value than on positive questions.

The contrasts between the replies by group and type of question are brought more sharply into focus in Table 2, which shows the average absolute difference between the percentage agreeing and the percentage disagreeing. Among health economists the extent of consensus for the positive questions is significantly larger than for the policy-value questions regardless of whether the comparison is between means or medians. Although the sample sizes are very small (7 and 13), the differences by type of question are so large we can reject the null hypothesis with considerable confidence.[27]

It is also worth noting that the extent of agreement among health economists on the positive questions is much higher than is usually found in surveys of economists covering a wide variety of fields. For example,

Table 2—Average Absolute Difference Between Percentage Agreeing and Percentage Disagreeing by Type of Question

	HEALTH ECONOMISTS	ECONOMIC THEORISTS	PRACTICING PHYSICIANS
Mean absolute difference:			
7 positive questions	71.6	64.3	30.9
13 policy-value questions	33.8	36.5	45.0
Difference in means	37.8	27.8	−14.1
Median absolute difference:			
7 positive questions	73.9	66.7	31.7
13 policy-value questions	27.3	33.3	45.0
Difference in medians	46.6	33.3	−13.3
Standard error of the mean:			
7 positive questions	6.8	7.1	3.5
13 policy-value questions	5.9	6.5	6.4
Standard error of the difference in means	9.0	9.6	7.3
Difference in means divided by standard error of the difference	4.2	2.9	−1.9
Chi-square of the difference between type of question	5.5	5.5	2.0

in a survey conducted by Richard M. Alston et al. (1992) the authors identify ten questions as "micro-positive" and seven as "micro-normative."[28] In order to achieve comparability between their survey and mine, I combined their "agree, with provisos" with their "agree," and then calculated the mean absolute difference between percentage agreeing and percentage disagreeing.[29] This difference (22 percentage points) was much smaller (and less statistically significant) than the difference I found for the health economists.[30]

Why is there so little agreement among economists regarding policy-value questions when there is so much agreement on the positive questions? One possible explanation is differences in values. Most health policy decisions have significant implications for freedom, efficiency, justice, and security. Health economists (like other Americans) probably desire all these goals, but (again like other Americans) they probably differ in the values they attach to them, or in the way they define them,[31] and these differences could lead to sharply different views about policy.

Another possible explanation is that there are positive questions embedded in the policy-value questions and that health economists disagree with respect to those positive questions. This is the view taken by Milton Friedman in 1953[32] although he subsequently modified his position in 1966 and 1995.[33] In order to gain some insights concerning the roles of values and embedded positive issues in policy differences I take a closer look at the policy-value questions bearing on national health insurance (3, 7, 14, 15) and on insurance company underwriting (8, 17, 20).

Consider, for instance, question 3 which calls for some national plan to cover the entire population. The 62–38 percent split among health economists may well reflect differences in values, with those who agree placing a high value on providing all Americans with the right to have access to health care. On the other hand, it is readily apparent that there are many positive questions embedded in this policy-value question. For instance, most economists see a loss in efficiency from requiring everyone to have the same health insurance, but they probably differ in their estimates of the extent of the loss. Some may even believe there is a net gain in efficiency because of imperfections in the private market for health insurance. Strongly held differences about this positive question could produce different answers to question 3 even among respondents with similar values.

Some of the positive questions embedded in question 3 may be beyond the scope of conventional economics. For instance, Professor A may favor national health insurance in part because she believes it will contribute to a more stable and harmonious society.[34] Professor B may disagree with that prediction, and is therefore less inclined to support national health insurance.

The role of embedded positive questions can also be easily discerned in the three questions (8, 17, 20) dealing with insurance company underwriting. Health economists strongly support charging higher premiums for smokers than for nonsmokers, but are strongly opposed to charging higher premiums to individuals born with genetic defects. On question 8, dealing with requiring insurance companies to insure the sick with no premium surcharge, the health economists are evenly split. One of the positive questions embedded in question 8 is the reason for people's illness. If a respondent thought that most illness was the result of genetic differences, the reply would presumably be consistent with the answer to question 20. On the other hand, if most illness was assumed to be the result of personal behaviors like cigarette smoking, the reply would probably be consistent with the one given to question 17. Inasmuch as leading medical scientists have strongly divergent views about the importance of genetic factors in disease, it is hardly surprising that health economists are unable to reach agreement. The state of knowledge about the links between genes and disease is constantly changing. Thus, if cigarette smoking were found to be determined primarily by genetic factors, the answers to question 17 would probably change even in the absence of any change in values.

Positive economic questions are also embedded in the insurance company underwriting issues. Most economists realize that requiring health insurance companies to charge healthy people the same premium as those with a genetic disease will deter healthy individuals from purchasing insurance. But economists may well differ as to how large that effect will be and how large a welfare loss it implies.

It is easy to see that there are positive questions embedded in the policy-value questions, but it is more difficult to believe that disagreement over them, rather than differences in values, explains the low level of consensus among health economists with respect to the policy-value questions. Note that the physicians have a higher level of consensus about the policy-value questions than do the health economists. This probably reflects more homogeneous values among physicians rather than agreement about the embedded positive questions. (Note the low level of agreement among physicians on the explicit positive questions.)

It may be that it is not so much *disagreement* among health economists about the embedded positive questions as it is *uncertainty* about them that make differences in values the driving force in replies to the policy-value questions. Many psychologists and economists have observed that uncertainty about a datum causes most individuals to give it less weight when making choices.[35]

Uncertainty among health economists concerning the positive questions that are embedded in the policy-value questions is suggested by their use of the "no opinion" option. Unlike the theorists, who chose "no opinion" twice as often for the positive questions as for the policy-value questions (28 percent versus 15 percent), the health economists chose "no opinion" less often for the positive questions than for the policy-value questions (8 percent versus 11 percent).[36] The role of uncertainty was mentioned by Milton Friedman in 1966 as a reason for qualifying his position about the relative importance of scientific judgment and value differences (Friedman, 1966 p. 6).

In order to investigate further the relationship between policy-value and positive questions, I developed two indexes based on the answers to the national health insurance and insurance underwriting questions. The first index measures each respondent's support for national health insurance. It is constructed by assigning a value of 1 to agreement with each of questions 3, 7, 14, and 15, a value of 0 for disagreement with those questions, and a value of 0.5 for no opinion. The sum of the values was divided by 4, giving a range for the index of 1 (indicating agreement with all four questions) to 0 (indicating disagreement with all four questions). The "actuarial"[37] model index was based on answers to questions 8, 17, and 20. In the case of question 8, "disagree" was given a value of 1, and for questions 17 and 20 "agree" was given a value of 1. The total score for each individual is divided by 3, again yielding a range for the index from 1 to 0 (indicating complete support or complete rejection of the actuarial approach).

The results are presented in Table 3. We see that with respect to national health insurance the support among the three groups is virtually identical. There is considerable variation around the mean for each group, and the amount of variation is similar across the groups. Thirteen percent of all respondents had an index value of 1, while 15 percent completely rejected the notion of national health insurance with an index value of 0. Not surprisingly, there is a negative correlation between the national health insurance index and the actuarial model index. But there is a

Table 3—Indexes of Support for National Health Insurance[a] and for an
Actuarial Model of Private Insurance Underwriting[b]

	HEALTH ECONOMISTS	ECONOMIC THEORISTS	PRACTICING PHYSICIANS	ALL
National health insurance index:				
Mean	0.48	0.48	0.49	0.48
Standard error of the mean	0.05	0.05	0.05	0.03
Coefficient of variation (percent)	71	70	67	69
Percentage with index = 1	15	9	14	13
Percentage with index = 0	13	18	14	15
Actuarial model index:				
Mean	0.46	0.61	0.44	0.50
Standard error of the mean	0.05	0.04	0.04	0.03
Coefficient of variation (percent)	71	42	64	60
Percentage with index = 1	7	16	7	10
Percentage with index = 0	22	5	14	14
Coefficient of correlation between the two indexes	$-0.37^\dagger$	$-0.34^\dagger$	$-0.37^\dagger$	-0.35**

[a] National health insurance index is based on answers to survey questions 3, 7, 14 and 15.
[b] Actuarial model index is based on answers to survey questions 8, 17 and 20.
$\dagger$ Significant at $p < 0.02$.
** Significant at $p < 0.01$.

significant difference between the groups in the extent of support for the actuarial model index. The economic theorists have a value of 0.61, compared with 0.46 for the health economists and 0.44 for the practicing physicians. The theorists are as supportive of national health insurance as are the other groups, but if insurance is to be provided through the private market, the theorists are more inclined than the other two groups to have premiums reflect expected loss. One reasonable interpretation of this result is that the theorists give more weight to the efficiency aspects of the actuarial model, whereas the health economists and the practicing physicians give more weight to the distributional aspects.

Is there a close relationship between the respondents' scores on the indexes and their responses to the positive questions? Low correlation coefficients show that the answer is overwhelmingly in the negative. For the national health insurance index there is only one positive question (10) for one group (the health economists) that reaches statistical significance with $p < 0.05$. For the actuarial model index, only questions 9 and 10 show a significant relationship for the health economists, and questions 10 and 12 for all groups taken together. Whatever it is that is determining the respondents' positions with regard to national health insurance or the actuarial approach, it is not their views on the seven positive questions.

Correlations between the indexes and the six policy-value questions not utilized in their construction also are typically low, with one striking exception. Respondents agreeing with question 5, which calls for national standardized health insurance benefit packages, also support national health insurance and just as clearly reject the actuarial approach for private insurance underwriting. The actuarial model index is also negatively correlated with agreement with question 1.

The weak relationship between the positive questions and the two indexes is also revealed in regressions of the indexes on the positive questions.[38] In the national health insurance regression the only statistically significant coefficient is for question 10 for health economists. Other things being equal, those who agree with the induced-demand hypothesis are more supportive of national health insurance than those who disagree, but the effect on the index (0.239) is less than changing one of the four answers from disagree to agree. The actuarial model regressions result in a few additional significant coefficients but, in general, the respondents' replies to the explicit positive questions do not explain their position with respect to such major policy issues as national health insurance or insurance company underwriting changes. It seems unlikely, then, that their position on these policy issues can be explained by differences in the embedded positive questions.

Although I believe that differences in values lie at the heart of the disagreement about policy-value questions, I recognize that there is scope for work on the embedded positive questions and this work could contribute to a narrowing of policy differences. One indication of where research is needed is the percent of health economists answering "no opinion" on the individual policy-value questions. This option was chosen most frequently (35 percent of the time) for question 11 concerning the optimality of expenditures on medical R&D.[39] Given the importance of technologic change in medicine both from the point of view of health outcomes and of expenditures, this is clearly a high-priority area for research. Two other questions elicited a "no opinion" response from one-fifth of the health economists. They are question 1 concerning the subsidies for health insurance by size of firm (a key part of the Clinton plan) and question 20 (about differential premiums for persons born with genetic defects). In the latter case the high percentage responding "no opinion" may reflect uncertainty regarding the magnitudes of the efficiency and distributional implications of eliminating premium differentials. Or, it may reflect a reluctance to choose between conflicting values.

Before leaving the survey it is worth considering what it reveals about the ability of health economists to disseminate their conclusions about the positive questions to a wider audience. Overall, one must conclude that they have not been very successful, as revealed by the political debate of 1993–1994 and the media coverage of policy issues. Consider, for example, question 19 concerning whether in the long run employers bear the primary burden of their contributions to their employees' health insurance. Although 87 percent of the health economists disagreed with that statement, politicians on both sides of the debate assumed, erroneously, that it was correct. Moreover, nearly all of the media made the same error. Most of the politicians and most of the media also showed little understanding of questions 4, 12, 13, and 18.

I am as ready as the next economist to criticize politicians and journalists, but the survey results suggest that their poor understanding of health economics is not entirely their fault. First, the economic theorists and the practicing physicians, two groups with above-average ability and opportunity to absorb the conclusions of the health economists, did not show good command of the positive questions. In my judgment the health economists answered 80 percent correctly, but the average theorist answered only 52 percent correctly and the mean score for the physicians was only 53 percent. The differences in the distributions of scores is striking: 45 of the 46 health economists had more correct answers than the average theorist or the average physician.

A second possible reason for the poor understanding of health economics displayed by the politicians and the media in 1993–1994 is the wide disagreement among health economists over the policy-value questions. When health economists interact with politicians and journalists, their discussions probably focus on the policy-value questions; in the absence of a professional consensus on many of these questions, it is not surprising that politicians and journalists fall back on their own values to shape their positions.

Returning to the question posed at the beginning of this section about why economic research failed to result in a more informed and productive health care policy debate, the survey results provide some provisional answers. First, although health economists are in substantial agreement about the positive questions, they have major disagreements about policy-value questions. Second, health economists were not successful in getting their conclusions on positive questions accepted by the politicians or the media, and even had difficulty in communicating their results to economic theorists and practicing physicians. Third, the health economists' disagreements over policy probably reflect differences in values, although it is clear that there are many positive questions embedded in the policy-value questions. In my judgment the problem is not so much that the health economists disagree about the embedded questions as that they are uncertain about them. In the face of such uncertainty, they tend to let their values drive their policy recommendations.

The Future

If values play such an important role in policy disputes, what are the implications for economics and economists? First, we should endeavor to make explicit the differences in values, and seek ways to resolve them. Value differences can take many different forms. Economists are most familiar with the distinction between efficiency and distributional issues, especially greater equality of income versus greater total income.[40] But comprehensive changes in health policy can have other important distributional effects. Even for individuals at the same income level, the costs and the benefits of care could change along many dimensions: rural areas versus central cities, the elderly versus the young, smokers versus nonsmokers, savers versus nonsavers, men versus women, and so on. Health economists who are unanimous in approving gains in efficiency might have very different views regarding the desirability of the distributional changes and might also differ in the weights they give to the changes in efficiency versus the distributional consequences.

Second, greater openness about value differences should force economists to make explicit the positive questions that are embedded in most policy-value questions. This would point the way to productive research. If the embedded questions are identified and studied, it should be possible to reduce the uncertainty about them and thus provide a basis for narrowing differences on policy-value questions.

A third agenda item for economists is to undertake research on the formation of values, especially insofar as they are the consequences of policy. Economists are understandably reluctant to prescribe values or to make normative judgments about them. But when economic policies affect values and preferences, and these in turn affect behavior, it is incumbent on economists to analyze the links between policies and values, and to examine the economic and social consequences of alternative value systems. I believe there is an analogy between the economics of values and the economics of technology. Over the past several decades some economists have begun to treat technology as at least partly endogenous.[41] Now, a similar effort must be undertaken for values (Henry J. Aaron, 1994; Becker, 1996; Albert O. Hirschman, 1986; Assar Lindbeck, 1994).

Finally, economists must develop more self-awareness of how our values color our judgment about policy, and more candor in making clear to others the respective roles of positive research and of values in our policy recommendations. Alice M. Rivlin, in her AEA presidential address in December 1986, warned economists against letting "their ideological position cloud their judgment about the likely effects of particular policies" (p. 4). She urged us "... to be more careful to sort out, for ourselves and others, what we really know from our ideological biases" (p. 9). In my view, there is a vast difference between a researcher and a reformer, between an analyst and a player in the policy arena. They are all socially valuable occupations, and the same individual may successfully wear different hats at different times. What is not likely to work well, either for economics or for policy, is trying to wear two hats at the same time.

In the remainder of this paper I present a summary of my policy recommendations for health system reform. The use of the bully pulpit by an AEA president to push personal policy choices has ample precedent, but I also want to use this opportunity to show how those choices are shaped by the interaction between my values and my understanding of health economics. Finally, I identify aspects of my policy recommendations that are problematic and which would clearly benefit from additional research. My three major recommendations are:

(i) a broad-based tax earmarked for health care to provide every American with a voucher for participation in a basic plan;

(ii) provision of care through integrated health systems that include hospitals, physician services, and prescription drugs. These systems would be led by physicians, would be reimbursed by capitation plus modest co-payment from patients at the time of use, and would be required to offer a wide variety of point-of-service options to be paid for by patients with after-tax dollars;

(iii) a large private center for technology assessment financed by a small industry-wide levy on all health care spending.

My desire to see all Americans insured for a basic health plan is clearly driven in part by values. Although medical care is often not a crucial factor in health outcomes, it is nearly always a source of utility through its caring and validation functions. In my judgment, it fully meets Adam Smith's 1776 definition of a *necessary*: "By necessaries I understand not only the commodities which are indispensably necessary for the support of life but whatever the custom of the country renders it indecent for creditable people, even of the lowest order, to be without" (1776; republished 1937 p. 821). To achieve universal coverage there must be subsidization for those who are too poor or too sick to acquire insurance, and there must be compulsion for the "free riders"[42] to pay their share.

There are only two ways to achieve systematic universal coverage: a broad-based general tax with implicit subsidies for the poor and the sick, or a system of mandates with explicit subsidies based on income. I prefer the former because the latter are extremely expensive to administer and seriously distort incentives; they result in the near-poor facing marginal tax rates that would be regarded as confiscatory if levied on the affluent.[43]

Both theory and experience show that integrated health care systems are usually the best way to deliver cost-effective care. The primary reason is the physician's central role in medical decision-making. Under any approach to care, it is the physician who admits patients to hospitals, orders tests and other procedures, and decides when to discharge. It is the physician who prescribes drugs and who refers patients to other physicians for consultation and treatment. Thus physicians' decisions are the major determinant of the cost of care. Only in an integrated system, however, do physicians have the *incentive*, the *information*, and the *infrastructure* needed to make these decisions in a cost-effective way. Integrated systems also have an advantage in avoiding excess capacity of high-cost equipment and personnel.

Given the central importance of physicians to medical care, I believe the integrated systems should be led by them and other health care professionals. At a minimum, health care professionals should have a prominent place in the governance of the systems. One of the greatest errors of health policy-makers today is their assumption that market competition or government regulation are the only instruments available to control health care. There is room for, indeed need for, a revitalization of professional norms as a third instrument of control.[44] The patient-physician relationship often is highly personal and intimate, similar in many ways to relationships within families or between teachers and pupils or ministers and congregants. This relationship is, in part, what economist Kenneth Boulding (1968) called an integrative system, one that depends on mutual recognition and acceptance of rights and responsibilities, enforced by traditional norms as well as market pressures and government regulations. As long as physicians control the use of complex technology in life and death situations, and as long as we expect them to perform priestly functions, they must be endowed with certain privileges and held to certain standards of behavior different from those assumed by models of market competition or government regulation.[45]

Comprehensive government control of medical care has not worked well in any setting. The essence of good care is an informed patient working cooperatively with a health professional who provides personalized attention and concern. The rules, regulations, and bureaucratic controls that almost always accompany governmental activities are inimical to high-quality cost-effective care. It is revealing that countries such as England and Sweden with deep government involvement in the financing of medical care have bent over backwards to leave physicians with a great deal of professional autonomy—indeed more autonomy than is possessed by many American physicians working in a "private" system.

Market competition also has its problems. It assumes a preoccupation with the bottom line and governance by a corporate mentality that judges the success of each division by its profit growth. Physician-led systems will also have to pay attention to costs, and physicians will also be interested in making a good income, but there is a vast difference between a profit-maximizing corporation and physicians who strive to balance their obligations to patients, the organization, and themselves.[46]

Reimbursement of these integrated systems should be primarily by capitation, adjusted for patient characteristics. In addition, patients should be required to make modest copayments at the time of use (e.g., $15 for each visit and $5 for each prescription). Such payments will generate some income but, more important, will help to discourage wasteful use of health care. The payments could be waived for patients living below the poverty level, and for essential preventive services such as vaccination.

The earmarked tax would provide every American with a voucher for a basic health care plan. Each integrated system would be required to offer the basic plan, plus a variety of options. These options are not alternative insurance plans; they are services to be paid for at time of use with after-tax dollars.[47] The options could take many forms: a private room in the hospital; a wider choice of physicians and hospitals than is available through

the basic plan; or access to new experimental technologies or older technologies not included in the basic plan because they have a low benefit-
to-cost ratio.[48]

These options would accommodate the demands of patients with
higher incomes or those who choose to spend more of their income on
medical care. The options would not constitute establishment of different plans. Everyone would be in the same plan and most persons would
stick to the basic plan most of the time. An option would be exercised
only when the patient desired and was willing to pay for it. This is the
quintessential American approach to balancing equality and freedom. On
the one hand, this approach avoids the egalitarianism of the English and
Canadian systems in which only a small elite have an escape valve. On
the other hand, it does not create a separate plan for the poor while the
great majority of Americans obtain care from a different system. The
experience with Medicaid shows that a separate system limited to the
poor is not likely to function well.

Where feasible, the integrated health care system would engage in managed
competition.[49] Having advocated policies similar to such an approach to
health care for more than 20 years, I am not unmindful of its virtues.
We cannot, however, rely on managed competition alone to contain costs.
In most rural areas, population density is too low to support several health
care systems. Even in some urban areas, competition is impossible or
undesirable because of economies of scale. For instance, only one hospital
is needed to serve a population of 100,000 efficiently. Similar constraints
apply to competition in physician specialty care, especially if the physicians
work full time at their specialties. A population of one million would
probably not justify enough independent maternity services or open-heart
surgery teams to create competitive conditions. Moreover, the public
interest is not best served by insisting that health professionals always
maintain rigorous arm's-length competition with one another. Patients
can benefit from cooperation among physicians and hospitals, both in
reduced costs and better service. Managed competition alone will not be
enough to contain costs; it must be supplemented by constraints on the
supply side, especially with respect to technology and the specialty mix
of physicians.

In 1995 Americans spent about one trillion dollars for health care,
broadly defined. If, during the past 30 years, health care spending had
grown at the rate of the rest of the economy, the health care bill in 1995
would have been only a little more than $400 billion. What accounts

for this extraordinary excess of almost $600 billion in annual spending? There has been a small increase in physician visits per capita, but use of acute care hospitals has decreased sharply. Patient-days per 1000 population are less than three fifths the level of 30 years ago. By far the most important factor accounting for the increase in health care's share of the GDP is the change in technology.[50] Physician visits and hospital-days cost more than they used to because the content has changed—the technologies used for diagnosis and treatment are more expensive than in the past. Much of this technol-ogical change is welcome; it contributes to enhancing the length and quality of life. Some of the change is less desirable because it adds more to cost than to patient benefit. Unfortunately, there is great uncertainty regarding the merits of many technologies. Moreover, even when the advantages and disadvantages are known, there are often significant barriers facing physicians who would like to practice in a cost-effective manner.

To deal with this problem, I propose the creation of a large, private center for technology assessment. Financing for this center would come from a small levy (less than one tenth of 1 percent) on all health care spending. A centralized approach is necessary, because health care is highly fragmented. Individual physicians and health plans lack the incentive and ability to commit the resources needed to assess new technologies. Even the largest insurance companies individually account for only a small percentage of the health care market; they are, there-fore, understandably reluctant to pay for large-scale assessments that would benefit all.[51] Government agencies try to fill the void, but the scale of effort is too small, and a private center would be able to avoid the political interference that often intrudes on government-run agencies.[52] Health care providers would fund and set the agenda for the center, much as the electric power companies do for the Electric Power Research Insti-tute. This institute is financed by a small levy on every public utility bill.

A health care technology assessment center would have two primary functions. First, it would help to develop and disseminate systematic knowledge about the cost-effectiveness of medical technology through support of research and through a comprehensive program of publica-tions and conferences. The center would have some intramural research capability, but most of the research would be conducted extramurally at medical schools, hospitals, and research institutes throughout the country. It would provide health professionals with essential information to eval-uate and improve their clinical practices and offer a rational basis for deciding what services should be included in the basic plan.

The second important function would be to provide legitimacy for the cost-effective practice of medicine. Currently, many directors of health plans and many individual physicians know they could be practicing in a more cost-effective way, but they are inhibited from doing so because they do not practice in a vacuum. Physicians are influenced by peers who have been trained in settings that emphasized the use of the latest technologies regardless of cost. Patients come with particular sets of expectations based on what they read or hear in the media and what their relatives and friends tell them has been their experience. The threat of malpractice suits lurks in the background. A major function of the center would be to give legitimacy and a stamp of authority to physicians who practice in a more cost-effective way.

My policy recommendations seek to achieve a balance among the diverse values of efficiency, justice, freedom, and security. The link between the earmarked tax and the basic plan would create a healthy tension between the desire to increase benefits and the need to pay for the increase in a responsible and equitable manner. Competition among health care systems in highly populated areas would widen choice and foster cost-effective practice. The private technology assessment center would help to contain costs without the imposition of controls or caps that might stifle innovation and progress.

Are these recommendations politically saleable? In the short run, certainly not. But neither are any other proposals for comprehensive reform. Indeed, for more than 20 years it has been my view that the United States would not enact comprehensive health care reform except in the wake of a major war, a depression, large-scale civil unrest, or some other event that completely changed the political climate. Why is the United States the only major industrialized nation without national health insurance? Many observers focus on the opposition of "special interests," and that certainly is a factor, but I do not find it a completely satisfactory explanation. After all, special interests are not unknown in Sweden, England, Canada, and other countries that do have national health insurance.

In 1976 I suggested four reasons for its absence in the United States: distrust of government, heterogeneity of the population, a weak sense of *noblesse oblige*, and strong private voluntary organizations such as nonprofit hospitals and Blue Cross and Blue Shield plans that carry out quasi-governmental functions with respect to the financing and delivery of health care. Upon revisiting this question in 1991, I concluded that the first three reasons were stronger than ever, but the fourth had weakened considerably. It is ironic that "the competition revolution" (Fuchs, 1988b), which erodes the ability of not-for-profit health care institutions to provide a modicum of social insurance through community rating and cost shifting, may in the long run push the country toward national health insurance.

My plan is certainly not a panacea; it would be difficult to implement and others might seek a different balance of values. Several aspects require additional research. For example, what should be the content of the basic plans? How should the content change over time? How should the plans be reimbursed from the funds raised by the earmarked tax, and especially how should reimbursement be risk adjusted to take account of differences in plan populations? Another problem is how to encourage competition among plans where it is feasible, while recognizing that a competitive approach will not be desirable or possible in areas of low population density. Considerable research is needed on how the out-of-plan options should be priced[53] and how the providers of such care should be reimbursed. Finally, much thought should be given to how to reinvigorate professional norms as a third instrument of control, along with market competition and government regulation.[54]

I conclude this tour of health economics—past, present, and future—on a mildly optimistic note. In the past three decades economics has made a positive contribution to health and medical care, and I believe that future contributions will be even greater. Now that the basic ideas of economics are gaining acceptance, it will be more important than ever for economists to master many of the intricacies of health care institutions and technologies. We will also have to consider the problems of dissemination in order to insure that when we agree on research results, these results are understood and accepted by all relevant audiences including the media, politicians, and health professionals. Moreover, we must pay more attention to values than we have in the past. Through skillful analysis of the interactions between values and the conclusions of positive research, we will be able to contribute more effectively to public policy debates. And, if health economists are successful in this demanding assignment, we can lead the way toward progress in areas such as child care and education that face similar problems of reconciling multiple goals and heterogeneity in values. To be useful to our society while deriving pleasure from our work—in the words of the old Gershwin tune, "Who could ask for anything more?"

REFERENCES

Aaron, Henry J. "Distinguished Lecture on Economics in Government: Public Policy, Values, and Consciousness." *Journal of Economic Perspectives*, Spring 1994, 8(2), pp. 3–21.

Alston, Richard M.; Kearl, J. R. and Vaughan, Michael B. "Is There a Consensus Among Economists in the 1990's?" *American Economic Review*, May 1992 (*Papers and Proceedings*), 82(2), pp. 203–9.

Arrow, Kenneth. "Uncertainty and the Welfare Economics of Medical Care." *American Economic Review*, December 1963, 53(5), pp. 941–73.

Bandura, Albert. "Self-Efficacy Mechanism in Physiological Activation and Health Promoting Behavior," in John Madden, ed., *Neural biology of learning, emotion, and affect*. New York: Raven Press, 1991.

Becker, Gary S. *Human capital: A theoretical and empirical analysis with special reference to education*. New York: National Bureau of Economic Research and Columbia University Press, 1964.

_____. *The making of preferences and values*. Cambridge, MA: Harvard University Press, 1996.

Boulding, Kenneth. *Beyond economics*. Ann Arbor: University of Michigan Press, 1968.

Brint, Steven. *In an age of experts: The changing role of professionals in politics and public life*. Princeton, NJ: Princeton University Press, 1994.

Brook, Robert H.; Ware, John E., Jr.; Rogers, William H.; Keeler, Emmett B.; Davies, Allyson R.; Donald, Cathy A.; Goldberg, George A.; Lohr, Kathleen N.; Masthay, Patricia C. and Newhouse, Joseph P. "Does Free Care Improve Adults' Health? Results from a Randomized Controlled Trial." *New England Journal of Medicine*, 8 December 1983, 309(23), pp. 1426–34.

Calltorp, Johan. "The 'Swedish Model' Under Pressure: How to Maintain Equity and Develop Quality?" *Quality Assurance in Health Care*, 1989, 1(1), pp. 13–22.

Camerer, C. F. and Weber, M. "Recent Developments in Modeling Preferences: Uncertainty and Ambiguity." *Journal of Risk and Uncertainty*, October 1992, 5(4), pp. 325–70.

Cutler, David M. and McClellan, Mark. "Technological Change in Medical Care." Unpublished manuscript presented at the National Bureau of

Economic Research conference on the Economics of Aging. Carefree, AZ, May 1995.

Davis, Michael M. and Rorem, C. Rufus. *The crisis in hospital finance.* Chicago: University of Chicago Press, 1932.

Dranove, David and Wehner, Paul. "Physician Induced Demand for Childbirths." *Journal of Health Economics*, March 1994, 13(1), pp. 61–73.

Eddy, David M. *Screening for cancer: Theory, analysis, and design.* Englewood, NJ: Prentice-Hall, 1980.

_____. "The Frequency of Cervical Cancer Screening: Comparison of a Mathematical Model with Empirical Data." *Cancer*, 1 September 1987, 60, pp. 1117–22.

_____. "Screening for Cervical Cancer." *Annals of Internal Medicine*, August 1990, 113(3), pp. 214–26.

Efron, Bradley. *An introduction to the bootstrap.* New York: Chapman and Hall, 1993.

Enthoven, Alain. "Managed Competition in Health Care and the Unfinished Agenda." *Health Care Financing Review Annual Supplement*, 1986, pp. 105–19.

_____. "Managed Competition: An Agenda for Action." *Health Affairs*, Summer 1988, 7(3), pp. 25–47.

Farrell, Phillip and Fuchs, Victor R. "Schooling and Health: The Cigarette Connection." *Journal of Health Economics*, December 1982, 1(3), pp. 217–30.

Feldstein, Martin. *Economic analysis for health service efficiency.* Amsterdam: North-Holland, 1967.

Frank, Robert H. "Consumption Externalities and the Financing of Social Services," in Victor R. Fuchs, ed., *Individual and social responsibility: Child care, education, medical care, and long-term care in America.* Chicago: University of Chicago Press, 1996.

Friedman, Milton. *Essays in positive economics.* Chicago: University of Chicago Press, 1953.

_____. *Dollars and deficits.* Englewood Cliffs, NJ: Prentice-Hall, 1966.

Fuchs, Victor R. "The Contribution of Health Services to the American Economy." *Milbank Memorial Fund Quarterly*, October 1966, 44(4, Part 2), pp. 65–101.

_____. *The service economy.* New York: National Bureau of Economic Research and Columbia University Press, 1968.

_____. ed. *Production and productivity in the service industries*. New York: National Bureau of Economic Research and Columbia University Press, 1969.

_____. "Some Economic Aspects of Mortality in Developed Countries," in Mark Perlman, ed., *The economics of health and medical care*. London: Macmillan, 1974, pp. 174–93.

_____. "Economics, Health, and Post-Industrial Society." Paper presented at the E. S. Woodward Lectures in Economics, University of British Columbia, November 1–2, 1978a; *Milbank Memorial Fund Quarterly/Health and Society*, Spring 1979, 57(2), pp. 153–82.

_____. "The Supply of Surgeons and the Demand for Operations." *Journal of Human Resources*, 1978b, 13 (Supplement), pp. 35–56.

_____. "Time Preference and Health: An Exploratory Study," in Victor R. Fuchs, ed., *Economic aspects of health*. Chicago: University of Chicago Press, 1982, pp. 93–120.

_____. *How we live*. Cambridge, MA: Harvard University Press, 1983.

_____. "Health Economics," in John Eatwell, Murray Milgate, and Peter Newman, eds., *The new Palgrave: Social economics*. New York: Macmillan, 1987, pp. 119–29.

_____. *Women's quest for economic equality*. Cambridge, MA: Harvard University Press, 1988a.

_____. "The 'Competition Revolution' in Health Care.' *Health Affairs*, Summer 1988b, 7(3), pp. 5–24.

_____. "The Health Sector's Share of the Gross National Product." *Science*, 2 February 1990, 247(4942), pp. 534–38.

Fuchs, Victor R. and Hahn, James S. "How Does Canada Do It? A Comparison of Expenditures for Physicians' Services in the United States and Canada." *New England Journal of Medicine*, 27 September 1990, 323 (13), pp. 884–90.

Fuchs, Victor R. and Kramer, Marcia. *Determinants of Expenditures for Physicians' Services in the United States 1948-1968*, Occasional Paper 116. New York: National Bureau of Economic Research and Department of Health, Education, and Welfare, 1973.

Garber, Alan M.; Fuchs, Victor R. and Silverman, James F. "Case Mix, Costs, and Outcomes: Differences Between Faculty and Community Services in a University Hospital." *New England Journal of Medicine*, 10 May 1984, 310(19), pp. 1231–37.

Grossman, Michael. *The demand for health: A theoretical and empirical investigation*. New York: National Bureau of Economic Research, 1972.

_____. "The Correlation Between Health and Schooling," in Nestor E. Terleckyj, ed., *Household production and consumption*, NBER Studies in Income and Wealth, Vol. 40. New York: National Bureau of Economic Research and Columbia University Press, 1975.

Gruber, Jonathan and Owings, Maria. "Physician Financial Incentives and Cesarean Section Delivery." *Rand Journal of Economics*, Spring 1996, 27(1), pp. 99–123.

Haack, Susan. "Puzzling Out Science." *Academic Questions*, Spring 1995, 8(2), pp. 20–31.

Hamilton, Walton. "Personal Statement," in *Medical care for the American people*. Chicago: University of Chicago Press, 1932, pp. 189–200.

Hirschman, Albert O. "Against Parsimony: Three Easy Ways of Complicating Some Categories of Economic Discourse," in Albert O. Hirschman, ed., *Rival views of market society and other recent essays*. Cambridge, MA: Harvard University Press, 1986.

Huxley, Thomas Henry. Preface to *Evidence as to man's place in nature*. London: Williams and Norgate, 1863.

Intriligator, Michael D. "The Impact of Arrow's Contribution to Economic Analysis," in George R. Feiwel, ed., *Arrow and the foundations of the theory of economic policy*. New York: New York University Press, 1987, pp. 683–91.

Klarman, Herbert. *The economics of health*. New York: Columbia University Press, 1965.

Lewis, Neil A. "Agency Facing Revolt After Report." *The New York Times*, 14 September 1995, p. A8.

Lindbeck, Assar. "Hazardous Welfare State Dynamics: Endogenous Habits and Norms." Mimeo, Institute for International Economic Studies, University of Stockholm, 1994.

Lundberg, George D. and Flanagin, Annette. "European Science in JAMA." *Journal of the American Medical Association*, 12 July 1995, 274(2), p. 180.

Maccoby, Nathan and Solomon, Douglas S. "Health Disease Prevention: Multicommunity Studies," in Ronald E. Rice and William J. Paisley, eds., *Public communication campaigns*. Beverly Hills, CA: Sage Publications, 1981.

Mark, D. B.; Hlatky, Mark A.; Califf, Robert M.; Naylor, C. David; Lee, Kerry L.; Armstrong, Paul W.; Barbash, Gabriel; White, Harvey; Simoons, Maarten L.; Nelson, Charlotte L.; Clapp-Channing, Nancy; Knight, J. David; Harrell, Frank E., Jr.; Simes, John and Topol,

Eric J. "Cost-Effectiveness of Thrombolytic Therapy with Tissue Plasminogen Activator as Compared with Streptokinase for Acute Myocardial Infarction." *New England Journal of Medicine*, 25 May 1995, 332(21), pp. 1418–24.

Mill, John Stuart. *Principles of political economy with some of their applications to social philosophy.* Boston: Little Brown, 1848; reprinted Fairfield, NJ: Augustus M. Kelley, 1987.

Mushkin, Selma J. "Health as an Investment." NBER Special Conference 15, *Journal of Political Economy*, October 1962 (Supplement), 70(5, part 2), pp. 129–57.

NBER Special Conference 15. "Investment in Human Beings." *Journal of Political Economy*, October 1962 (Supplement), 70(5, part 2), pp. 1–157.

Newhouse, Joseph P. "Medical Care Costs: How Much Welfare Loss?" *Journal of Economic Perspectives*, Summer 1992, 6(3), pp. 3–21.

Okun, Arthur. *Equality and efficiency: The big tradeoff.* Washington, DC: Brookings Institution, 1975.

Redelmeier, Donald A. and Fuchs, Victor R. "Hospital Expenditures in the United States and Canada." *New England Journal of Medicine*, 18 March 1993, 328 (11), pp. 772–78.

Rivlin, Alice M. "Economics and the Political Process." *American Economic Review*, March 1987, 77(1), pp. 1–9.

Romer, Paul M. "Implementing a National Technology Strategy with Self-Organizing Industry Investment Boards." *Brookings Papers on Economic Activity: Microeconomics*, 1993, (2), pp. 345–90, 398–99.

Roos, Leslie L.; Fisher, Elliott S.; Sharp, Sandra M.; Newhouse, Joseph P.; Anderson, Geoffrey and Buboiz, Thomas A. "Postsurgical Mortality in Manitoba and New England." *Journal of the American Medical Association*, 9 May 1990, 263 (18), pp. 2453–58.

Schwartz, William B. "The Inevitable Failure of Cost-Containment Strategies: Why They Can Provide Only Temporary Relief." *Journal of the American Medical Association*, 9 January 1987, 257(2), pp. 220–24.

Sen, Amartya. "Justice," in John Eatwell, Murray Milgate, and Peter Newman, eds., *The new Palgrave: A dictionary of economics.* New York: Stockton Press, 1987, pp. 1039–42.

Smith, Adam. *An inquiry into the nature and causes of the wealth of nations.* London: Strahan and Cadell, 1776; republished in Edwin Cannan, ed., *The wealth of nations.* New York: Modern Library, 1937.

Stigler, George J. "The Economist and the State." *American Economic Review*, March 1965, 55(1), pp. 1–18.

Thaler, Richard A. and Shefrin, H. M. "An Economic Theory of Self Control." *Journal of Political Economy*, April 1981, 89(2), pp. 392–406.

Townsend, Peter and Davidson, N., eds. *Inequalities in health: The Black report*. Hamondsworth, England: Penguin Books, 1982.

Weber, Max. "The social psychology of the world religions, 1915," in H. H. Gerth and C. Wright Mills, eds., *From Max Weber: Essays in sociology*. New York: Oxford University Press, 1946.

Weinberg, Steven. "The Methods of Science ... and Those by Which We Live." *Academic Questions*, Spring 1995, 8(2), pp. 7–13.

Weisbrod, Burton A. "The Health Care Quadrilemma: An Essay on Technological Change, Insurance, Quality of Care, and Cost-Containment." *Journal of Economic Literature*, June 1991, 29(2), pp. 523–52.

Wilkinson, Richard G. "Socioeconomic Differences in Mortality: Interpreting the Data on Their Size and Trends," in Richard G. Wilkinson, ed., *Class and health: Research and longitudinal data*. London and New York: Tavistock, 1986.

NOTES

INTRODUCTION: Health and Economics

1. Gordon McLachlan, "From Medical Science to Medical Care," *The Lancet*, no. 7491 (March 25, 1967): 630.

CHAPTER 1 Problems and Choices

1. Jonathan Spivak, "Where Do We Go from Here," in Robert D. Eilers and Sue S. Moyerman, eds., *National Health Insurance* (Homewood, Ill.: Richard D. Erwin, 1971), p. 272.
2. Raymond Aron, *Progress and Disillusion* (New York: Praeger, 1968), p. 3.
3. R. H. Tawney, *Religion and the Rise of Capitalism* (New York: Harcourt Brace, 1920), p. 270.
4. Henry Sigerist, *Medicine and Human Welfare* (New Haven: Yale University Press, 1941), p. 103.
5. J. Douglas Colman, "National Health Goals and Objectives" (speech delivered to the National Health Forum, Chicago, Illinois, March 20, 1967).

CHAPTER 2 Who Shall Live?

1. Sigismund Teller, "Birth and Death among Europe's Ruling Families since 1500," in D. V. Glass and D. E. C. Eversley, eds., *Population in History* (London: Edward Arnold, 1965), pp. 87–100.
2. Walsh McDermott, Kurt W. Deuschle, and Clifford R. Barnett, "Health Care Experiment at Many Farms," *Science* 175 (January 7, 1972): 23–31.
3. National Center for Health Statistics, *Comparison of Neo-Natal Mortality from Two Cohorts Studies*, Department of Health, Education, and Welfare Publication no. (HSM) 72–1056, Series 20, No. 13 (Rockville, Md., June 1972), p. 8.
4. Herbert G. Birch, "Health and the Education of Socially Disadvantaged Children," *Developmental Medicine and Child Neurology* 10 (1968): 582.
5. National Center for Health Statistics, *Infant Mortality Rates: Socioeconomic Factors*, Department of Health, Education, and Welfare, Series 22, No. 14 (Rockville, Md., March 1972).
6. Dugald Baird, "Infant Mortality and Social Class in Aberdeen, Scotland," *Annual Report of the Association for Crippled Children* (New York: 1971), p. 17.
7. *Infant Death: An Analysis by Maternal Risk* (Washington, D.C.: Institute of Medicine, 1973).
8. See, for instance, Victor R. Fuchs and Marcia J. Kramer, *Determinants of Expenditures for Physicians' Services in the United States, 1948–68* (New York: National Bureau of Economic Research, 1972).
9. Walsh McDermott, "Demography, Culture, and Economics and the Evolutionary Stages of Medicine," in E. D. Kilbourne and W. G. Smillie, eds., *Human Ecology and Public Health*, 4th ed. (London: Macmillan, 1969), p. 24.

10. Michael Grossman, "The Correlation Between Health and Schooling," Conference on Research in Income and Wealth, *Household Production and Consumption,* National Bureau of Economic Research, in press.

11. "Unexpected Deaths Increase for Women," *New York Times,* November 20, 1972, p. 34.

12. Grossman, "Correlation Between Health and Schooling."

13. From Sonnet XXIX of "Fatal Interview" by Edna St. Vincent Millay. *Collected Poems,* Harper & Row. Copyright © 1931, 1958 by Edna St. Vincent Millay and Norma Millay Ellis. By permission of Norma Millay Ellis.

14. René Dubos, *The Mirage of Health* (New York: Harper, 1959), p. 110.

CHAPTER 3   The Physician: The Captain of the Team

1. E. F. X. Hughes, E. M. Lewit, R. N. Watkins, and R. Handschin, "Utilization of Surgical Manpower in a Prepaid Group Practice," National Bureau of Economic Research Working Paper 19 (1974).

2. H. G. Mather, N. G. Pearson, et al., "Acute Myocardial Infarction: Home and Hospital Treatment," *British Medical Journal* 3 (1971): 334–338.

3. Eliott Friedson, *Professional Dominance: The Social Structure of Medical Care* (New York: Atherton, 1970), p. xi.

4. Kenneth Arrow, "Uncertainty and the Welfare Economics of Medical Care," *American Economic Review* 53, no. 5 (December 1963).

5. Walsh McDermott, in Edwin D. Kilbourne and Wilson G. Smillie, eds., *Human Ecology and Public Health,* 4th ed. (London: Macmillan, 1969), p. 9.

6. Ibid.

7. Sidney Garfield, "The Delivery of Medical Care," *Scientific American* 222, no. 4 (April 1970).

8. William P. Longmire, "Problems in the Training of Surgeons and in the Practice of Surgery," *American Journal of Surgery* 110 (1965): 16.

9. E. F. X. Hughes, V. R. Fuchs, J. E. Jacoby, and E. M. Lewit, "Surgical Work Loads in a Community Practice," *Surgery* 71, no. 3 (March 1972): 315–327.

10. E. F. X. Hughes and E. M. Lewit, National Bureau of Economic Research, paper in progress.

11. This problem was first discussed by Dr. Howard Taylor in connection with the training of obstetricians-gynecologists. See H. C. Taylor, "Objectives and Principles in the Training of the Obstetrician-Gynecologist," *American Journal of Surgery* 110 (1965): 35–42.

12. E. F. X. Hughes, E. M. Lewit, and E. H. Rand, "Operative Work Loads in One Hospital's General Surgical Residency Program," *New England Journal of Medicine* 289 (September 27, 1973): 660–666.

13. Such a plan was introduced by the United Store Workers Union in New York in 1973 in connection with the administration of their health and welfare fund. *New York Times,* June 19, 1973.

14. Department of Health, Education, and Welfare, *Medical Malpractice,* Report of the Secretary's Commission on Medical Practice (Washington, D.C.: Government Printing Office, January 16, 1973), p. 52.

15. Nathan Hershey and Walter S. Wheeler, "Health Personnel Regulation in the Public Interest: Questions and Answers on Institutional Licensure," California Hospital Association, 1973.

16. See Victor R. Fuchs, Elizabeth Rand, and Bonnie Garrett, "The Distribution of Earnings in Health and Other Industries," *Journal of Human Resources* 5, no. 3 (Summer 1970): 382–389.

17. Henry Sigerist, *Medicine and Human Welfare* (New Haven: Yale University Press, 1941), p. viii.

CHAPTER 4 The Hospital: The House of Hope

1. Anonymous, "An Interview with J. Douglas Colman," *Hospitals* 39 (April 16, 1965): 45–49.

2. W. John Carr and Paul J. Feldstein, "The Relationship of Cost to Hospital Size," *Inquiry* 4, no. 2 (June 1967): 64.

3. J. Gordon Scannell, et al., "Optimal Resources for Cardiac Surgery," *Circulation* 44 (September 1971), pp. A 221–236.

4. John H. Knowles, "The Medical Center and the Community Health Center," in *Social Policy for Health Care* (New York: New York Academy of Medicine, 1969), p. 158.

5. John S. Millis, *A Rational Public Policy for Medical Education and Its Financing* (New York: National Fund for Medical Education, 1971), p. 104.

6. See Victor R. Fuchs and Marcia J. Kramer, *Determinants of Expenditures for Physicians' Services in the United States, 1948–1968* (New York: National Bureau of Economic Research, 1973).

7. Herbert Klarman, "The Difference the Third Party Makes," *The Journal of Risk and Insurance* 36, no. 5 (December 1969): 553–566.

8. Bernard Friedman, "A Test of Alternative Demand-Shift Response to the Medicare Program" (Paper delivered at the International Economic Association Conference on Economics of Health and Medical Care, Tokyo, April 2–7, 1973).

9. Richard J. Radna, E. F. X. Hughes, and Eugene M. Lewit, "Determinants of Length of Stay in a Group of Neurosurgical Patients" (New York: National Bureau of Economics Research, unpublished).

10. G. R. Ford, "Innovations in Care: Treatment of Hernia and Varicose Veins," in G. McLachlan, ed., *Portfolio for Health* (London: Oxford University Press for Nuffield Provincial Hospitals Trust, 1971).

11. Paul T. Lahti, "Early Post-Operative Discharge of Patients from the Hospital," *Surgery* 63, no. 3 (March 1968): 410–415.

12. Adolph M. Hutter, Jr., Victor W. Sidel, Kenneth I. Shine, and Roman W. DeSanctis, "Early Hospital Discharge After Myocardial Infarction," *New England Journal of Medicine* 288, no. 22 (May 31, 1973): 1141–1144.

13. Sidney Lee, personal communication.

14. Victor R. Fuchs, "Improving the Delivery of Health Services," *The Journal of Bone and Joint Surgery* 51-A, no. 2 (March 1969): 407–412.

15. See Roger G. Noll, "The Consequences of Public Utility Regulation of Hospitals" (Paper delivered at the Conference on Regulation in the Health Industry, Institute of Medicine, Washington, D.C., January 7–9, 1974).

CHAPTER 5 Drugs: The Key to Modern Medicine

1. Allen Norton, *The New Dimensions of Medicine* (London: Hodder and Stoughton, 1969), p. 41.

2. See Reuben Kessel, "Price Discrimination in Medicine," *Journal of Law and Economics* 1 (October 1958): 20–53.

3. J. J. Burns, "Modern Drug Research," in Joseph D. Cooper, ed., *Economics of Drug Innovation* (Washington, D.C.: American University, 1970), p. 57.

4. Allan T. Demaree, "Ewing Kauffman Sold Himself Rich in Kansas City," *Fortune*, October 1972, pp. 98–103.

5. *The Medical Letter* 15, no. 10 (May 11, 1973): 42–44.

6. *Drug Topics,* March 5, 1973, p. 42.

7. Sam Peltzman, "An Evaluation of Consumer Protection Legislation: The 1962 Drug Amendments," *Journal of Political Economy* 81, no. 5 (September–October 1973): 1049–1091.

8. Ibid.

9. Louis Lasagna, "Research, Regulation and Development of New Pharmaceuticals: Past, Present, and Future—Part II," *American Journal of the Medical Sciences* 263, no. 2 (1972): 70.

10. Ibid., p. 72.

11. See W. McVicker, "New Drug Development Study," Industry Information Unit, Food and Drug Administration (Washington, D.C.: Government Printing Office, 1971).

12. William M. Wardell, "Introduction of New Therapeutic Drugs in the United States and Great Britain: An International Comparison," *Clinical Pharmacology and Therapeutics* 14, no. 5 (September–October 1973): 773–790.

13. William M. Wardell, "British Usage and American Awareness of Some New Therapeutic Drugs," *Clinical Pharmacology and Therapeutics* 14, no. 6 (November–December 1973): 1022–1034.

14. William M. Wardell, "Fluroxene and the Penicillin Lesson," *Anesthesiology* 38, no. 4 (April 1973): 309–312.

15. L. E. Cluff, "Problems with Drugs," Paper presented at the Conference on Continuing Education for Physicians in the Use of Drugs, quoted in Donald C. Brodie, *Drug Utilization and Drug Utilization Review and Control,* National Center for Health Services, Research and Development, Department of HEW Publication no. (HSM)72–3002 (1971).

16. John M. Firestone, *Trends In Prescription Drug Prices* (Washington, D.C.: Enterprise Institute for Public Policy Research, 1970).

CHAPTER 6   Paying for Medical Care

1. See Martin S. Feldstein, "The Feldstein Plan," in Robert D. Eilers and Sue S. Moyerman, eds., *National Health Insurance* (Homewood, Ill.: Richard D. Erwin, 1971) and "The Welfare Loss of Excess Health Insurance," *Journal of Political Economy* 81, no. 2, part 1 (March–April 1973).

2. Mark V. Pauly, "Discussion of Fein [Rashi] Paper," in Eilers and Moyerman, *National Health Insurance,* p. 108.

3. Ibid., p. 109.

4. Paul M. Elwood, Jr., "Restructuring the Health Delivery System: Will the Health Maintenance Strategy Work?" in *Health Maintenance Organizations: A Reconfiguration of the Health Services System* (Chicago: Center for Health Administration Studies, University of Chicago, May, 1971), p. 3.

5. Ray E. Brown, "Implications of the Health Maintenance Organization Concept," in *Health Maintenance Organizations,* p. 70.

6. August Heckscher, "Medicine and Society," *New England Journal of Medicine* 262, no. 1 (January 7, 1960): 19.

7. Daniel S. Hirschfield, *The Lost Reform* (Cambridge: Harvard University Press, 1970).

8. Jonathan Spivak, "Where Do We Go from Here," in Eilers and Moyerman, *National Health Insurance,* p. 273.

CONCLUSION   Health and Social Choice

1. John Maurice Clark, "Economic Means—To What Ends?" in *The Teaching of Undergraduate Economics, American Economic Review Supplement* (December 1950): 36.

What Every Philosopher Should Know About Health Economics

1. S. Woolhandler and D. U. Himmelstein, "The Deteriorating Administrative Efficiency of the U.S. Health Care System," *New England Journal of Medicine* 324 (1991): 1253–1258; U.S. General Accounting Office, *Canadian Health Insurance: Lessons for the United States*, Washington, DC: U.S. Government Printing Office, GAO/HRD-91-90 (1991).

2. Victor R. Fuchs and James S. Hahn, "How Does Canada Do It? A Comparison of Expenditures for Physicians' Services in the United States and Canada," *New England Journal of Medicine* 323, No. 13 (1990):884–890; and Donald A. Redelmeier and Victor R. Fuchs, "Hospital Expenditures in the United States and Canada," *New England Journal of Medicine* 328, No. 11 (1993): 772–778.

3. M. L. Berk and A. C. Monheit, "The Concentration of Health Expenditures: An Update," *Health Affairs* 11, No. 1 (1992): 145–149.

Poverty and Health: Asking the Right Questions

1. Comments from Alan Garber, M.D., John Hornberger, M.D., and Douglas Owens, M.D., are gratefully acknowledged.

2. See J. L. Palmer, T. Smeeding, and C. Jenks, "The Uses and Limits of Income Comparisons," in J. L. Palmer, T. Smeeding, and B. Boyle Torrey, eds., *The Vulnerable* (Washington, D.C.: Urban Institute Press, 1988), pp. 9–27.

3. V. R. Fuchs, "Toward a Theory of Poverty," in Task Force on Economic Growth and Opportunity, *The Concept of Poverty* (Washington, D.C.: Chamber of Commerce of the United States, 1965), pp. 71–91.

4. A. Smith, *The Wealth of Nations* (New York: Random House, Modern Library edition, 1937), p. 821.

5. O. Andersen, "Occupational Impacts on Mortality Declines in the Nordic Countries," in W. Lutz, ed., *Future Demographic Trends in Europe and North America* (New York: Academic Press, Harcourt Brace Jovanovich, 1991), p. 46.

6. J. Calltorp, "The 'Swedish Model' Under Pressure: How to Maintain Equity and Develop Quality," *Quality Assurance in Health Care* 1, no. 1 (1989): 13–22.

7. See, for example, A. J. Fox, *Social Class and Occupational Mobility Shortly Before Men Become Fathers*, OPCS Series LS No. 2 (London: HMSO, 1984); J. Stern, "Social Mobility and the Interpretation of Social Class Mortality Differentials," *Journal of Social Policy* 12(1983):27–49; and M. E. J. Wadsworth, "Serious Illness in Childhood and Its Association with Later Life Achievement," in R. G. Wilkinson, ed., *Class and Health: Research and Longitudinal Data* (London: Tavistock, 1986).

8. R. G. Wilkinson, "Socioeconomic Differences in Mortality: Interpreting the Data on Their Size and Trends," in Wilkinson, ed., *Class and Health*, p. 10.

9. R. Carr-Hill, "The Inequalities in Health Debate: A Critical Review of the Issues," *Journal of Social Policy* 16(1987):527.

10. See, for example, M. C. Berger and J. P. Leigh, "Schooling, Self-Selection, and Health," *Journal of Human Resources* 24(1989):435–455; P. Farrell and V. R. Fuchs, "Schooling and Health: The Cigarette Connection," *Journal of Health Economics* 1(1982):217–230; M. Grossman, "The Correlation Between Health and Schooling," in N. E. Terleckyj, ed., *Household Production and Consumption* (New York: Columbia University Press for NBER,

1976); and D. S. Kenkel, "Health Behavior, Health Knowledge, and Schooling," *Journal of Political Economy* 99(1991):287–304.

11. R. Auster, I. Leveson, and D. Sarachek, "The Production of Health: An Exploratory Study," *Journal of Human Resources* 4(1969):412–436.

12. M. Grossman, "The Correlation Between Health and Schooling."

13. V. R. Fuchs, "Time Preference and Health: An Exploratory Study," in V. R. Fuchs, ed., *Economic Aspects of Health* (Chicago: University of Chicago Press, 1982), pp. 93–120; and A. Bandura, "Self-Efficacy Mechanism in Physiological Activation and Health-Promoting Behavior," in J. Madden IV, ed., *Neural Biology of Learning, Emotion and Affect* (New York: Raven Press, 1991), pp. 229–269.

14. B. C. Vladeck, "Unhealthy Rations," *The American Prospect* (Summer 1991):102.

15. For other explanations by economic theorists for tied transfers, see N. Bruce and M. Waldman, "Transfers in Kind: Why They Can Be Efficient and Nonpaternalistic," *American Economic Review* 81(1991):1345–1351.

16. See S. Coate, S. Johnson, and R. Zeckhauser, "Robin-Hooding Rents: Exploiting the Pecuniary Effects of In-Kind Programs," (Cambridge, Mass.: Harvard University, March 1992, mimeo).

17. Personal communication from Ruth Watson Lubic, December 9, 1991.

From Bismarck to Woodcock:
The "Irrational" Pursuit of National Health Insurance

1. Brian Abel-Smith, "Major Patterns of Financing and Organization of Medical Care in Countries Other Than the United States," Bull. N.Y. Acad. Med. 40 (2 ser. 1964): 540.

2. For a discussion of why the United States is the last to adopt national health insurance, see p. 189 infra.

3. Martin S. Feldstein, "The Welfare Loss of Excess Health Insurance," *J. Pol. Econ.* 81 (1973): 251.

4. Milton Friedman, "Leonard Woodcock's Free Lunch," *Newsweek*, Apr. 21, 1975, 84.

5. George J. Stigler, "The Citizen and the State: Essays on Regulation," x (1975).

6. George J. Stigler, "The Economies of Scale," *J. Law & Econ.* 1 (1958): 54–71.

7. Lester C. Thurow, "Cash Versus In-Kind Transfers," *Am. Econ. Rev.* 64 No. 2 (Papers & Proceedings of the 86th Annual Meeting, May 1974): 190–95.

8. Mark V. Pauly, *Medical Care at Public Expense: A Study in Applied Welfare Economics* (1971).

9. Arthur M. Okun, *Equality and Efficiency: The Big Tradeoff* (1975).

10. Peter Townsend, "Inequality and the Health Service," Lancet 1 (1974): 1179–90.

11. John & Sylvia Jewkes, *Value for Money in Medicine* 60 (1963).

12. Cotton M. Lindsay, "Medical Care and the Economics of Sharing," *Economica* 36 (n.s. 1969): 351–362.

13. Gary S. Becker & Nigel Tomes, "Child Endowments, and the Quantity and Quality of Children," *J. Pol. Econ.* 84 No. 4 Part 2 (1976): S143–S162.

14. I am grateful to Sherman Maisel for suggestions concerning this section.

15. Lester C. Thurow, supra note 7, p. 193.

16. Kenneth J. Arrow, "Government Decision Making and the Preciousness of Life," in *Ethics of Health Care 33*, (Papers of the Conference on Health Care and Changing Values, Institute of Medicine, Laurence R. Tancredi ed., 1973).

17. Albert Breton, *The Economic Theory of Representative Government* (1974).

18. I am grateful to Seth Kreimer for suggestions concerning this section.

19. See Maurice LeClair, "The Canadian Health Care System, in National Health Insurance: Can We Learn from Canada?" 11, 16 (Proc. of Sun Valley Forum on Nat'l Health 1974 Symposium, Spyros Andreopoulos ed., 1975). LeClair writes that the experience in Saskatchewan clearly indicated economies of scale in the administration of a virtually universal plan. See also further comment on this point by LeClair, *id.* 24.

20. Mark G. Field, *Soviet Socialized Medicine* 14 (1967).

21. Brian Abel-Smith, supra note 1.

22. Daniel S. Hirshfield, *The Lost Reform: The Campaign for Compulsory Health Insurance in the United States* (1970) p. 16.

National Health Insurance Revisited

1. The author gratefully acknowledges comments from Andrew Batavia, Alan Garber, Donald Redelmeier, and Joanne Spetz.

2. National health insurance can take many forms. Emphasis here is on a national system that provides universal coverage with equitable financing and strong cost control.

3. D. Chollet, "Update: Americans without Health Insurance," *EBRI Issue Brief* (Washington, D.C.: Employee Benefit Research Institute, July 1990).

4. Health Insurance Association of America, *Providing Employee Health Benefits: How Firms Differ* (Washington, D.C.: HIAA, 1990).

5. See, for example, G. Dejong, A. I. Batavia, and R. Griss, "America's Neglected Health Minority: Working-Age Persons with Disabilities," *The Milbank Quarterly* 67 (Supplement 2 Part 2, 1989): 311–351.

6. The United States has some compulsion and some subsidization in large companies. In the typical case, all workers participate, and the firm rarely adjusts the individual worker's wages or premiums to take full account of differences in expected utilization.

7. The RAND Health Insurance Experiment clearly showed that utilization is greater when patients do not bear some of the cost of care. See W. G. Manning *et al.*, "Health Insurance and the Demand for Medical Care: Evidence from a Randomized Experiment," *The American Economic Review* (June 1987): 251–277.

8. J. Rawls, *A Theory of Justice* (Cambridge, Mass.: Harvard University Press, 1971).

9. V. R. Fuchs and J. S. Hahn, "How Does Canada Do It? A Comparison of Expenditures for Physicians' Services in the United States and Canada," *The New England Journal of Medicine* (27 September 1990): 884–890.

10. Ibid.

11. J. Boswell, *Life of Johnson* (1791; reprint, New York: Oxford University Press, 1953).

12. The effect of national health insurance on health depends on the product of two elasticities: (1) the responsiveness of the quantity of medical care to national health insurance, and (2) the responsiveness of health to changes in the quantity of medical care. In developed countries, the product of these terms is apparently very small.

13. P. Townsend and N. Davidson, eds., *Inequalities in Health: The Black Report* (Harmondsworth, England: Penguin Books, 1982).

14. O. Andersen, ''Occupational Impacts on Mortality Declines in the Nordic Countries,'' in *Future Demographic Trends in Europe and North America*, ed. W. Lutz, International Institute for Applied Systems Analysis, Laxenburg, Austria (New York: Academic Press, Harcourt-Brace-Jovanovich, 1991), 46.

15. J. Calltorp, ''The 'Swedish Model' Under Pressure: How to Maintain Equity and Develop Quality,'' *Quality Assurance in Health Care* 1, no. 1 (1989): 13–22.

16. B. C. Vladeck, ''Unhealthy Rations,'' *The American Prospect* (Summer 1991):102.

17. R. H. Tawney, *Religion and the Rise of Capitalism* (New York: Harcourt Brace, 1926).

18. V. R. Fuchs, ''The 'Competition Revolution' in Health Care,'' *Health Affairs* (Summer 1988): 5–24.

The Clinton Plan: A Researcher Examines Reform

1. G. J. Stigler, *Chicago Today* (University of Chicago Press, Winter 1966), 30.

2. The 10 percent figure derives from the fact that the employer's share is set at 80 percent and the employee's share at 20 percent, and the employer's share is capped at 7.9 percent of payroll.

3. *Economic Report of the President* (January 1993), 451.

4. Ibid., 396.

5. J. B. Quinn, ''Paying for Universal Care,'' *Newsweek* (29 November 1993): 59 (quoting Uwe Reinhardt).

6. W. G. Manning et al., ''Health Insurance and the Demand for Medical Care: Evidence from a Randomized Experiment,'' *American Economic Review* (June 1987): 251–277.

7. L. B. Russell, ''The Role of Prevention in Health Reform,'' *The New England Journal of Medicine* 329 (1993): 353.

8. See R. H. Brook et al., ''Does Free Care Improve Adults' Health? Results from a Randomized Controlled Trial,'' *The New England Journal of Medicine* 309 (1983): 1426–1434; J. Calltorp, ''The 'Swedish Model' Under Pressure: How to Maintain Equity and Develop Quality?'' *Quality Assurance in Health Care* 1, no. 1 (1989): 13–22; L. L. Roos et al., ''Postsurgical Mortality in Manitoba and New England,'' *Journal of the American Medical Association* 263 (1990): 2453–2458; P. Townsend and N. Davidson, eds., *Inequalities in Health: The Black Report* (Harmondsworth, England: Penguin Books, 1982); and R. G. Wilkinson, ''Socioeconomic Differences in Mortality: Interpreting the Data on Their Size and Trends,'' in *Class and Health: Research and Longitudinal Data*, ed. R. G. Wilkinson (London and New York: Tavistock, 1986).

9. Some of the difference may be the result of higher U.S. death rates at younger ages— leaving only the most robust individuals to reach age eighty. This is the so-called crossover effect.

10. A value-added tax is viewed as regressive by some critics, but that is because they mistakenly look at data for a given year, when income tends to fluctuate more than spending. Over a family's life cycle, spending tends to be proportional to income. Also, household data on income and spending exaggerate regressivity because they ignore family gifts and bequests. It is useful to note two truisms about money: ''You can't spend what you don't have,'' and ''You can't take it with you.''

11. This bias is attributable to the absence of certain markets for contingent claims. John Pratt and Richard Zeckhauser show that if such markets were complete, willingness-

to-pay for a given amount of risk reduction would be independent of the concentration of risk among individuals. J. Pratt and R. Zeckhauser, ''Willingness to Pay and the Concentration of Risk'' (Mimeo, Harvard University, 1993).

12. V. R. Fuchs and A. M. Garber, ''The New Technology Assessment,'' *The New England Journal of Medicine* 323 (1990): 673–677.

Economics, Values, and Health Care Reform

1. For a short introduction to the field of health economics, see Fuchs (1987). For a thorough review of the health economics literature prior to 1963, see Herbert Klarman (1965).

2. There were 132 dissertations completed in 1990–1994, compared with only 12 in 1960-1964. The number of dissertations in all fields of economics increased by 2.5 times during that 30-year interval.

3. Examples include the Congressional Budget Office, the General Accounting Office, the Office of Management and Budget, and the Office of Technology Assessment.

4. This is Arrow's most frequently cited single-authored paper (Michael D. Intriligator, 1987, p. 687).

5. In an extension of the crossword puzzle analogy suggested by Richard J. Zeckhauser in a 1995 personal communication, it seems that economics might make more progress if theorists didn't tend to concentrate on the lower left-hand corner of the puzzle while empiricists work the upper right-hand corner.

6. The relatively new International Health Economics Association held its inaugural conference in Vancouver in May 1996.

7. The *Journal of the American Medical Association* has twenty international editions published weekly in eleven languages, with 40 percent more recipients than the regular U.S.-based edition (George D. Lundberg and Annette Flanagin, 1995).

8. For an explanation, see Fuchs (1974); Robert H. Brook et al. (1983); Johan Calltorp (1989); Leslie L. Roos et al. (1990); Peter Townsend and N. Davidson (1982); and Richard G. Wilkinson (1986).

9. See Fuchs and Marcia Kramer (1973), Fuchs (1978b, 1990), Alan M. Garber, Fuchs and James F. Silverman (1984), Fuchs and James S. Hahn (1990), Donald A. Redelmeier and Fuchs (1993).

10. See David Dranove and Paul Wehner (1994).

11. See Jonathan Gruber and Maria Owings (1996).

12. As a sign of the times, Sweden, Norway, Finland, and the World Health Organization sponsored the first international conference on priorities in health care in October 1996.

13. Economists fall into their own monotechnic trap when they offer policy advice under the assumption that efficiency is society's only goal.

14. See Feldstein (1967).

15. To put this in perspective, consider the choice between tissue plasminogen activator (TPA) and its cheaper alternative, streptokinase, as the treatment to dissolve a clot during a heart attack. The latest studies suggest that the incremental cost of TPA rather than streptokinase is $33,000 per year of life extended (D. B. Mark et al., 1995). In the United States TPA is usually the treatment of choice, but Canadians use streptokinase.

16. Eddy's analysis focuses on the incremental benefit and cost of more services to all the patients in a population. Another important example of margin is the cost and benefit

of extending a (usually) once-in-a-lifetime service such as coronary bypass surgery to more and more patients.

17. Antibiotics, drugs for hypertension, surgery for trauma, and care of infants born prematurely are examples of outstanding successes.

18. Standard errors of the regression coefficients shown in parentheses. Mortality rates are 3-year averages centered on the years shown. Regressions are weighted by state population.

19. This is in sharp contrast to the effects of income and medical care on health—their marginal products diminish rapidly over the ranges usually found in high-income countries.

20. It is worth noting that the negative relation between schooling and smoking is only evident for cohorts that reached age 17 after the information about the effects of smoking on health became available. It is also of interest that the relationship has not diminished for more recent cohorts even though the information about the negative consequences of smoking has become more widely available.

21. There are alternative or complementary "third variable" explanations possible; compare Albert Bandura's (1991) concept of self-efficacy.

22. Stigler's optimism regarding the impact of empirical research on policy may have had more vindication in other fields, but my research into family issues (Fuchs, 1983) and gender issues (Fuchs, 1988a) do not lead me to such a conclusion.

23. In order to keep a clear distinction between health economists and theorists, I excluded any theorist who had done a substantial amount of work on health care.

24. An empirical researcher who specializes in public economics, a law professor who teaches a course in health policy and who has read widely in philosophy, and a theorist who specializes in law and economics.

25. The fact that there is perfect unanimity for only one of the seven positive questions should not be a cause for surprise. Even physics has its dissenters. Steven Weinberg (1995), winner of the Nobel Prize in physics, has noted "If you had a lawsuit that hinged on the validity of the unified weak and electromagnetic theory, you could probably find an expert witness who was a Ph.D. physicist with a good academic position who would testify that he didn't believe in the theory" (p. 12).

26. I believe the health economists' majority responses are correct for all seven questions.

27. This was confirmed by Byron Wm. Brown, who examined the data using the bootstrap method (Bradley Efron, 1993).

28. The identification is in a longer, unpublished version of their paper.

29. I also tried treating "agree, with provisos" as "no opinion"; this reduced the difference between the positive and normative questions with respect to consensus.

30. Comparisons based on the entropy index used by Alston et al. (1992) are even more striking. The mean entropy (a measure of lack of consensus) was 0.70 for their micro-positive questions, but only 0.52 for the health economists' answers to our positive questions. The mean for their micro-normative questions (0.80) was just about the same as for the health economists' policy-value questions (0.77).

31. For a discussion of alternative conceptions of justice, see Amartya Sen (1987).

32. In "*Essays in Positive Economics*", Friedman (1953) wrote "Differences about economic policy among disinterested citizens derive predominantly from different predictions about the economic consequences of taking action..." (p. 5).

33. See *Dollars and Deficits* (1966 p. 6); personal communication in 1995.

34. In 1974 I recommended universal comprehensive insurance for several reasons, one of which was the speculation that ''a national health insurance plan to which all (or nearly all) Americans belong could have considerable symbolic value as one step in an effort to forge a link between classes, regions, races, and age groups.'' I also thought it important to add ''It will be more likely to serve that function well if not too much is expected of it—if it is not oversold—particularly with respect to its probable impact on health''.

35. For a comprehensive review of the role of uncertainty in decision-making, see C. F. Camerer and M. Weber (1992).

36. The physicians also differed from the health economists, choosing ''no opinion'' more often for the positive than for the policy-value questions (15 percent versus 9 percent).

37. In actuarially-based insurance it is presumed that premiums will be determined (to the extent feasible) by expected loss. Health insurance did not begin with that assumption; the early Blue Cross/Blue Shield premiums were typically ''community rated,'' with healthy individuals paying the same premiums as those who were ill.

38. The reliability of the OLS regressions was checked in several ways: values for each respondent were predicted from each regression and found to be always between zero and one; regressions run with the dependent variable transformed to the odds ratio or to a dichotomous variable estimated with a logistic specification that showed even less predictive value than the OLS regressions.

39. This one question accounted for one-fourth of the health economists' ''no opinion'' replies to the 13 policy-value questions.

40. See Arthur Okun (1975).

41. For example, Kenneth Arrow, Zvi Griliches, Ed Mansfield, Richard Nelson, Nathan Rosenberg, and Jacob Schmookler.

42. It is true that most of the uninsured currently receive some care, but it is financed through a haphazard hodgepodge of self-pay, cost shifting, government subsidies, and philanthropy.

43. The choice of the tax base is primarily a problem of public finance, not health economics. I prefer a value-added tax because it is more efficient than a payroll tax (it does not tax labor while ignoring capital), and I prefer it to an income tax because it encourages saving and discourages consumption (a value judgment). The VAT appeals to my sense of fairness because it is more difficult to escape its impact through tax loopholes or tax evasion, and when taken in conjunction with the benefit that it provides, is clearly progressive.

44. See Arrow (1963) for a discussion of professional control in medicine.

45. The patient-physician relationship presents an extreme case of the principal-agent problem; research by specialists on that topic is badly needed.

46. The effects on television network news departments of the subordination of professional norms to the pursuit of profits shows what could happen in medical care.

47. Readers whose values lead them to prefer a more egalitarian system might consider how individuals now have options to use their income to live in safer neighborhoods, drive safer cars, avoid unhealthy occupations, and make other choices that have larger and more predictable effects on health than the options available in my recommendation for health care.

48. Many advances in medicine do not spring full-blown from the test tube. They require long periods of development through trial and error and incremental improvements. In my judgment it is desirable to have a system in which technologic opportunities can be explored on a reasonably large scale with the costs borne by those patients who are most

willing and able to pay for a chance at unproven benefits. Government- or industry-financed randomized clinical trials with small samples of selected patients treated in selected environments are not always a satisfactory substitute for larger scale efforts to establish the effectiveness, and especially the cost-effectiveness, of a medical technology.

49. See Alain Enthoven (1986, 1988).

50. For general discussions, see Joseph P. Newhouse (1992), William B. Schwartz (1987), and Burton A. Weisbrod (1991). For a detailed examination of the role of technology in increasing expenditures on heart attack patients, see David M. Cutler and Mark McClellan (1995).

51. See Paul M. Romer (1993).

52. The federal government's Agency for Health Care Policy and Research has shown that even a modest budget can produce valuable information about medical technologies, but the agency now faces extinction because of the opposition from politically influential medical and surgical specialists who expect to be adversely affected by its findings. See Neil A. Lewis (1995).

53. For an interesting discussion of the "topping off problem", see Robert H. Frank (1996).

54. This would undoubtedly require research to uncover the reasons for the erosion of professional control. See, for example, Steven Brint (1994).

INDEX